# A SONG FOR SATAWAL

# A SONG FOR SATAWAL

## Kenneth Brower

1817

**HARPER & ROW, PUBLISHERS,** New York

Cambridge, Philadelphia, San Francisco, London
Mexico City, São Paulo, Sydney

*For Corrine*

FIRST EDITION

Designer: C. Linda Dingler

Library of Congress Cataloging in Publication Data

Brower, Kenneth, 1944-
    A song for Satawal.

    1. Pacific Islands (Trust Territory)—Description and travel. 2. Natural history—Pacific Islands (Trust Territory) 3. Brower, Kenneth, 1944-  . I. Title.
DU500.B763 1983    996'.5    82-48110
ISBN 0-06-015093-9

83 84 85 86 87 10 9 8 7 6 5 4 3 2 1

# CONTENTS

# 1

# *THIS SMALL PLACE YAP*

———————

Yap Village

The original Yap Institute of Natural Science sits overgrown by jungle on a hilltop above Colonia, capital village of Yap. It is an odd and precarious site for an institute of science. Yap is an archipelago of sorcerers, ghosts, and red-lipped men in loincloths. The grandmothers of Yap are tattooed. The monetary system is Stone Age. The money is actual stone, in fact, calcium-carbonate disks the size of millstones, the most massive currency on this planet. On ancient Yap a pinball machine, or a pay phone, or a parking meter, would have been a monument the size of the Pyramid of Cheops or the Ziggurat of Ur. A gangster on Yap could send a rival to the bottom with a nickel in his pocket.

A great breaking wave of vines rolls over the back of the old institute, and a backwash of vines rolls over the front. A visitor is nearly to the door before he sees the institute's right front tire, half-obscured by vegetation. He realizes that the backwash of vines is boiling up through an empty engine compartment. He takes a big step up, pauses, and in some backroom of his memory he fumbles for a dime.

The original Yap Institute was pre-originally a schoolbus. Stenciled in white on the bus's gray side is "TTPI YAP," and affixed under that is the round emblem of the United States Trust Territory of the Pacific Islands. The emblem shows a coconut palm bending in a sea wind, encircled by six white stars. Each star once represented an archipelago in the old Micronesian protectorate, but no more, for in the little galaxy of Micronesia there has been a big bang. Palau and the Marshalls, the stars at either end, have opted for independence and are speeding off in their own directions. The Marianas, Micronesia's northwesternmost chain, have entered into a separate covenant with the United States. Only three of the old stars, Yap, Truk, and Ponape, remain in the middle. Joined by a nova, the island of Kosrae, they make up a new sovereignty, the Federated States of Micronesia. The new configuration is not particularly stable, and it may change again.

The jungle overwhelming the old Yap Institute is not the unruly sort that overwhelms temples in Yucatán or Cambodia. Much of this jungle is potted and labeled. From an awning over the bus windows, spider plants and succulents hang in planters made from coconut halves or sections of bamboo. On the ground below sit rows of starter boxes, in which the label stakes read, "White Okra, Aconcagua, Yolo Wonder, Jumamoto Eggplant, Chinese Cabbage Michihli, Wong Bok, Chinese Cabbage Santoh, Chinese Cabbage Nokaoka, Mustard Tendergreens, Chinese Chives." Beyond the bus are a small taro garden, a melon patch, rows of assorted vegetables, and a sapling breadfruit. The rest of the hilltop is wild and thigmotactic. Growing wherever experimental crops do not is a carpet of mimosa, a bipinnate, acacia-like, cowardly plant which shrivels when touched.

Three buildings stand on that sensitive slope: The *new* Yap Institute, a square one-room structure raised on cinder-block pilings, with an outrigger paddling canoe parked in the shadow beneath. A weathered outhouse, entwined and pulled partway over by vines. The modest tin-roofed home of Marjorie Cushing Falanruw, founder of the institute, director, staff scientist, and gardener.

"Sometimes, when I'm at a meeting in a city, I get restless," Mrs. Falanruw said, her arms folded, surveying her handiwork. "Nothing seems to apply. All my concerns are with Yap, this small place. None of what I'm hearing applies, and I get restless. When I get home and see the garden, I get excited and run all around and see how much everything has grown.

"Other times I come back—from San Francisco, say—and I just

say, 'Oh.' I see it for what it really is. Those excited times, I was seeing the ideal, the garden as it will be in the future."

"A conservatory?" I asked. "An arboretum?"

"Yes," she said. She laughed at the size of her own ambition.

It is an ambition that might have surprised her father, Captain Mars.

Margie Falanruw, a product of Captain Mars's union with the Sky Lady, was not born to natural science—to the microscope and the smell of formalin. She was born to the balancing pole and the smell of greasepaint. Her parents had high-wire hopes for her.

Captain Mars himself was born Frank Cushing in Durango, Mexico, to a European-American father and a Basque-Apache mother. He grew up to be a sailor, a prize fighter, a soldier of fortune flying Jennies in China, the inventor of the first toggle switch, a barnstormer, a motorcycle stuntman, a human-torch highdiver, a human cannonball. In 1947, as a protest against what he considered injustices in the administration of the GI Bill, he jumped off the Golden Gate Bridge, the first man to do so and survive. Margie's mother, Marjorie Bailey, known professionally as Vernita Bird, Grace Darling, or the Sky Lady, was a high-wire artist. Margie herself began as a trapeze artist and motorcycle stuntgirl with the family show, Death's Holiday Thrill Circus. She grew up at the family's base on Guam and on the road.

"My first memories are of the Philippines," she says, "Borneo. Malaya. I don't remember that much about the United States. I met an orangutan in Borneo. That really impressed me."

On Guam, the Cushing family first had pets, then too many pets, then a private menagerie, finally GUAM ZOO AND SEA LIFE PARK, open to the public and "Featuring live sharks, Giant Sea Turtle, Monsterous Moray Eel, Saltwater crocodile, Tropical fish, Huge Python snake, Llama, leopard, Raven, Monkey, Guam deer, wildboars, Monitor lizards, Fruit bats, Snakes, and others plus displays, refreshments, and souvenir stand."

Perhaps Margie's moment of destiny came as she fed the family crocodile, or cleaned up after the python or the boars. Perhaps it arrived as she looked into the wise, rueful face of that orangutan in Borneo. However it was, she is irrevocably now a biologist. The brand of bush science that she practices is a hard way to make a living, but the family act has long since disbanded, and there is no going back to the circus.

You can take the biologist out of the circus—you can even close the circus down—but you can't take all the circus out of the biologist. Her skills as an acrobat are rusty, but Margie is able to revive them occasionally in the interests of science. She once surprised a botanist colleague, the story goes, by running barefoot up a tree to pluck a specimen of epiphyte with her toes.

I had met her once before, in 1975, at the end of an unmarked dirt road in Guam's humid interior. She had returned that year to her old home island for a brief visit from Yap. She was on vacation, but her natural inclinations had taken her into what the people of Guam call "the Boonies," and she was skinning out an enormous leatherback turtle. The smell was terrible. There was a blizzard of flies. Her strong arms were shiny with turtle oil to the elbows and above. Her hair was pulled back in a bun, Yapese-style, but stray strands were escaping and her forehead glistened in spots where, with the back of her bent wrist, she had pushed them away. Her neck glistened where she had dabbed at flies. She was sifting flour on the inside of the leatherback's shell to soak up the oil; sifting by the sackful, for the turtle was big as a rowboat. Under the shine of the turtle grease and her powdering of flour, she was a young and good-looking woman, I thought. It was hard to know for sure. Between her front teeth was the interval that black Americans call a "lie gap." The Yapese probably call it something else. Her high cheekbones, her color, and something about her eyes all hinted at a trace of native blood. The trace may have been her eighth part Apache, about which I was ignorant at the time. The trace may have been less nature than nurture, some individual accommodation of physiognomy to her lifetime among the Malayo-Polynesians of Micronesia. She displayed her greasy fingers and apologized for not shaking my hand.

The leatherback she was beflouring was a wonderful animal, or a wonderful wreck of one. It looked like a survivor from the opening epochs of the Age of Reptiles, and it very nearly was. Other sea turtles—green turtles, loggerheads, hawksbills, ridleys—are ancient forms too, but they suggest some small refinement of the prototype. The leatherback does not. Its leathery plates, thick, brontosaur-colored, antediluvian, could pass for original equipment. Leatherbacks grow increasingly rare, and this one was the first of its species that Margie had encountered. It lay in the Guam clearing like one of those guesswork saurians of an artist's reconstruction, a reconstruction magically come alive and then, through some tragic mischance, killed again.

The forest grew thick to the edges of the clearing. It was scrub, second-growth jungle, but dense enough to have hidden, until 1972, the second-to-last known straggler from the Japanese Imperial Army. That lost Japanese soldier is irrelevant, probably. It is only that he *should* belong. In her background and qualifications, Captain Mars's daughter is out of Edgar Rice Burroughs or a Saturday-matinée serial, and a lost Japanese soldier should fit in there somewhere.

Margie Falanruw, born about the time the Japanese soldier went into hiding, came to Guam six years later, as he was settling into his forest routine, and she was the mother of a four-year-old by the time he came out. The Japanese soldier was there the whole time, a rumor, a shadowy lurker in the insect hum of the forest and the id of the islanders, a legendary stealer of all lost lunch pails and sheets missing from the line. Is it possible that the Japanese soldier, that infinitely stubborn and patient man, that celibate by fate and introvert by necessity, happened, while trapping the freshwater shrimp that sustained him, and amassing his thousands of *yen* in back pay, to peer out from his jungle concealment and see her, a lithe and professionally coordinated girl, collecting specimens for the family zoo? It is possible. Sergeant Yokoi mentions no such encounter in his memoirs.

Working on the far side of the leatherback was Margie's brother, Frank Cushing, Jr., another graduate of Death's Holiday Thrill Circus. Frank was now a technician with the University of Guam Marine Lab, and the turtle was his responsibility. Captured 1,250 miles away, off the island of Ponape, halfway across Micronesia, it had arrived on Guam very ripe, and Frank, whose chore was to prepare it as a museum specimen, was working fast.

Frank Jr. has a certain renown on Guam. It came about like

this: In April 1965, the two Frank Cushings, Senior and Junior, were out on their raft collecting fish on the reef. Tropical fish were a family sideline; Captain Mars sold them to hotels, which put them in aquariums. Night fell. Not wanting to risk the trip home in darkness, the two Cushings anchored in a small cove and slept. In the morning they woke to find themselves adrift, no land in sight. They survived by their wits and were picked up a month later off the tip of Luzon Island, at the northern end of the Philippines, 1,800 miles to the west.

Skeptics on Guam hint that the long drift was less accident than performance. It was an ordeal, they suggest, in the same sense that Captain Mars's 1947 leap off the Golden Gate Bridge was a suicide attempt. Captain Mars denied this. "It was all for real and a terrible experience for me and my son," he told the press. "If you want to live all your sins over again, just take a trip like that."

Ten years afterward, as he skinned out his leatherback, Frank Jr. did not look particularly blighted. A slim, laconic man, he labored without expression. He and his sister coordinated their efforts wordlessly. They had had practice at that—in the Death's Holiday trapeze act, she had been his catcher. He was a nicer brother than most, she says. That was sensible of him. His life depended on her good hands and good humor. Clearly Frank Jr. knew all about butchering turtles. It was a skill acquired, perhaps, on that long drift to the Philippines.

The turtle skinners took a break, and Margie sat down with me just outside the blizzard of flies. She had recently finished a stint as a staff ecologist for the Trust Territory Environmental Protection Board, and I had some ecological questions to ask her. I was curious about oil. An enormous oil transshipment port had been proposed for Micronesia, and I was writing a story on it. I wanted her opinions as former staff ecologist and as Yap's resident scientist.

There had been frequent small oil spills on Yap, she told me, most of them accidents by the U.S. Coast Guard, which maintains a LORAN station on Yap. It had fallen to Margie herself to report the spills. If she failed to, then they went unreported, for the Yapese were a people who kept low profiles and avoided making waves.

I noticed her accent. There was a smidgen of pidgin there—

none of the crazy grammar or syntax, just the inflection and the rhythm.

"The first one was a perfect mini-oil-spill," she said. "Everything was just like a real U.S. spill. We even had a bird kill—one frigate bird. Someone had him as a pet, with a streamer to show it. That's a custom we have in Yap—there's even a pet bat with a streamer. It says, 'Please don't shoot me.' The frigate bird wasn't flying too good to begin with, and then he landed in the wrong place."

She told me of the Yapese women who had come to her complaining about the spills. Their children got itchy when they went swimming, the women said, and the clams they caught tasted oily. The women were upset, but not belligerent. They would not sign spill reports, out of that Yapese desire to keep a low profile. Margie admitted to a growing reluctance to sign them herself.

Toward the middle of the interview, that first day of our acquaintance, I began to have a peculiar sensation. I felt Mrs. Falanruw receding from me. We both remained seated exactly where we were, twenty feet from the shell of the turtle. The movement away was in spirit, then, I guessed, but I would have sworn for a moment that it was physical.

She was telling me that the U.S. Coast Guard, the worst oil spiller on Yap, happened also to be the agency responsible for enforcing Federal oil-spill regulations. This sort of irony can make mainland ecologists apoplectic, but Mrs. Falanruw's tone, if anything, grew milder. She named no Coast Guard names. She assigned no personal blame. The Yapese style was not to make waves, she had said, and that, I guessed, was it. Mrs. Falanruw was withdrawing, in the way of her adopted islands, from controversy. She was withdrawing from interviews like this one.

Her seven-year-old, half-Yapese daughter, Leetun, played nearby, chattering to herself in Yapese. In Mrs. Falanruw's own accent there was that trace of Pacific Island pidgin, and I noticed again her high cheekbones and her vaguely Oriental eyes. It all made for something like vertigo: Margie Falanruw receding yet remaining where she sat, Leetun chattering in that strange, complex language, the flies vortexing around the great shell of the turtle, alighting in swarms, then buzzing off to join the vortex again.

"All I really want to do," I remember her saying toward the end, "is live a sensible island life."

Now, five years later, as we studied her Yap Institute garden, I saw Margie Falanruw for the first time unanointed by oil of leatherback, and she was a good-looking woman indeed. She still has the lie gap. She still speaks with a smidgen of pidgin. I reminded her of the leatherback, and she smiled.

"I fell in love with that leathery turtle," she said. "They're so *different* from other sea turtles."

She had chartered the Yap Institute in 1975, she said, the year of the leatherback. "The first office was that bus over there. It served very well, but it got too hot. Now we've got a ventilator on it."

The roof of the bus was painted white, and the ventilator perched on top. It was a solar ventilator, one of several solar demonstration projects on the hilltop. The Yap Institute of Natural Science is, in the words of its founder, "A small local nonprofit organisation dedicated to the idea of maintaining indigenous integrity through wise sustainable use of local resources, and the search for a valid ethno-ecological lifestyle in the Yap Islands ecosystem." (A sensible island life.) On Yap sunlight is a local resource of mother-lode magnitude, and the ventilator is an attempt to use it wisely. The device is supposed to cool the bus by convection, removing the heated air near the roof so it can be replaced by cooler air sucked up by accordion tubes hanging close to the ground. Through those pleated tubes—its several trunks—the old gray elephant of the bus roots and snuffles in the ferns of Margie's potted jungle.

She lifted one of the tubes, held the end near her cheek, and looked skyward thoughtfully.

"I don't know. Do I feel anything? I always wonder if it's my imagination."

She handed me the tube and I held it to my own cheek. I thought I felt a coolness and the tiniest of breezes. I was not sure. If it existed at all, it was the ghostly sort of convection that three or four harnessed bees might have generated, tethered somewhere in the bus interior. I returned the tube without a verdict, and Margie set its snout down in some ferns a short distance from where it originally had rested, hopeful, I suppose, that it might draw better in the new spot.

From the green fountain of vines that welled out of the empty engine compartment and up over the windshield, one tendril diverged. The tendril had a mind of its own. It grew around to the side, entered the bus door, and climbed the three stairs nearly to the driver's seat. When Margie excused herself to take care of other business, I followed the tendril inside.

The bus seats had been removed. An aisle still ran to the back, but it was bounded now by file cabinets, wooden desks, coils of wire, sacks of animal feed. The old institute had become a storage place for the new. One of the feed sacks had fallen and split open, and on the floor at the edge of the spilled grain was a single chicken dropping. I idly wondered for a moment why, next to that cornucopia of feed, the chicken had lingered only long enough for a single dropping. It was not much of a mystery, really. As I stared down at the dropping, a drop of sweat rolled off my nose, plummeted, and hit to make a dark spot on the floor. A second drop followed instantly, then a third. The rat-tat-tat of my productivity made me happy for a moment, in a goofy way, like a boy who has hit a jackpot on a gumball machine. Then I realized that my hand was sticking to my notebook's open page. The interior of the bus was a passive solar oven. The solar ventilator on top was not doing the job. The ventilator was sending back an infinitesimal fraction of the ferocity that the Yapese sun was beaming down. The test was unfair, of course—a sealed bus at a dead standstill at two in the afternoon nine degrees north of the equator.

There were shelves of books. *So Human an Animal* by René Dubos. *Science and Survival* by Barry Commoner. *Mushrooms, Moulds, and Miracles* by Lucy Kavaler. *Defoliation* by Thomas Whiteside. I noted the titles quickly, careful to keep the damp heel of my hand off the notepad. Halfway through, the heat became too much. I escaped the bus at a half trot and sat down outside. Cooling off, I devised a plan. Taking a deep breath, I put the plan into effect: I plunged inside, memorized several titles, ran out, dried my writing hand on my shirt, committed the titles to my notebook, then

plunged in once more. In this way I inventoried the entire contents
of the bus, making efficient use of my time inside, like a diver
working deep.

There were *The Population Bomb* by Paul Ehrlich, and *On Population*, a book of essays by Malthus, Julian Huxley, and Frederick
Osbourn, and *The Prevalence of People* by Marston Bates. There was
*Population Explosion: Abundance or Famine*, a longish title whose author I was unable to memorize before the heat drove me from the
bus again. The emphasis on population surprised me. Oceania is
one of the few places on earth where *de*population has been the
problem, and the depopulation of Yap is studied as a classic case.
There were once 50,000 people on Yap, according to archaeological
estimates. Today there are 5,000.

At the back of the bus, pinned to the wall, was a torn and
yellowed clipping from the March 3, 1978, edition of *Pacific Daily
News*, Guam's newspaper. "Over Troubled Waters," ran the head,
and underneath a photograph showed Margie walking a tightrope
over an open tank of water. "Margie Cushing Falanruw no longer
earns a living as a professional daredevil, but she likes to keep her
hand in," the story went. "She's been tightrope walking since she
was a child. But she's no ordinary child; she was born into the
Cushing family, an assortment of daredevils with father Frank's
'Death's Holiday Thrill Circus.'" In the photo, Margie is grinning.
Directly below her, shadowy, its broad pectoral fins outspread, is an
eight-foot tiger shark from the family's menagerie.

Beneath the clipping, a long plank workbench lay where the
rear seat once had been. The bench was clean and well organized,
with plenty of working space. On top was a big bottle of alcohol, a
small enamel bowl full of metal clamps and calipers, and a large
enamel bowl covered by an improvised lid—a block of wood. The
surface of the wood block was sprinkled lightly with gecko droppings. The droppings were strong evidence that the old Yap Institute is still used occasionally at night. Geckos are nocturnal lizards.
In the twentieth century they have become specialists at hunting
insects drawn to electric lights. One or more of the pale, primitive
reptiles, walking upside down on the rounded adhesive pads that
tip their toes, had stalked the illuminated ceiling while some scientist burned midnight oil below.

Margie entered. "Let me show you something incredible," she said, walking rapidly down the aisle to join me at the workbench.

She lifted the gecko-bombed wood block from the big enamel bowl.

The smell of alcohol was sudden and cloying in the superheated air. Lying on the bottom of the bowl, in a pool of clear alcohol, were two gray-pink fetal animals. One was much larger than the other. Both had long, doglike muzzles. Small triangular ears were beginning to form, not on the sides of the heads, but on top, like horns. Both creatures had translucent fetal wings, from the middle joints of which grew single long, gripping claw-fingers. There were no arms, but feet were taking shape, huge feet, *mammalian* feet, clearly, yet feet crisped into claws as if gripping a branch. In the toes, the nails had darkened, hardened, and defined themselves sharply. Great orbs showed dark under translucent lids—oversized infants' eyes sleeping now forever without once having wakened. The two creatures had the eeriest dual look of innocence and evil. If mortal woman had been impregnated somehow by Satan, and, despairing of finding a mainland physician unorthodox or priest arcane enough to help her, she had journeyed to Yap in search of a sorceress, and with the aid of that wrinkled, black-toothed woman had aborted, then she might have left something like this in the bowl.

The fetuses were twins, Margie said, looking down on them fondly. She had never encountered twins in the literature of fruit bats, nor in real life until this pair was brought to her. In her fruit-bat autopsies she had made another discovery—female fruit bats pregnant and lactating at the same time. This suggested, she said, that the fruit bats of Yap breed faster than she had previously figured. She admitted that she was in no hurry to publish revised calculations. Her reluctance was partly professional caution—the scientist wanting to make sure she was right—and partly environmental politics, for the hunting pressure on Yap's fruit bats is heavy, and a slightly higher birthrate would render slightly less telling her arguments in their defense.

"Yap's only indigenous mammals are fruitbats of the genus *Pteropus*," Margie Falanruw has written. "These large bats live mainly in the forest and eat a wide variety of fruits and nectar.

Ecologically they are believed important in pollination and seed distribution. On Yap, fruitbats have legendary significance and are also a source of food. Traditional food taboos, however, restrict the eating of fruitbats to but a portion of Yap's population. Thus, even today, the hunting of fruitbats for local consumption is limited.

"On the nearby island of Guam, however, fruitbats are much sought after. There, habitat destruction and overhunting have exhausted the populations of fruitbats to a point where one species is probably extinct, and the other endangered. The demand for this Chamorro delicacy remains high, however, and frozen fruitbats command a very high price on the Guam and Northern Marianas markets. In recent times, frozen fruitbats have been imported from the Trust Territory and even the Solomons and New Guinea in response to this demand. Because of their similar smell to Guam animals, fruitbats from the Trust Territory are preferred.

"The expansion of Yap's road system in recent years has given hunters easy access to fruitbat habitat and flightlines, and guns and bullets are increasingly available.

"If current trends and odds against fruitbats continue, Yap will emulate Guam and lose a component of its ecological system, source of legend, food item, and any prospect of harvesting Yap's highest priced export commodity on a sustainable basis. Furthermore, the children of Yap and of the world will lose the company of an especially intelligent and sensitive expression of life."

"The new office is passively cooled," she told me, as we left the bus. "It's what I call Neo-Palauan design. The configuration of the two-by-fours in the walls is different from normal, in that the air spaces run the whole height of the walls."

"Does it *work?*" I asked.

"Well, it's no hotter inside than outside, and that's something."

After the furnace of the bus, the climate of the new institute seemed boreal. At one desk sat Margie's assistant, a young Yapese woman named Loofen Saweyog. Margie's desk adjoined. On top was a stereoscope, through which Margie had spent the morning studying aerial photographs and identifying vegetation types.

On the wall hung a copy of the "Yap Almanac Calendar" that

Margie and the Yap Institute produce each year. This year's cover, drawn by a Yapese artist, John Ruw, showed a smiling sun shining down on a bird in a bush and on a coconut palm. Propped at the foot of the palm were two huge disks of Yapese stone money. It looked as if it was going to be a good year.

The calendar text began humbly, as is Margie's wont:

"A journey of a thousand miles begins with a single step."
—LAO-TSE

We hope to improve this calendar each year.
Thank you.

Then the calendar got down to business. "It is illegal to capture sea turtles Dec. 1–Jan. 31," it warned, in the two blank squares before January 1, which happened that year to fall on a Tuesday. In each of the daily squares that followed, Margie had provided tide tables, and in the appropriate squares she had noted phases of the moon, important anniversaries and holidays, and occasional turtle-season and fire-hazard warnings. Above, in the place where, on a less purposeful calendar, the naked girl or the autumn scene would have gone, she displayed "bits of information useful in living on Yap." March offered ideas for solar devices, May offered ideas for gardening, June some tips for using cacao and for building a fireless cooker.

The calendar was eclectic. Scattered throughout were quotations from Lao-tse, the Bible, Gautama Buddha, Abe Lincoln. "The human brain, so frail, so perishable, so full of inexhaustible dreams and hungers, burns by the power of the leaf," mused Loren Eiseley, for the edification of the people of Yap. "Never lose an opportunity of seeing anything that is beautiful, for beauty is God's handwriting—a wayside sacrament," Ralph Waldo Emerson advised them.

The word "small" recurred: "Most persons would succeed in small things if they were not troubled with great ambitions," said Henry Wadsworth Longfellow. "The greatest fine art of the future will be the making of a comfortable living from a small piece of land," predicted Abraham Lincoln. There was even a smallness quote from Rudyard Kipling, not a poet much associated with that theme, nor a poet especially popular on Third World walls. Kipling wrote:

> God gives all man all earth to love,
> But since man's heart is small,
> Ordains for each one spot should prove
> Beloved over all.

It is not hard to guess which spot Margie Falanruw had in mind.

Beneath the calendar were shelves of books and monographs. After a moment of hesitation, she pulled one book out for me. It was the black spiral-bound binder she calls "The Dream Book."

The Dream Book lists the projects she plans to do someday. She has marine dreams and terrestrial dreams. In the sea, she would like to study the feasibility of mariculture for Micronesia, and of artesinal deep-water bottom fishing, and of lagoons as tuna traps, and of a trochus-shell cottage industry, and of reintroducing sailing canoes as commercial fishing vessels. She would like to estimate sea-turtle populations and to evaluate the wisdom of channel blasting. On land, she plans studies on the ethnobotany of Yap; on vegetative changes on Yap; on the relationship between geology, land use, and savannah land on Yap; and on biodynamic vegetable gardening on Yap. She plans a piggery project, a poultry project, and a coconut-crab project. She would like to "Do Something Effective to Reduce Siltation." She would like to conduct a survey of traditional Yapese subsistence agriculture and write a "History of Yap as Recorded in Chant." She wants to do a fruit-bat survey.

Some Dream Book projects have come to pass. "A Newspaper for Yap," one item on the list, was published for eleven issues. The "Yap Institute of Natural Science Facility" and the "Falanruw Self-sufficient Home" both came to be—came to be nearly indistinguishable, in fact, as they expanded across the hilltop. And the fruit-bat survey is underway.

"Preliminary talks with Yapese elders," she writes, in her *Study Plan: Ecology and Ethnobiology of the Fruitbats of Yap*, "indicate that in the past, there were areas where fruitbats were plentiful and even places where they were routinely captured with hand nets. Although the eating of fruitbats was limited to but a portion of Yap's population, still the human population of this small island of but 39 square miles is estimated to have been as high as 50,000 in precontact times. That fruitbats could continue to co-exist with such dense human populations suggests that traditional patterns of use were effective in allowing for sustained harvest of this resource. This provides hope for wise management of fruitbats in modern times."

Her fruit-bat plan calls for a review of fruit-bat literature ("This task has been initiated through use of the Yap Institute of Natural Science Fruitbat Files"), and for the compilation of information on traditional management of fruit bats in the Pacific ("It is interesting, for example, that while on Yap the eating of fruitbats is confined to lower ranks, fruitbat hunting is a prerogative of the chiefly class on Tonga"). Her plan calls for taxonomical analysis of the fruit bats of Yap and the neighboring atoll of Ulithi; field counts and observations of wild fruit bats, including habitat preference, foods, reproduction, and effects of changing environmental conditions; compilation of statistics on fruit-bat exports, population characteristics, and measurements of harvested fruit bats; compilation of environmental data relevant to fruit bats; and for training local personnel and assisting Yap State in setting up a fruit-bat management program and a "Smokey the Fruitbat" campaign.

Of this "Smokey" campaign, Margie elaborates: "Talks with educators indicate that short, self-contained units on conservation would be welcomed in Micronesian schools. This effort might well be assisted through the use of a local conservation symbol similar to the 'Smokey the Bear' image so popular in the continental United States. The available local animal candidates are limited to the rat, monitor lizard, and fruitbat. Of these the indigenous, clean, flower- and fruit-eating, forest-dwelling, intelligent, big-eyed fruitbat is the obvious choice!"

These fruit-bat plans are big plans, and when I finished I read them dryly back to Margie.

She smiled. "I hope I haven't bitten off more than I can chew," she said. She paused to look out the door at the forested skyline.

"They are definitely decreasing. The other evening, I went out to look for them. It was a nice time of day. The food they like was ripe and ready. I waited. They didn't show up."

If the people of the archipelago of Yap, of the western Caroline Islands, of Micronesia, of the west-central Pacific Ocean, were to be pressed suddenly for some summary of their place, three thousand words or less to be entrusted to a capsule destined for a distant time or galaxy, then the Yap Almanac Calendar would probably have to do. There is a lot of Yap in Margie's calendar. It weighs just two and a half ounces and would roll up easily to fit inside.

On the verso of the cover is a simple schema of the "Hello! We are here!" sort that space scientists like to put in probes fated for interstellar space. A line drawing shows Earth's sun in its twelve positions around the year. Inside the ellipse of those twelve suns, the artist John Ruw has drawn four larger suns, complete with rays, to represent the two equinoxes and the two solstices. For each of those points of the ecliptic, Margie has noted the date and the Yapese name for the star or constellation that marks it for Yap. At the summer solstice, the sun rises in the same spot where Magirgir, the Pleiades, rises. At the winter solstice it rises with Thumur, or Antares in Scorpio. Outside the twelve suns, concentric circles of information describe what happens on Yap over the course of a year. An extraterrestrial intelligence, opening the capsule and twisting its head, or heads, to read around those circles, would learn that in January the sun shines on Yap, the trade winds blow, and the main orange season begins. In March through May, the migratory birds leave Yap for their northern breeding grounds. The mango season runs from March through June, the breadfruit season from April to August. Winds are calm from May through July. In August comes the rainy season, and fishing is good, and the migratory birds begin returning from their breeding grounds. The yam season begins in October. In November the typhoon season begins, but passes quickly, and the trade winds return, and the year begins all over again.

Should an extraterrestrial navigator want to see firsthand this place where the typhoon season is brief, and where in a given month either oranges, breadfruit, mangoes, or yams are bearing, he could, with the calendar before him and a little rudimentary deduction, home right in on Yap. The information is all there. He would come looking for a place near the eastern edge of the monsoon area where, influenced by the intertropical convergence, the rainfall is variable, but on average peaks at about seventeen inches in July and drops to around five or six inches a month in January through April; a place with a mean temperature of about 81 degrees Fahrenheit, a relative humidity of 80 percent in the driest months and 85 percent in the dampest; a place where the difference between the longest and shortest day of the year is only an hour and eleven minutes. If he wants to time his visit to coincide with the summer solstice, he should fly in with the sun's first rays from the direction of Magirgir, the Pleiades, and look for the first archipelago where mango trees are bearing. At the winter solstice he should fly straight in from Thumur and look for oranges.

He would arrive well informed. He would know from the calendar that the gestation period for the pig, a Yapese animal, is sixteen Earth weeks, for the dog nine, the cat eight, the duck thirty Earth days, the chicken just twenty-one days. He would know that using a clothesline instead of an electric dryer saves as much energy per hour as turning off 1,739 100-watt light bulbs, and that a tadpole turns into a toad faster if its puddle is drying up. He would be aware that in recent years more egrets are coming to Yap, and that some seem to want to forget migration and stay on Yap full time. He would know how to build a ferro-cement water-catchment tank. He would know better than to drop a trolling line on his approach run, having been warned that "fishing by foreign vessels is illegal within 12 miles of the Federated States of Micronesia," and that "fishing within 200 miles is legal only with a valid permit from FSM Micronesian Maritime Authority."

The visitor would know the birthdays of a number of Earth's luminaries: Washington, Lincoln, St. Valentine, St. Patrick, Frank Cushing (this last figure apparently most luminous, for the year of his birth, 1902, is given, not just the day).

About Yapese agriculture, the visitor would be best informed, for the calendar is, after all, an almanac. He would have learned that on an island of variable rainfall a diversified agriculture is best, and that the old Yapese had developed one: artificial mixed forests of breadfruit, coconut, buoy nut, and rowal fruit; yam gardens growing back into those forests; mixed vegetable gardens in high drained areas; taro gardens down low. He would know that in the taro gardens stagnant water was avoided by clever irrigation systems that kept a slow current moving through. He would know that the Yapese still grow all those things. He would know that in recent times a people called the Japanese introduced open-land monoculture, but that this caused soil degradation and was not nearly so good.

He would have learned about the recent introductions that *were* good: Bush spinach, *Abelmoschus manihot* in Latin, *mbele* in Fijian, a relative of okra common to Melanesia and other parts of the Pacific, its young leaves good lightly boiled or fried with sardines. The vine called *ikemas*, brought by Spanish galleon from Mexico, where it was called *jícama*, by way of Guam, where it was called *sinkamas*; a bean by any name, but—more important—the producer of a tuber, like the sweet potato; a tuber sweet and crunchy when young, good for pickling or for use in chop suey and with one virtue nearly miraculous: Yapese children like to eat it raw, but Yapese rats have not discovered it yet. The wingbean, a native of southeast Asia and New Guinea, called *sigidillas* on Guam. According to the calendar, scientists, having recently "discovered" the high protein content of the bean, in their excitement were recommending that it be spread. It already had been on Yap for eight years, the calendar noted, "evidence that really good things travel fast among 'just plain folk.'" The wingbean is illustrated in the calendar by a murky photograph of a small child perched on a stepladder and holding a pod half as long as himself. The child is Margie's four-year-old son, Lubuw. The weight of the wingbean seems about to topple Lubuw from his ladder.

A bar graph shows the productivity of various Yapese crops over a recent year. The graph has a nice informality. It is titled

"Yap's Concert of Food," and its measures of abundance are simply "some" or "lots." Pineapples and mangoes produce only in the first half of the year, with peaks in June. Oranges produce all year long, with peaks at either end. Sweet potatoes and yams peak at either end, but produce not at all in the middle. Breadfruit makes several peaks in the middle of the year, but produces nothing at the ends. Taro, down at the bottom of the graph, looks at first glance like a mistake. It is frozen at "lots," making a broad band from January straight through December, without a single peak or valley.

But the most remarkable vegetable in the almanac calendar is the apparently primitive tree that accompanies the month of September. John Ruw's line drawing is another of those simple schemas that might have been intended for another star system, or for a Third World classroom, or for some other place where written language might prove a barrier to communication. Leaf scars girdle the tree's trunk all the way to the top, as on some fossil plant from the Carboniferous. From different parts of the tree, Ruw has drawn chains of products leading outward. From old flower stalks fallen around the base come kindling, brooms, and a device for removing the intestines from roasted boxfish. From the leaf-scarred trunk comes lumber. From the huge pinnate leaves come thatch for roofs, baskets, bowls, hats, fans, whistles, pinwheels, and packages. From the midribs of the leaves come tongs and other utensils and tiny nooses for catching shrimp. From the unopened flower buds comes a sap drunk straight as a nutritious beverage, or boiled for molasses, then spun for sugar, or made into a pudding, or used to make rice cakes rise, or allowed to ferment into a beverage that makes you dance. That dancing beverage—palm wine, or *tuba*—if allowed to sour turns to vinegar. From the "gauze" growing at the base of the fronds come sieves, "tea bags" for medicines, and sandals. From the young green nuts that clustered under the crowns comes a third beverage and a sterile medium. The green husks of the young nuts provide fiber for rope and string. The brown husks of mature nuts are burned as fuel, and from the white meat at the mature core come copra, copra oil, soap, medicines, and hair oil. The meat can be grated and squeezed for cream, and that cream then boiled for still another grade of oil. In a fallen and sprouting nut, the core hardens into an "apple," from which cups, shakers, spoons, and other utensils come.

An extraterrestrial botanist, tracing these product lines outward with a finger or some other appendage, might be forgiven for believing that here, at last, is a planet on which genetic engineering has been attempted and really works. Reading a sidebar to the drawing, he would learn more, perhaps, about the miracle tree than he wanted to know: That the tallest on record was a Ceylon specimen 117 feet high. That early-germinating nuts usually grow into vigorous, early-bearing trees. That some short varieties flower before three years, most tall varieties around eight years. That a new leaf usually emerges each month; or up to thirteen or fourteen new leaves each year. That the leaves are arranged spirally every 140 degrees around the trunk so that each gets maximum sun, thereby lining up every fifth leaf scar. That to estimate the age of a tree, one should count leaf scars and divide by thirteen. "Coconut=Tree of Life," the drawing was titled. So grateful were the inhabitants, according to the calendar, that they had consecrated a day, March 30, as "Palm Sunday."

The principal lessons of the calendar have to do with natural history, but there are other things to glean from it. An extraterrestrial intelligence officer, reading between the lines, could learn a good deal about the pace of human life on Yap. In September, the calendar states, "School generally starts." In October it says, "Generally U.N. Day celebration."

To call Yap small, provincial, and a backwater is not to convey the place. The islands of Margie Falanruw's voluntary exile are small and provincial in nearly ultimate senses of those words. The Yap phone book is a pamphlet five pages long. There are sixty-one residential listings. Louis Moongog, Edward Pungod, Tony Yug, Beyad Untun, Joe Sham, John Caad, Luke Tman, Sam Falanruw, and fifty-three others are inhabitants important enough to have phones. There are two hotels. The E.S.A. Hotel stands on the south shore of Colonia Lagoon, its initials those of the owner, Erina Silbester Alfonso, a Palau Islander who has made good on Yap. Mr.

Alfonso is a Christian, and no alcoholic beverages are served in his place. On the north side of the lagoon stands the Rai View Hotel, whose owner has no such compunctions, and the Rai View has a bar. You can eat in either hotel, or at a place called Island Flavor Restaurant. The phone book lists a Family Chain Restaurant, as well, but I have never been able to find the place. I could be wrong, but I believe it to be the Island Flavor by another name. "Holy Land Lamb Meat" was the Saturday special chalked on the Island Flavor's menu board the last time I visited. The real origin of the lamb was almost certainly New Zealand, and all of it was gone by the time I arrived.

Adjoining the Island Flavor is a private bar. One enters the bar through the restaurant by way of a door plastered with warnings. "Leave your basket with the cashier before entering," says one. (The "basket" is the palm-frond purse in which Yapese men and women keep their betelnut.) Another sign warns that admission is limited to outsiders and to Yapese with membership cards. It's an odd admission policy—strangers welcome—but it makes perfect sense on a remote island where new faces are rare. The bar's hours are irregular. "Closed!" the bored barmaid is apt to say, flipping the OPEN sign over suddenly. "Sorry, you have half hour to finish your drink and leave."

R-rated movies are screened occasionally on one wall of the private bar. They are never the sort of films that show in Cannes. One night the selection was an Italian B movie with a cast of Amazonian women in helmets from some vaguely Grecian time. It was dubbed in English, or seemed to be—the sound was too murky and out of synch to know for sure. None of the bar's habitués bothered to watch at all until the nude wrestling scene, for which a few turned their attention to the wall. One young barmaid watched blankly, as jaded as Juno, her elbows on the bar. Several Coast Guardsmen from the LORAN station watched stolidly from their tables, and several Yapese men in Western dress watched from theirs. Only one customer showed anything like animation—a middle-aged Yapese woman who was new to R movies. She watched with mounting horror.

The Amazons, bodies oiled, grappled on the bar wall. They

were leggier than Pacific women, who are built close to the taro; paler too and less voluptuous. The exposed breasts of the Amazons did not trouble the middle-aged Yapese woman, for in the traditional cultures of the Pacific, breasts are not erotic. Thighs are another matter, and as the camera panned below the wrestlers' waists, the Yapese woman ducked her head in embarrassment. Twice she looked sharply around at the men of the tables behind, to see if they had seen. Finally, unable to stand it, she jumped up and walked rapidly from the bar, her head down, her hand to her eyes, like a woman walking into a driving rain.

There are no research libraries on Yap. There are no biology labs. There are no coffeehouses where graduate students in zoology or botany gather to share observations or test theories. There are no coffeehouses. There are no graduate students. There are no professors or seminars or faculty teas.

In her isolation on Yap, Margie Falanruw once raised tadpoles in an aquarium. She discovered by accident that if tadpoles of *Bufo marinus* had no "land" in their tanks, they never underwent their metamorphoses into toads. They had not metamorphosed, at any rate, by the end of three months, when her class's interest in the experiment began to wane, or by the end of four, at which point the aquarium was accidentally broken. They lived and died as tadpoles. The tadpoles of her control group were provided with land, and in a short time they sprouted back legs and began their great change. Once begun, the metamorphosis could not be halted. If, after the back legs had grown, she removed the land, the front legs went on to sprout, the tail resorbed, the tadpoles became toads, and they drowned. Some biologist, Margie is nearly certain, must have discovered all this before her, but she cannot remember reading it anywhere. No book in her own small library alludes to the phenomenon, and she has no toad specialist to ask. She may indeed be the discoverer. If so, she has not discovered it yet.

There are no computer terminals in Yap. There are no art galleries. There is no opera.

"Where can I find Margie?" I asked a passerby once, on arriving in Colonia. The man knew who I meant—no last name was necessary. He directed me to the Yap Department of Education's

Audio-Visual Center, where Margie was working that morning. It was, I realize now, a nice test of the archipelago's size. Yap is not much of a place.

And yet Yap is enormous. If you have spent all your previous life on a coral atoll of 150 inhabitants—and there are many such atolls in Micronesia—then Colonia becomes a metropolis. If, for you, *terra firma* has been an islet of coralline sand eight feet high at its greatest elevation and half a mile long, then Yap's thirty-nine square miles of green volcanic hills become an Australia or an Asia.

In the Micronesian scheme of things, Yap is anything but provincial. Dozens of tiny coral satellites once paid tribute to Yap's volcanic central cluster, and today true provincials from those outer islands are still drawn to the Rome that is Colonia. Fortunately, their exposure to vastness on the scale of Yap's usually has been by stages. Most young atoll dwellers go first to high school on Ulithi. Ulithi is a big atoll, for the western Carolines. Ulithi has a road, an airstrip, and 1.799 square miles of sandy soil. After a year or so on Ulithi, a student's eyes have stopped popping and he is half prepared for Yap's thirty-nine square miles and five-page phone book.

The outer islanders live along the shore of Tomil Harbor in an attenuated, spacious, thatchy ghetto called Madrich. In Madrich there are people from Elato and Faraulep and Lamotrek. There are people from Fais, an island of shark eaters. (To the Romans of the central cluster, shark is unfit food and a shark diet comical, but to the reefless people of Fais, who have little else, shark is a necessity and they have come to prefer it. The Fais shark-fishing technique is hair-raising. The Fais fisherman goes to sea alone, paddling out on a log. Bobbing on the swells of the open Pacific, he splashes to attract the big pelagic sharks that cruise there, offering himself as bait. He nooses the shark as it swims in to investigate, then ties it to the log and paddles back to shore.) In Madrich dwell people from Satawal, an island of great navigators, and people from Mogmog and Eauripik and Ifaluk. The outer islanders are low folk in Yap's social order, yet they are the noblest looking. They travel in family groups along the dirt streets of town, the men wearing the *thu*, the loincloth of the Carolines, the women topless and wearing *lava-lavas* striped in broad horizontal bands of black and gray. The men are strong and well made, even the grandfathers. The women are sturdy and lovely, their long black hair pulled back in buns or cropped short in mourning.

There are no biological labs or libraries in Yap, but there is plenty of biology. Yap has forests, savannahs, mangrove swamps, rivers, patch reefs, fringing reefs, and barrier reefs, all beautiful and all full of life. There are no graduate students or professors with whom Margie Falanruw can compare notes, but there are colleagues. Yap is full of naturalists. In the subtlety of their concepts, in the sheer number of items of biological information stored in their memories, the outer-island men in loincloths, and many inner-island men in shorts and ragged T-shirts, are the equals or superiors of Western Ph.D.s in zoology. It is hard for Westerners to believe this, but it is true.

In 1968, when she was a student at the University of Guam, Margie collaborated with Sam Falanruw, her new Yapese husband, and with Mo'on Nigat, an old Yapese folk professor of marine biology, to produce a paper she titled *The Ethnoichthyology of Yap*. Her study was then, and remains today, the only ethnoichthyological work ever written about Yap. It was an ambitious project for an undergraduate, full of information on the genius of the men in loincloths. It earned only an A-minus, for reasons mainly cosmetic.

"The typing was bad because the first copy got chewed up and crawled over and peed on by my daughter," Margie explains. "She was that age." The spelling was bad, too—a Cushing family trait, demonstrated abundantly, for anyone who cares, by the signs at the family's zoo on Guam.

Yapese biology does not classify fish phylogenetically. There are other sensible ways of grouping animals, and the islanders use several of them. Yapese classification, as Margie reports it, is less detached and cerebral than our own. The Yapese taxonomist makes use of all his senses, not just his brain. "Fishes are ecologically classified on Yap by their home areas, habits, taste and smell," she writes. "Fish which inhabit coral areas, or eat algae, or inhabit the top of the open sea, or the bottom, can be distinguished by their smell and taste even if the fish was not previously seen or known.

Schools of fish which cannot be seen from above the water are identified by the way they break the water and the orientation of their shadows on the sand."

The Yapese have genus names and species names for fish. The brown triggerfish is genus *wuu*, species *nguff*. The bump-head parrotfish is genus *choi*, species *gamegul*. The gray parrotfish is genus *choi*, species *nguiwe*. Sometimes in scientific Yapese, as in scientific Latin, both names are the same. Thus the ray is genus *rol*, species *rol*. The jack is genus *ngol*, species *ngol*. Yapese taxonomists are lumpers more than splitters. Uninterested in making distinctions much finer than they can taste, they fall into repetition more often than do their Western counterparts. Thus in Yap, butterfly fish are genus *gap*, species *gap*. Damselfish are genus *dak*, species *dak*. Sharks—all except the hammerhead—are genus *aeeng*, species *aeeng*. The hammerhead, that fast, acrobatic, queer, ballpeen form, has a class to itself, and that makes sense to anyone who has seen one.

The index of fish names in Margie's *Ethnoichthyology* is a failure, by the standards of Western science. Margie's index makes the mistake of being interesting. Whenever she has a good bit of lore or information, she throws it in. She notes, after her entry on the bright-painted surgeonfish *Acanthurus lineatus* (Yapese genus *achingal*, species *aringal*), that "Girls who decorate themselves up a great deal are called 'aringal.'" She explains that the Yapese name for seahorse, *lik e bu'oy*, means "like the roots of the Tahitian chestnut." She hints that the large dark-brown triggerfish, *nguff*, has a delicious liver. She observes that *tugo*, the yellowfin tuna, does not have worms in its stomach lining, as the bluefin does. Of the cornetfish or flutemouth, Yapese *sgnop*, she says, "Generally the head of this fish is broken off and thrown away, as it is empty and no good to cook. Thereof comes the insult, 'The sgnop's head is better than yours.'"

(*Sgnop* is a fish as bold as it is empty-headed. Fishermen-scientists in Yap and elsewhere in Oceania have long known of that boldness; Western science was in the dark until 1981, the year an acquaintance of Margie's, Robert Johannes, published *Words of the Lagoon*, an account of the fishing lore of Palau, Yap's southern neighbor. Johannes's Palauan informants told him that the cornet-fish, a reef dweller with an attenuated body and a long snout, has the habit of approaching the moray eel as the eel rests, jaws agape, at the entrance to its hole. The eel stares, in the blank way of mor-ays, right through the cornetfish. The cornetfish is beneath its con-cern. The eel's open jaws continue articulating slightly as it passes water over its gills. Suddenly the cornetfish darts forward and rams its snout down the throat of the eel. It is the last thing the eel expected—or the human observer either, the first time he sees this happen. The eel appears paralyzed. It is unable to close its jaws or use the razors of its teeth. Somehow, somewhere back in evolution-ary history, some proto-cornetfish learned the secret pressure point of the moray eel. The cornetfish roots around for a while in the moray's gullet, then withdraws with bits of eel flesh sticking to the abrasive tip of its flute. The eel is so weak-kneed after the experi-ence that it is sometimes unable to crawl back into its hole.

("While in Yap," Johannes writes, "an island 300 miles from Palau inhabited by people of a quite different culture and language, I asked five different fishermen whether they had ever seen a cor-netfish and a moray eel do something strange together. All five immediately volunteered that they had witnessed cornetfish ram-ming their snouts down the throats of moray eels. Yapese accounts differed from most Palauan accounts only in one way. The Yapese surmised that the cornetfish was eating the intestines of the eel, whereas most Palauans said they believed that the cornetfish was 'vacuuming' out the stomach contents of the eel.")

Margie Falanruw's unorthodox fish index includes a mystery animal. For the creature that the Yapese call *galuf nu medai* she lists no English common name. "'Monitor lizard of the sea,'" she trans-lates. "Lives in mangroves, head like a crocodile, caught at night, has lizard-like skin and red meat that tastes like salmon. Three to four feet long."

No asterisk or footnote further explains this entry. I decided, worrying over it, that if the *galuf nu medai* was not merely a myth, then something like the Galápagos marine iguana must have mi-grated, unknown to Western science, deep into the Indo-Pacific. I put the question to Margie. The *galuf nu medai*, she said, only *looked* like a lizard. It was really a fish, and it really existed.

The Yapese scheme for reef zonation is, except for the names, much like the scheme Western marine biologists use. First, fringing land, is the dark-green margin of mangrove forest called *melil*, a transitional zone, half-terrestrial, half marine. Then comes the shallow offshore depression called *lupuu*, a zone full of algae, except where Yapese reef managers have cleaned it out. Then comes a slight rise that ends in the sandy plateau called *ey*; then the steeper descending slope called *tele makeff*, a zone of corals and seaweed; then, at the bottom of that slope, a moderately deep channel floor called *makeff*; then another *tele makeff*, its slope ascending this time; then *lane yan*, the reef flat, a zone dotted with seaweed and coral; then *naa*, a thin zone where breakers beat against the spine of the reef; and finally *regur*, the open ocean. *Daken e dai* is the ocean's surface, *toru wan dai* the midwater depths, and *t'ai e regur* the ocean floor.

In her *Ethnoichthyology* Margie graphs this reef topography with a wandering black line. Presented in a boardroom, her graph would cause consternation. Reef sales hold their own out to the *ey*, then frighten the directors in the mild drop of the *makeff*, then build again gradually to peak in the zone of breakers, *naa*, and finally plunge sickeningly down the reef front to crash abyssally in the total black bankruptcy of the *t'ai e regur*.

Reef zonation is applied science in Yap. The Yapese fisherman knows which fish live in which zone, and when he wants a certain species he visits its milieu. In the mangrove zone he finds tangs, halfbeaks, archerfish, mudskippers, freshwater eels, and saltwater eels (for the mangroves are the transition zone between salt and fresh), and cornetfish and monitor lizards of the sea, should he really want to find those. He finds *angar*, too, and *g'lad achoow'*, *gariung*, and *galginman*, fish for which Margie's index neglects to provide the English or Latin. From the *lupuu* zone to the *ey*, he finds tangs, surgeonfish, jacks, and mullet. From the landward *tele makeff* down to the channel bottom of the *makeff* and up the slope of the seaward *tele makeff* he finds jacks, triggerfish, and surgeonfish. From the *lane yan* to the *naa*—on the reef flat, in other words—he finds triggerfish, jacks, parrotfish, surgeonfish, and damselfish. On the *daken e dai,* the open ocean beyond the reef, he fishes for bluefin and yellowfin tuna, bonito, swordfish, marlin, and sharks.

The Yapese are astute fish behaviorists, and here too their science is meant to be applied.

"Bottom fishing on moonlit nights yields red snappers and *wachamul* (Big-eyes)," Margie writes. "To catch *wachamul,* trochus bait is used. Catching this fish requires a sensitive hand to detect the right time to jerk, as this is a tricky fish. It first blows on the bait and then takes it and spits it out. The line must be jerked at just the right moment, when the bait is in its mouth.

"Off certain places in the reef, the labrid *nmam* (a parrotfish) may be caught at early morning or sunset with a bait of a live land crab. The crab's legs are tied to its body and as it is lowered into the water it gives off a stream of bubbles which attract the parrotfish to eat it.

"If a swordfish is caught, a mat woven of coconut leaves about 3X3 feet in area is strung on the line and let drag until it comes to lie over the fish's eyes. Then the fish doesn't fight so hard and is easier to bring in. This works to a lesser degree with marlin."

The real genius of Yapese ichthyologists rests less in swordfish blinders and bubbling bait, however, than in the reef-management principles they invented—principles that succeeded in preserving, through many centuries, on a small, densely populated archipelago, a prolific and healthy reef. The Yapese system worked mainly by preventing what Garrett Hardin has called the Tragedy of the Commons. Waters within the reef were owned privately. The owners had an interest in seeing that their stretches of reef remained productive, and their permission was required to fish there. Margie's *Ethnoichthyology* reports, for example, that when the owners of a particular stretch of the *lupuu* zone decided that their fish were becoming too small or too scarce, they erected a *bungud,* a stick with a flag of coconut fronds attached, which signaled to the public that these waters were off limits. Sometimes the *bungud* remained in place for as long as two years before the owners determined that the recovery was complete. Waters beyond the reef were owned by the municipality inland from them. Citizens of other municipalities could fish there only by trolling. Stopping to fish with spear or line was forbidden.

Taboos often had the effect of conservation law. "Restrictions on eating certain kinds of fish affect people whose *nik*, or family totem, happens to be a fish, in the belief that people will aquire the characteristics of the fish they eat," Margie writes. "Thus sharks and rays are not eaten least the eateer get weak bones, marine eels less he become sluggish and fawning, or freshwater eels, which are associated with spirits. People from Okau village aspiring to be fine dancers should not eat barracuda, lest they aquire the dumb stare of that fish."

("Eateer" is a fine word but not in any dictionary, and Margie tried three versions of "lest" before getting it right, and "aquire" is missing a "c." This is one of those passages in which she lapses into the circus-child spelling that often afflicted her early academic career. At the moment of composition, Leetun the baby was screaming, probably, or tipping something over.)

Yap's caste system, like the taboo system, worked to balance the hunting pressures on the various animal populations. "The Pimelingai, the lowest class, owned no land and had no fishing grounds other than streams and rivers," she writes. "They were restricted from owning any fishing equipment. They had to report any 'high class' fish caught. They lived on land animals, like crabs, and on marine eels, octopi, sharks and rays and other fish which could not be eaten by the higher classes. In former times, only the Pimelingai fished with poisons, and only in the limited areas available to them—mainly rivers and near mangroves. No coral grow in these areas and there were only eels and small fish. No one was allowed to use poison in any other location."

Of all matters she covered in her old study, this business of reef management is of greatest interest to Margie Falanruw today. Many of Yap's old reef-management principles remain in effect, but the system is eroding. The old principles worked. The new, Western principles—really the absence of principles—do not, and now the reef itself is eroding.

"We've got to neo-traditionalize the system," she says. Having said that, she frowns and concedes that neo-traditionalizing won't be easy.

Margie is unhappy with the sketchiness of her *Ethnoichthyology*. All its subjects deserve fuller treatment, she thinks, and a rounding out of the study is one of the projects listed in her Dream Book. She is not certain that she is the ethnoichthyologist to do the job, or that any woman is. "Women are definitely taboo to fishermen," she writes in her section on taboos. "The sea is a woman and a jealous one, and a man must have no smell of a woman when he goes to sea." On Yap fishing knowledge is not women's knowledge. "Some of my informants don't mind," she says today. "They're understanding. They've told me, 'You're a scientist, this is your business.' Others, I'm not so sure."

These doubts have not stopped her from noting bits of information when they chance to fall her way, and the old typescript of the *Ethnoichthyology* is now scribbly with penciled corrections and amplifications. Where the original states, for instance, that "In at least three places in the waters of Rull Municipality there are large schools of barracuda to be found at all times; they swim vertically, appearing like coconut leaflets in the water, about thirty feet down," she has crossed out the "vertically" and penciled in this revision: " . . . At an *angle*. According to Sam they 'park' with head higher than tail but not even as much as 30° off *horizontal*. Not vertical." With small refinements like that, science in the Yap Archipelago advances.

Magic remains a great force in Yap. For all the accomplishments of Yap's fishermen-scientists, the archipelago is better known for its sorcerers. Yapese folk science is not the kind of discipline that banishes dark arts and the supernatural. On Yap, in fact, sorcerer and scientist are often the same man.

The Palau Islanders, Yap's nearest high-island neighbors, have adopted the Yapese word for magic, *masmas,* and they concede, uncharacteristically, that in this one department Yapese practice is superior to their own. The Palauans are an aggressive, adaptable people who have attacked the twentieth century with more enthusiasm than have the Yapese. Palauans generally make better businessmen, even on Yap, where a number live as expatriates, and Palauans make tougher street fighters. Yet Palauans are a bit spooked by the Yapese. The standard advice from a Palauan man, on hearing that you are traveling to Yap, is that you should never walk up behind a Yapese man and tap him on the shoulder. The Yapese will spin, screaming and flailing his arms. The correct *Palauan* reaction, one of my Palauan advisors explained, would be to turn slowly and coolly, face impassive. My advisor then shook his head. There was something unmanly in the Yapese reaction, he suggested, but more than that, something strange.

The reputation of the Yapese for spookiness has traveled from Palau, at the western end of Micronesia, to the Marshall Islands at the eastern end. In the Marshallese language, Yap is *Iaab* and the Yapese *Rilaab*. The sample sentence in the Marshallese dictionary reads: *Rilaab rokkuranran,* "The Yapese get startled easily."

Westerners in Yap feel Yap's strangeness, too. Americans stationed in the archipelago seem to go native at a higher rate than Americans stationed in other Micronesian groups. There is something compelling in Yap's culture, or Yap's atmosphere, or Yap's soil. Americans in Yap tend to stray quickly from the world view of Newton and Descartes.

Not everyone, of course. I once knew a Peace Corps Volunteer on Yap, a Cartesian, more or less, a solid sort who had not exchanged his pants for a *thu* or got himself tattooed, as Peace Corpsmen in Yap tend to do. Riding his bicycle one day between villages, he pedaled up a rise in the savannah and at the summit encountered a fireball. It hung stationary just above the ground, a glowing sphere of light about eight feet in diameter, and then it rolled through the air after him, chasing the bicycle most of the way home. "St. Elmo's fire?" he wondered, months later, as we tried to imagine what the fireball might have been. His "father" in Yap— the head of the household in which he lived—was not the least puzzled nor was he much interested. On hearing the story, the old Yapese asked whether the fireball had appeared on a certain hill. His American son admitted that it had. The father nodded; that hill was notorious for its ghost, the old man said, and he went back to weaving his thatch.

If the hill of the fireball has an antipode in Yap, it is Margie's hill of the old schoolbus. The Yap Institute of Natural Science, on its cluttered green prominence above Colonia, is an outpost at the very frontier of Western rationality.

Irrationality in Yap, if that's what it is, has its clinical side. Yap has more than its share of crazies. The problem, in the opinion of the Peace Corps Volunteers, is culture shock. Yapese society is the most traditional and conservative in Micronesia, and the trauma of the encounter with the Western world, according to this theory, runs deeper in Yap and is more abiding than in most archipelagos. Perhaps there is, as well, some residual dislocation from Yap's great depopulation. Perhaps all the magic practiced in Yap has had a disorienting effect. Perhaps there is some X-factor in the Yapese soil. Whatever the cause, a disproportionate number of Yapese seem to have run off their trollies.

Ten years ago, a good part of Yap's feel of ubiquitous lunacy was generated by a single man, an islander called Doublecheck. Doublecheck was the man whose semaphores guided your taxiing plane in, and the driver who sped out in the airfield truck to pick up your baggage, and the celebrant you saw at all three of the bars you visited that night, a shirtless man singing to himself, drinking, and dancing alone; and he was the tour guide who greeted you soberly after dawn that morning for a trip to see the stick dancers of Maap Island, and he was the boatman who ferried you there. He spoke seven Pacific languages, it was said; he had been married four times, and he had once served as fire chief of the island of Saipan, in the Marianas. He was named for his habit of shouting, at more or less regular intervals, "Check! Double-check!" It was the opinion of the Peace Corps Volunteers that Doublecheck was very intelligent, and their diagnosis was that he was a casualty of culture shock in something like its tertiary stage. My own notion, similar but fuzzier and grander, was that Doublecheck, with his frantic pace and interminable checklist, was taking on himself, Christlike, all the sins of modern man, as if that might smooth the passage of his people into the twentieth century.

It is possible, of course, that I simply travel in eccentric circles in Yap and that my impressions are skewed. In fairness, I should describe my sampling method. One night it went like this: I walked down to the private bar at the Island Flavor Restaurant, in search of a beer, with which I intended to unwind from the rigors of science on Margie's hilltop.

At the next table, talking to herself in English, was a Yapese woman in her mid-twenties. Her eyes were bright and troubled. Her soliloquy was full of exclamations, sudden laughter, and nervous asides, none of which made sense. We talked a while, I and the several of her, for in conversation she was like a committee. I got her story in bits and pieces and finally isolated what I thought was the problem. Several years before, it seemed, she had traveled to the United States with an American man. *He had taken her to Los Angeles.*

I stepped outside and walked uphill, under the sobering influence of the Southern Cross, to the bar of the Rai View Hotel. A few Coast Guardsmen from the LORAN station were sitting inside with Yapese girls, and small groups of Yapese were drinking beer quietly. A Yapese woman in her early forties sat down at my table. She was a pretty woman except for her eyes, which were slightly exophthalmic, with a pronounced cast. She was mildly drunk and had a strange high voice. Her English was Biblical. She carried a Bible. When she learned that I was a writer, she opened the Good Book and had me write my name in the back. "I want you to put a line in *your* book thanking Americans for the goodness of their tax dollars," she said.

She was being ironic, I suggested. (The United States, while it has not done worse than other colonial powers in the Pacific, has not done any better, and no Micronesian I had ever met, until that moment, had been happy with America's performance.)

The lady was indignant. It was goodness, she insisted, that America had been practicing in its thirty-five years of governing Yap, a goodness that originally had come down from God, and which Americans were sharing.

"But you'll admit, at least, that those tax dollars are a mixed blessing," I said.

"Mixed babies? Why do you say that?"

"No, no. Mixed *blessings.*"

The Christian lady did not hear me. She was sweeping the dim room with her unblinking, slightly bulbous eyes. She lingered on the Coast Guardsmen and their Yapese girls. There were potential mixed babies there, all right, and I guessed that the woman was contemplating those, but I was wrong. "Yesterday I saw nothing but enemies here," she murmured. "Today I see no enemies, just . . . confusion. Or maybe one enemy."

I looked around the room, trying to guess the enemy. No one looked particularly sinister, so I gave up.

The Christian lady told me a story. A week before she had met a Jehovah's Witness, she said, a young American man. "What are you doing in Yap?" she had asked the young missionary pleasantly. "I'm preaching," he had answered. "And what do you preach?" she had asked. The missionary had explained the principles of the Jehovah's Witness faith. "It must be expensive, coming over here—how do you afford it?" she had wondered. The young man had answered that his parents gave him money.

"*American* dollars?" she had asked, her voice rising.

"Yes."

"Don't you know that Our Lady is the Queen of America? You are spending her dollars to spread your false message. Get out of Yap! I don't want you interfering with my people. *Get out of Yap!*"

The Catholic lady's lips thinned with rage in the Rai View bar as she repeated this warning for me. Her eyes snapped, then narrowed without losing their cast, so that she was looking wrathfully in two places at once. In the old days, I was certain, the Catholic lady would have been a sorceress. Had *I* been the Jehovah's Witness, I decided, I would have got myself out of Yap.

A slender, drunken Yapese man with stunned eyes and electric hair was drifting among the tables, talking to himself in Yapese, in Palauan, and in English. Stopping at our table, he spread his arms wide. "Ladies and gentlemen, lend me your ears," he said. "I come not to praise Caesar, but to bury him." He paused for the attribution, then delivered it, "—MacArthur." We laughed, and the Yapese man laughed bitterly with us before moving on.

The Catholic lady and I watched his erratic course through the tables. "Wouldn't you agree, though," I suggested, wanting to clear up an earlier matter, "that our tax dollars have been a mixed *blessing*? Is a cash economy really so good for Yap? Are all the things it buys? Is alcohol good? Is television?"

"We should be thankful for alcohol," she said. "God put alcohol here so we can drink and enjoy ourselves. What are you worried about? We know how the end of the world will come. The Bible says, 'Nation will war against nation.' It doesn't say anything about television. It doesn't say anything about radio."

"You don't agree with Margie, then," I said. (If the Christian lady was right, then all Margie's experimentation with solar ovens and ventilators was wasted effort.)

"*Margie?*" asked the Catholic lady. She smiled broadly. "You know Margie? She's my very good friend. She's a very gifted and talented lady. I went to her house and she had this . . . *serpent* in a box. To take care of wild animals like that . . . it's a gift."

GUAM ZOO & SEA LIFE, OPEN DAILY, TUMON BEACH, reads the sign outside Margie's old home on Guam. A second sign lists the zoo's ingredients: "Live sharks, Giant Sea Turtle, Monsterous Moray Eel, Saltwater crocodile . . ."

Margie's talent for wild animals may be a gift, as the Catholic lady said, but surely it is also a skill acquired here in the family's backyard.

The zoo has no paths or walkways. The cages and enclosures are scattered over a big lawn, and you walk from one to another with grass underfoot. Ducks and ducklings run free on the lawn, waddling away just ahead of you. The animal inmates seem happier than the inmates of most zoos. The frigate bird looks dispirited, but how else could that greatest of soarers look, grounded and caged? The leopard lies on its side, panting in the heat but appearing reasonably content. It seems to have resigned itself somehow to the strangeness of its fate here in the middle of Oceania, so far from the Dark Continent. There are monitor lizards and a rear-fanged rat snake. There are macaques and a llama. There are Guam deer, shy, melting toward the rear of their enclosure as you approach. There is an eight-foot saltwater crocodile from the Palau Islands named Freddie.

The smaller sea creatures live in aquariums, the larger ones in metal tanks. In the first of the tanks swim a green turtle, a hawksbill turtle, some unicorn fish, surgeonfish, big-eyed squirrelfish, angelfish, and cowfish. In the second tank swim more unicorn fish, two big nurse sharks, and a small nurse shark. In the third tank a moray eel sits all by itself. It looks unsociably up toward the surface, its jaws opening and closing ceaselessly as it passes water over its gills.

The zoo's signs are pleasantly informal, ungrammatical, and faulty in punctuation.

"There are two stone fish in here. Look carefully," says the sign beside one aquarium. At the bottom, camouflaged, lie two specimens of that remarkably ugly and poisonous fish.

"Don't touch his back or he will spit, but don't worry he doesn't bite," advises the sign by the llama pen.

"Jojo is an American Raven," says the sign by the raven. "He is an intelligent bird and likes to play. He can even 'talk' when he's in the right mood. Don't be surprise if your walking by his cage and he'll say hello."

Stashed here and there on the zoo grounds is gear left over from various Captain Mars enterprises. Under the roof of one shed lie three homemade outrigger paddling canoes. The Cushing family used the canoes in their fish collecting, perhaps. Behind the marine tanks, draped over the fence, is a gill net and an old-fashioned heavy-canvas diving suit with metal helmet. Against the same fence, farther down, rests a one-man yellow submarine. Captain Mars built the sub himself. The yellow paint is flaking badly, exposing dark metal beneath. Farther up the fence, near the crocodile pool, sits what looks like a full-scale lunar lander. (According to his wife, the Sky Lady, Captain Mars was interested in rocket propulsion back when the Army Air Corps said it was impossible. Maybe the thing near the crocodile pool *is* a lunar lander.) The zoo could be the hideout of some mad boy inventor. With its stored canoes and odd apparatus, Captain Mars's backyard has much the same feel, though less of the topography, of his daughter's hilltop in Yap.

When it rains on the zoo, the place changes. The frigate bird perks up in the downpour. The ducklings sprint toward the marine tanks, brake, and bill furiously in the long puddle of rainwater that appears instantaneously under the edge of the roof. Jojo the raven curses—in raven language, not in English. He hops down from his perch and takes refuge under the tree in his little aviary. Freddie the saltwater crocodile slips backward and out of sight into his pool. It is a surprise to see him go. Rain should have few terrors for a saltwater crocodile—maybe the smack of the first drops just surprises him. After a while, Freddie's nostrils reappear at the surface. His head emerges, and then the forward third of the crocodile slides out to enjoy the storm.

Hands outspread on her desk in Yap, Marjorie Cushing Falanruw leaned into the eyepieces of her stereoscope. Between her fingers was a red pencil. The desk top was covered with aerial photographs, on which she had delineated in red the various biomes—mangrove, agriforest, savannah. The aerial photograph is a new tool at the Yap Institute, and Margie is still refining her technique with it.

"We may be able to distinguish savannah that's predominantly grassy from savannah that's mostly ferns," she said, raising her eyes for a moment's rest. "By subtle differences in shading." She winced doubtfully at the difficulty of that and screwed her eyes back into the stereoscope.

The photos were not of Yap, she said, her voice refracting again from the tabletop; they were of the Palauan island of Angaur, where she recently had conducted a survey for the Forest Service.

"The Forest Service has a presence here?" I asked, surprised.

"I'm it," she said.

She had taken her daughter Leetun on that trip to Palau, she added, and in their spare time they had driven all over the big Palauan island of Babeldaob on a motorbike. It was a good thing for them, Margie thought. Leetun is twelve, a difficult, fractious age in Yap, as it is most everywhere else, and she and her mother had begun to grow apart. Until the dust and speed of that Palau trip, her mother's circus days as a motorcycle stuntgirl had been just a rumor—ancient history. When, in the course of the trip, Margie confessed to her daughter that for a time on Guam she had been a member of a motorcycle gang, Leetun's rising estimation of her mother soared. Later, visiting Guam and telling her grandfather Cushing about the little Honda motorbike her mom had raced over the dirt roads of Palau, Leetun got very excited. Captain Mars, remembering the big Harley-Davidsons of the family's old stunts, just smiled.

Recently, a severe local storm had hit Angaur, Margie continued, as her red pencil accented some features on the black-and-white Angaur below her. The storm had been sent by the Yapese. She explained that most Palauan expatriates in Yap hail from Angaur and from Peleliu, its neighbor island in southern Palau. Some of those expatriates had been misbehaving, and Yapese magicians had sent the storm to their homeland as punishment. Margie's inflection was flat. There was no telling from her voice whether or not she believed this bit of Yapese meteorology.

Lubuw, her four-year-old, was playing on the Yap Institute floor as his mother worked, and from time to time he asked a question. There was scarcely any lag time in her answers. She was preoccupied with the stereoscope, yet she succeeded in making the answers sound like conversation. It seemed to me that I had never heard that done before.

"What are you doing?" Lubuw asked.

Margie began keeping him informed. "Now mommy's drawing a red line around these mangroves," she said. She sketched a while. "Now mommy's drawing a red line around these coconut trees." Lubuw grew interested, and when Margie turned away to make some notes, he took over at the stereoscope.

"Why can't I see anything?" he wondered.

Her answer for the first time was several milliseconds slow in coming.

"Maybe it's because you're only using one eye." Lubuw could tell from the lag, or from an absent quality in his mother's voice, or from its misdirection, that she was not paying attention, and he looked over at her indignantly.

"Can Japanese people see anything through it?" he asked, louder. "Because their eyes go like this." With his fingers in the corners of his eyes, Lubuw showed how Japanese people's eyes go.

Margie laughed and returned to her writing. "I don't know," she said, "but I think they can probably see it perfectly well."

Practicing what Margie calls "indigenous science" has its ups and downs. In Yap and places like it, there is little work for local scientists. The Yap Institute was a full-time job for the first three years of its existence, then came a dry period with too few commissions and assignments. Today Margie works for the institute half time and spends the other half making a living. One of several money-making jobs is her forestry work. "For the Forest Service we're mapping vegetation," she says. "Their interest is agriforestry—food forests, multipurpose forests—and we're trying to study that. We're doing Forest Service fruit-bat studies, too—looking at the fruit bat as a forest product, and looking for information that will help us manage them. A while ago the Forest Service were bad guys, I think. Now I think they're trying to be good guys."

("The forest," Gautama Buddha says, in the Yap Almanac Calendar, "is a peculiar organism of unlimited kindness and benevolence that makes no demands for its sustenance and extends generously the products of its life activity: it affords protection to all beings, offering shade even to the axeman who destroys it.")

Margie's employment as staff ecologist for the Trust Territory Environmental Protection Board helped make ends meet and was a good thing while it lasted, but it ended explosively.

"I quit," she says. "I suppose it was over channel bombing. The channel bombing here in Yap, and on Kayangel Atoll in Palau, was supposed to be reviewed by me first, but it wasn't. It was gross. I had thought it was an art. I thought somebody went down and carefully placed a small charge. But what they did was use a whole lot of old bombs. They hired a lot of outer islanders to help, I guess because outer islanders wouldn't realize they were working with bombs. It was a peaceful day on the lagoon, nobody there. *Boom!* Instantly the place was full of people, birds, sharks. I wondered where they all came from."

("Hurt not the Earth, neither the sea nor the trees," God says, in Revelation 7:3 and the Yap Almanac Calendar.)

Channel bombing, the enlargement by explosives of natural passes through the reef, is intended to improve navigation. Reef scientists don't like it, for the reef's passes, with their good tidal circulation, are rich places biologically. The blast destroys corals and the concussion kills fish by the ton in the pass and beyond. Sharks, birds, and people come, attracted to the dead and dying fish. There is a big interspecific party, briefly, but afterward a mess.

"The water was yellow. There were depth charges among the bombs, and there is picric acid in the depth charges—that was why they were cleaning them up. I have this photograph of ninety-eight people in brilliant yellow water. I kept some of that pretty yellow water. It kept changing colors in the jar. I wound up with a little pile of black stuff on the bottom.

"But Steve Aetkin, the bomber, is a good guy. He didn't do every channel they asked him to. And I've worked happily since with the TTEPB. This place is too small for us all not to get along. It doesn't do any good to attack the TTEPB. They're all we've got."

Indigenous science in a place like Yap can be lonely. For a time, Margie had professional company in Michael McCoy, a Peace Corps fisheries scientist who co-founded the Yap Institute along with Sam Falanruw and Margie. But then McCoy became director of Marine Resources for the Federated States of Micronesia and he moved from Yap to the island of Ponape, the new nation's capital.

McCoy told me, when I spoke with him there, that he and Margie still meet occasionally at conferences on the mainland. They like to wear their "Yap Institute of Natural Science" pins, he said, partly from loyalty to the institute and partly for the confusion that the pins produce in their zoologist colleagues. None of the zoologists have heard of the Yap Institute. None of the zoologists have heard of Yap. (This, at least, is McCoy's interpretation: that the mainland scientists, squinting hard, are trying to decipher the pins. It is just as likely, I think, that the zoologists are trying to decipher McCoy himself. He is, like Melville's Queequeg, a large man "full of odd little parti-colored squares and triangles . . . and this arm of his tattooed all over with an interminable Cretan labyrinth of a figure," tattoos, in McCoy's case, from the island of Satawal.) From Margie Falanruw's point of view, of course, those rare reunions with McCoy on the mainland are not the same as having a co-worker in the field.

Indigenous science has its moments. Margie has the freedom to take her research anywhere she wants without angering some department head. She can study fruit bats or forestry or frogs. She has the support of a few good mainland men, like the botanist Raymond Fosberg. ("Until Fosberg came to Yap, I had a lot of botanical names floating in my head but nothing to connect them to. We're good for Fosberg. He has us out here in the field, and we have him and his stature. If you're going to be an indigenous scientist, you have got to work with top guys.") She has even had a few fiscal triumphs, like the Janss Foundation grant that permitted the Yap Institute to send her assistant, Loofen Saweyog, to school in Fiji. But if Margie is sore about anything, on balance, it is the way the world treats its indigenous scientists.

"I figured out recently that I could earn more as a tour guide, or by renting my Jeep, than I can as a scientist. That's discouraging. It's not good for your ego. We *need* local scientists. The way the system works now, outside scientists get the work. They do their studies and leave, and it has no impact on Yap. Sometimes they don't even send us a copy of the paper they did."

She gestured out the doorway, at the slope of Mimosa and solar experiments and the old Yap Institute bus.

"I'm not so bright," she said, "but I sure am *here* a lot."

One of the odd jobs Margie hustled for herself was a piece of literary work for the South Pacific Commission, an international outfit based in Nouméa, New Caledonia. Working half time for six months and aided by three Yapese artists, she produced the SPC's *Environmental Education Handbook* and an accompanying set of what she calls "environmental mini-lessons."

"I wanted to do it for Yap," she says, "but there were no takers. Art Dahl from the SPC came through, and he agreed to do it. The SPC sent me around to show it to kids. They sent out a memo: 'We've got an environmental-education consultant, if you want one.' I went to Samoa, Fiji, Tarawa, the Solomons, anyplace they would have me. In Tuvalo they said, 'We're not ready,' God bless 'em—people usually just put up with consultants.

"The kids loved the pictures. I was told by one group of educators that I had to make the pictures simpler—I had too much detail—and I felt bad. 'You've got dinosaurs,' they said. 'Kids in the Pacific won't know about dinosaurs.' In the Solomons, in a third-grade class I visited, they said, 'Oh, look, dinosaurs.'"

Margie's handbook is romantic.

"To the teacher," she begins. "This booklet is for you to use with your class. First, though, read it outside, under a tree, on a mountain-top or by the sea. Think about it."

Margie's handbook is lyrical.

"If there is a certain kind of seagrass in your lagoon, you may one day see a 'seagrass flowering festival,'" she writes. "This event seems timed to the tide. Male *Enhalus* flowers are shed into the water and float about like tiny white-skirted dancers. During a big 'seagrass flowering festival' there are thousands and thousands of tiny white flowers skimming along on the water. If you join them in their dance on the incoming tide, you find more and more swirling together as if they all were converging on little mounds of still-exposed sand for a big event. Eventually rising tide and winds will wash you ashore amid great drifts of slightly soiled dancers!"

That the ocean sometimes flowers was a new one on me, and I asked Margie about it.

"Oh, it's beautiful," she said. "I want to do a project on it with the kids. Get the students in on it, as a network of watchers. We already put an article on it in *The New Nation*. I thought it would be nice to put it in a children's magazine, so that if anyone did research on the flowers, he'd have to refer to it.

"As the tide rises, there are little currents that occur because of high spots and low spots in the lagoon, and they concentrate the flowers in certain places. I went out with the kids one day. I'd seen the flowers before, but never like that. You put your hand through, and some of them stick. Like snow? I don't really know what snow is like, that much. *Light snow*? Confetti? I don't know what instigates it. That's one of the things we've got to do. I'm surprised there isn't any more published on it—it should happen wherever there are big beds of seagrass. I mentioned it to an expert from Alaska, and he was interested, but he didn't know that much. That's why I'd like to get the kids to write it up. I'd like to set up a station here to study it."

The handbook shamelessly reflects the author's loves and biases. Its section on leatherback turtles, for example, is much longer than its sections on other sea turtles. "Leatherback turtles are different from all other sea turtles," the handbook states. "They are a very old kind of turtle and they don't have a bony back shell. These turtles are not usually eaten. They are rare because they have only a few places to nest, and in those places their eggs are taken by people. Some people need these eggs for food, but most eat them because of the mistaken idea that they make them more manly. This is not true."

Of sea turtles in general, the handbook advises, "Use turtles only in traditional ways. Sea turtles are too important to islanders to be shared with the rest of the world. By selling turtles, people break tradition. The money they get can't even buy much other meat to replace the turtle meat they sold."

The handbook is full of exclamation points. "It all starts with sunshine! Use people power! Let's pass on this good life to our children! Of the 105 known species to have become extinct since 1600, 97 were island forms! The rarest sea turtle is the Leatherback, a beautiful animal that can grow to 1,200 pounds or 540 kg! If we are wise and take care of turtles today, our children and their children will have a wonderful way to turn seagrass into turtle meat in the future! We must control our own population growth! There's just not enough to go around! Perhaps 20 million people will starve to death this year! Next time you look at a plant, breathe in the oxygen it is producing and think about what's happening! See how many useful things you and your friends can make out of junk! You can make a slow steam cooker using sunpower! If we make a way to catch this water vapour, we can turn salt water into fresh water! Then turn the cooker toward the sunset and put on your supper pot! Then open the bag carefully and taste the water that has collected on the bottom! Best of all, wind is free! Turn it to the wind and watch it spin! Wouldn't it be good if we could use sunpower to cool! We can! Next, start carrying out your plan! Good luck, the future of the world is up to you!"

The handbook is full of things to do. It tells you how to make a simple solar water heater from a length of black hose. If you want to build something more sophisticated, it provides an address in Quebec to write for plans. The handbook tells you how to make a centrifuge from a bottle and a piece of string. It tells you how to make a microscope from a penlight bulb, eight small screws, one big nail, a small piece of mirror, a ninety-millimeter length of wire, a strip of sheet metal, some wood, some black paint, a glass slide or piece of cellophane tape, and some glue—either wood glue, model airplane glue, glass cement, or Oceania's traditional cure-all, bread-fruit sap and lime.

"That microscope of yours," I asked her once. "Does it really work?"

"The kids on Yap prefer it to big, thousand-power, expensive scopes," she replied. "Those fancy scopes are too delicate. The humidity is high in the tropics, so you get fungus, and the thing gets frosted, and it has all those knobs. The homemade kind, you can do anything with them. The guy who taught me to make one used it in his orchid research."

The first thing the beginning microscopist should do with his new scope, the handbook suggests, is "Catch the smallest animal you can find. It shouldn't be any bigger than a tiny ant. A very small head louse is a good thing to look at." The microscopist is advised how to adjust the mirror, then told how to roll the big nail back and forth until the louse comes into focus. "Draw what you see. Did you know that head lice have such hairy legs? If you get a small transparent one, you may be able to see its stomach moving as it digests the blood it sucks from our heads!"

The head louse is a handy insect for children of the tropics, surely, but I wondered about its featured role in the handbook. How would the louse go over in the new Pacific nations, with all their developing pride? "Did you have any reservations about the head louse?" I asked.

"We had a picture of a head louse, but we took that out. A Peace Corps photographer took the picture through the microscope lens. Another thing we did was make a little movie theater with a big cardboard box. We projected the louse. They're neat animals. You can see the intestines."

"But you had reservations?"

"I thought about these proper British places, like Fiji, but I put it in anyway. If they want to take it out, they can. A louse is easy to look at. If you don't get the right thing under the mike, you're not impressed by it."

"Spend one hour, alone, in a forest, savannah, mangrove, reef, or other wild place," Margie suggests in mini-lesson 25. "In your notebook write where you went and what impressed you."

I went southward with my notebook along the mangrove shoreline of Tomil Harbor. What impressed me, first, were the tin cans and old Clorox bottles the tide had deposited among the mangroves at the edge of town. That was not, I was certain, the kind of impression Margie meant. She is interested in flotsam, but only as something to clean up. ("Drink coconuts instead of cola," her handbook advises. It praises the State of Yap for its tax on nonreturnable cans, and it shows drawings of all the useful things—bailers, funnels, planters—that can be made from old Clorox bottles.)

To put distance between me and the town litter, I took to the road. As I walked, I watched for a likely patch of mangroves. I was not interested in the deep mangrove swamp, with its gloom, obscure plopping sounds, and thick mosquitoes. For my hour in the mangroves I wanted forest where sunlight penetrated and a view of the sea.

The road was dirt, a simple bulldozer track through the forest. It led me past high, abandoned house platforms of stone. The wood and thatch of the houses themselves were long gone, but the fitted-stone foundations remained, the cobbling on top still perfectly level. Saplings had grown up through the cobbles and turned aside a stone or two, but the rest were in place. At the platform corners sat the backward-leaning, smooth-tapering, pointed little monoliths that Yapese men used for backrests.

The meanders of the bulldozer road intersected, again and again, with the meanders of ancient stone paths. The old paths were much the narrower, built to accommodate a single file of humans, not a machine. The rounded flagstones had been fitted skillfully, and time and the forest had failed to pop loose more than a few. Down the middle of the flagstones ran a darker path within the path, a trail worn smooth by century upon century of bare feet. The inner path had a sheen like glacier polish. The glacier here had been

at body temperature, a brisk stream of callused soles. The forest
grew thick, all vines and big tropical leaves, and the eye could seldom follow the paths for more than a few dozen yards, but they
ended, I knew from having followed similar paths by foot, in more
clusters of abandoned house platforms. From those abandoned villages, new paths would ramify, leading off through farther forests to
still more abandoned villages. The inhabitants of modern Yap are
survivors camped on the ruins of a grander and more populous past.

I found a sandy point of land where the belt of mangroves was
less than thirty feet deep and dappled by sunlight. I sat, opened my
notebook, and set my pocket watch on the sand beside me. It was
3:00 in the afternoon.

At 3:02, a mosquito landed on my arm. I waved it off.

At 3:04, a small dark bird with a vermilion hood, a silent flier,
landed in the mangrove canopy near me. It looked down at me,
preened, and then flew silently on.

At 3:05, there was a splash near the base of one mangrove
trunk. I could not tell what made it.

At 3:07, a second mosquito landed. I slapped and missed.

At 3:08, I gave up trying to record my mangrove impressions
this way—in order and by the clock. The impressions were coming
too fast for that, no matter which direction I looked. The beach
under me was layered. Topmost were shells—clam shells, snail
shells, cones—for the most part whole or only slightly broken up
by the surf. Under the shell layer was coarse sand, and lowermost
was fine sand. I had never studied a Micronesian beach profile
quite so closely, never having had a reason. The beach sloped down
to the lagoon, and land and sea met placidly, the lagoon's wavelets
so stilled by the breakwater of the mangroves that around the landward trunks the water was pond flat. Many of the mangrove
trunks were riven, as if by lightning. Actual bolts could not have
struck so often in one grove. The lightning here, then, was all in
the genes of the mangroves. Reflected light danced on the under-
sides of the mangrove leaves. Birds called from deeper in the forest.
A single mangrove branch creaked, high-pitched and querulous.
The boom of the surf sounded distantly from the barrier reef.

The riven trunks of the mangrove forest were rising up
through a lesser forest of pneumatophores, the specialized vertical

roots through which mangrove trees respire. Seaward, the pneumatophores grew thick as a bed of nails. In places, they crowded so upon one another that I could not see the water for them. Each breathing root was conical yet gnarled, and collectively they looked, I thought, like an army of hooded gnome-soldiers advancing on the beach. A small fish, a halfbeak, swam into the gnome ranks, just under the surface, then turned and swam back toward the lagoon. Pop-eyed blennies—mudskippers—moved among the gnomes, flipping from gnome shoulder to gnome shoulder. They propped themselves, bodies arched, on their stubby pectoral fins, one mudskipper to a pneumatophore, and they watched me with bulging eyes. I stood suddenly and took a big step seaward. The mudskippers scattered backward into the gnome ranks.

Approaching land, the pneumatophore army withered. As the gnomes marched up on the beach, their ranks thinned and the individual pneumatophores grew stunted. They attacked, feebly, the ramparts of a long windrow of dead eelgrass. A few breached the line, but above, on the shell-sand beach, they disappeared entirely.

I turned my attention to the windrow of eelgrass. Here and there along it lay peculiar woody batons. They were shaped like attenuated bowling pins with points at either end. Clearly they were mangrove productions—the wood looked mangrovy—but I could not imagine what part of the tree they came from, nor could I guess their function. I had never seen them before, or I had never noticed. I decided to ask Margie about them.

Not all the shells on the beach had reached their angles of repose. At wide intervals, snail shells of various species were wandering about with an odd jiggly motion. Each time I approached one of these motile shells, it would jiggle one last time, then lie still. Inside, I knew from experience, were hermit crabs. These were born-again snail shells. They were reincarnated, repossessed.

"Remove a hermit crab from its shell," Margie suggests in mini-lesson 6. "This can be done in two ways."

The first way requires a moist sponge and a heated object, of which I had neither. The second requires a drop of water and a steady hand, and this was the method I attempted. Going to my lips, like a spitball artist loading up, I doctored the crab, placing the drop at the top edge of the shell just above the opening, as Margie advises. I held the shell *very still*—emphasis Margie's—and I waited.

"When the crab comes out, grasp it behind the head and pull it gently from the shell." I did so. It is necessary to grasp quickly, for a hermit crab has quick reflexes and the last thing it wants is to be grasped behind the head. Pulling the crab gently out, I saw with a shock that the long, soft abdomen was covered with pink, spiral clusters of roe. Margie had not warned me about that. I felt guilty but continued the experiment, setting the crab down on the beach as instructed. The crab huddled there so miserably that I quickly returned her shell to her. At first she refused to take it. She no longer trusted this house that had betrayed her. Then reluctantly she grasped the forward edge with her claws and front legs, hesitated again, then backed herself in, flipped the shell over, and jiggled away.

I removed a second crab. This one had no roe and it refused to take its shell back. I pursued it down the beach, importuning, but it wanted no part of me or anything I had touched.

I had learned, already, the main thing about hermit crabs: There is in Nature no animal more dichotomous. From the thorax forward the hermit is all chitinous armor and overmuscled crushing claws; from the abdomen back it is all flaccid and pale and vulnerable. Protected by its shell, it is feisty and irritable—crablike. Naked on a beach, it is as dispirited and unheroic as a grub evicted from its log. The crab's hindmost pair of legs, modified for holding on inside the shell, look white and devolutionary, like appendages on some blind cave animal. The shame of a hermit crab, when sunlight strikes its secret, is deeper than any shame humans know. In the affairs of men there is no embarrassment rosier.

I removed a third crab. As I held it in my fingers, houseless, its long, prehensile abdomen searched and spiraled backward in the air, deep into the convolutions of the shell it wished were there. I could *see* that shell, just as one sees the nonexistent wall a good mime leans against. I set the crab down on the beach, and it backed away abjectly. It tried to back downward as well, but matter—the beach's sand and old broken shells—resisted. In its chagrin the crab was trying to violate the laws of physics. It was attempting through pure wishfulness to back out of existence entirely.

I continued extracting crabs, then returning their houses to them. Micronesian hermits come in all colors, I can report, from a dark purple to a pale ivory. Their roe comes in several colors too, red, pink, salmon, yellow. Mini-lesson 6 suggests a number of hermit-crab experiments, but I was happy just extracting and I never got around to them. In one experiment, I was supposed to place a naked hermit in a tray with several empty shells. "Does it go into the first shell it comes to, or does it make a careful selection?" The experiment was not really necessary, for I was familiar enough by now with hermit shame to know the answer: The crab goes into the first shell. I was supposed to place several naked crabs in the tray with a single shell and see what happened. I could imagine. I was supposed to run hermit races. In the races I could urge my crab onward with words, but nothing more. If my crab lost, I was to discuss the reasons with the child who owned the winner.

"For example," Margie hints, "'my crab has too heavy a shell to run fast, but the heavy shell protects it from being crushed by big crabs.' Or, 'My crab lost because it didn't move. It thinks it's better to stay still and look like a stone so a passing bird won't peck at it.'"

Both of these sound, to me, like arguments no Oceanic child will ever attempt after losing a hermit-crab race. The whole notion of a hermit race sounds doubtful. A number of entries are left at the starting gate, apparently, where they hide from passing birds and pretend to be stones. More than a few of the games Margie has invented for the handbook will never work, in my opinion. I suggested this once to her, and she cheerfully agreed.

I might have undressed all the hermits at the beach, had not my crabbing taken me down to the windrow of eelgrass. I picked up one of those odd batons, the double-pointed mangrove bowling pins lying there. I realized suddenly what it was. It was a pneumatophore, an uprooted one—the whole thing. With a living, breathing pneumatophore, the root's tip is all you see, protruding from mud or water. I had assumed that the girth remained roughly the same under the mud. It does not. A pneumatophore swells dramatically just under the surface, for some reason, and then, just before it meets its collecting system, it tapers off sharply again.

"Search through drift seaweed," mini-lesson 25 suggests. "How many kinds of living things can you find there? Drift seaweed offers hiding places and protection from sun, wind, and birds. It provides food and hunting grounds for many creatures. Just think of the story you could write about what goes on here!"

That sounded like the assignment for me. I found a spider shell, and with its long tines I began combing through the windrow of eelgrass. The combing was uncomfortable, for I was wearing cut-off jeans, and the shell beach was sharp under my bare knees. From the windrow I selected two mangrove leaves, big and leathery, and I knelt on those. Mini-lesson 25 says nothing about mangrove kneepads; I offer the idea as my own contribution.

The windrow was only a foot wide and several inches deep, yet it made an ecological province to be reckoned with, for in length it was nearly interminable, contouring the points of land to the north and south and going on to encircle, for all I knew, the entire archipelago of Yap. The eelgrass in the top layers of the windrow was sun-dried, light-colored, and deserted. I found nothing alive inside. The tines of my spider shell rousted a single amphipod—a sand flea. It hopped for its life and then skittered away, like a dog trying to turn a corner on a waxed floor. Margie had promised many creatures, and I had an uneasy moment: Maybe Margie was wrong.

Bending closer to the windrow, I combed down through the sun-dried layers to where the eelgrass was still wet, slick, dense, and dark. It was here, in its depths, that the windrow lived. I discovered a fluorescent-orange mite. The mite was tiny, and I would have missed it entirely except for the striking contrast its color made against the dull, kelpy brown of the wet eelgrass. The mite had antennae that were just discernible when I held it close to my eye. It had a stretchable, questing body, like an earthworm's, yet it also had legs. The legs were too small to see, actually, but I could deduce them from the mite's motion. Digging down, I came upon more of the mites in dense concentrations. They hated sunlight and fled deeper into the windrow's dark. The smallest of the mites were nearly white—the Day-Glo orange seemed to come with age. Was it true fluorescence? Perhaps it was, and perhaps in the darkness the mites found one another that way.

The tines of my spider shell disrupted a gathering of sand fleas. They hopped and skittered away. I came upon ants. One species was small and black, built something like a carpenter ant. Another species was new to me, unlike any ant I had ever seen and more beautiful, with legs so long that I mistook the first of its kind for a spider. The reddish abdomen was elegant and tear-shaped, the head mantislike and regal. If the black ants were the pygmies of the windrow, then these new ants were the Watusi. My hour in the mangroves was up. On my own time, now, I dug deeper into the sea smell and dank secrets of the eelgrass.

Margie stood at the head of the classroom, addressing a scattered audience of Yapese schoolteachers.

"In the old days, if we took *wel*, turtles, they went to the chief," she said, "and you couldn't take turtles just any time. Now people are talking about anybody should be able to take *wel*, any time. That way, pretty soon no more turtles."

She forced a laugh, a nervous habit she inherited from her mother. Laughing nervously, Marjorie Bailey Cushing and Marjorie Bailey Cushing Falanruw, the two former high-wire artists, sound exactly the same. The Yapese teachers smiled along with Margie— out of politeness, I thought. They did not want her laughing alone.

The schoolhouse roof was bare corrugated metal, steep-pitched and lofty. The beams up there were natural logs. The wall paint, an institutional green, was chipped up high near the beams and smudged down low by small passing hands. Ebbing out to recess, the hands in their multitude had left a band as straight and true as the one the tide leaves on mangrove aerial roots, or on the coral riprap of a jetty. Above that line, the walls were bare, except for a few spelling posters. Some of the spelling was Yapese, some Neo-Yapese. "Waay," said one poster, and its drawing showed a betel-nut purse. "Kaarroo," said a second, and it showed a car. "Fook," said a third, and it showed a fork. The desks and benches, scaled down for elementary schoolchildren, jammed the teachers' knees and jammed my own. Here and there on the desk tops the children had carved figures. They were unlike the scratchings that American schoolchildren leave on desk tops. The Yapese marks were simple, conventionalized, and unfamiliar, like symbols from some alien astrology.

"Cash," Margie said. "Fossil energy. Non-biodegradable products. Big technology. Some of it is nice. It's nice to run around in cars. But there are also problems with it. Pollution. When people concentrate too much on money, it's not so good. The world runs on sun—that's our money."

With this lecture, the lessons of the *Environmental Handbook* were returning home to Yap. Margie had toured the South Pacific with the handbook, testing the ideas and drawings on the children of far islands; now it had come full circle and she was asking the Yapese teachers for help in adapting it to local classrooms.

Despite all the practice of her Pacific tour, she seemed ill at ease at the front of the class. She has never learned to like lecturing. ("I'd much rather do a workshop than a talkshop.") Part of her unease that day, she would admit to me later, was in having to speak so much English, out of politeness to me. Part of it too, I suspect, was uneasiness with the role. She was teaching the sensible island life to the people who invented it, and the author of the *Ethnoichthyology of Yap* would have seen the irony in that better than anyone. "Maintaining traditions that work," she said. "This is where all of you have to help. If the old way doesn't quite fit, we have to fix it so it does fit."

There were nine male teachers in the audience and a single woman. All were dressed informally. Several of the men were shirtless, and one, a young teacher from a small village, wore only a red loincloth. The lone woman teacher, who was in her late middle age, was Margie's most animated listener. The woman's teeth were blackened from chewing betel, a mark of eccentricity or stubbornness, for today most Yapese use Japanese-brand abrasive toothpastes to erase the stain. The woman teacher wore glasses on a chain, like some sort of Republican dowager—or like that dowager's nightmare of herself. Her glasses were dime-store glasses and the chain was the sort that the U.S. Army uses for dog tags. Whenever Margie said something agreeable, the woman teacher would glance up from her knitting and grunt "Ummm-ummm," in support.

The woman looked up while Margie sketched some quick population graphs on the blackboard.

"Medicines keep people from dying so much," Margie said, "and pretty soon we'll have too many people. We've got to start teaching about that." The woman grunted approvingly before Margie had finished her thought, and there were murmurs of assent from the men. It surprised me anew that the Yapese, a people so savagely depopulated by European diseases, should be so amenable to population-control arguments. Margie Falanruw's own interest in the population issue owes, she thinks, to a former professor, Raymond Coles, and to her circus childhood in the teeming Philippines. These Yapese teachers had known neither. They had grown up in an archipelago of abandoned villages and untraveled stone highways. Yap's depopulation has been too recent, perhaps, for old Yapese cultural attitudes about population to have changed, and those old attitudes were stern: in pre-contact times, human numbers on Yap were controlled by abortifacients, infanticide, suicidal voyages, and war. Or perhaps the explanation lies more in the common-sense perceptions of individual modern-day Yapese. When all the land you know amounts to thirty-nine square miles, the notion of terrestrial finiteness, and the need to control human fertility on it, must be easier to grasp.

Margie passed out some breadfruit she had solar-dried in a single day, and she followed that with some solar-dried cacao. The woman teacher was impressed. She gestured with the plastic bag of cacao at the young teacher sitting next to her. She described the virtues of this quick-dried cacao in emphatic Yapese. The young man was not at all inclined to argue. He turned the cacao bag over dutifully in his hands, then passed it on.

"One job we have today is to translate these concepts into Yapese," Margie said. "I really don't know some of them, and I need help on this." The teachers were willing, and as they warmed to the translation, the class ceased being a lecture; it became a workshop, just as Margie had wanted.

"Sun" was easy to translate. "Sunlight" was not. The teachers' ancestors had seen no need, apparently, to distinguish the sun from its light. The teachers debated the matter until one stocky man in his forties announced, authoritatively, *"Roan e yal'."* The teachers moved on. The English word "Nature" became *Ba' nan ni kepii ekan,* "Something that gave spirit." There was no agreement, oddly, on a word for atoll. The Yapese phrase "Not high island" was the best the teachers could do. For "fossil fuels" there was no good translation. The teachers all realized this from the start and quickly moved on to the next word. For "bulldozer technology" the word *babiy*, which originally meant "pig" and now also means "bulldozer," was deemed sufficient. For "strong chemicals" the teachers agreed that the Yapese word *f'lay*, which is like our "medicine" but broader, would be good, or the Neo-Yapese word *clorox*.

"We don't completely want to go back to the old style, because it's hard," Margie told the teachers. "What do we do? Nobody knows. But we have to start looking. And in this course that's what we do. We're on a voyage into a better island in the future. What's involved in this future for the Pacific? We don't know. But we've got to seek. The Bible says, 'Seek and ye shall find.'"

The teachers laughed. Were they amused at hearing Margie quote the Bible, or was it simply pleasure at hearing a phrase in English that was actually old and familiar? Margie laughed along with them, and then she finished.

"We've got to seek," she said again.

Lubuw Falanruw stood outside the door of the new Yap Institute office. He looked mournful. At his shoulder was the solar dehydrator/oven that Margie calls "the Hotbox." At his feet, moving hardly at all, was a huge toad.

The sky poured down solar energy, but not, for the moment, on Lubuw. His sister, Leetun, stood between the boy and the light. Leetun was developing fast, as girls do in the tropics. She was well on her way to womanhood, she towered over him, and she was angry. She had sent his day into temporary eclipse.

"You got that frog, you eat it," she said.

"Boom Boom got it," Lubuw admitted, sadly. Boom Boom is Lubuw's nickname.

"You eat it, or get sick on it," said Leetun.

Harsh punishment, Leetun! This toad at Lubuw's feet was not a native species; it was the West Indian toad, introduced to Yap in the Japanese occupation, and it had adrenal glands in its head. If Lubuw had eaten the toad, as instructed, he would have died in hideous convulsions.

The Hotbox, the device that completed this little tableau, had been engineered, and for the most part built, by Lubuw's uncle on Guam, the celebrated castaway Frank Cushing, Jr. The Hotbox rests on a round table that revolves on rollers to follow the sun. The interior is lined with crumpled beer cans that have been painted black. Two sides and the top are drilled with holes, and the holes are plugged by a thicket of corks. Removed and inserted in various combinations, the corks regulate air flow and temperature. Margie has got the Hotbox up to 275 degrees. She hopes, with improvements, to raise that to 350 degrees.

I found her inside the office at her desk. "What happened to the toad?" I asked.

"My son put him in the Hotbox." She laughed and cringed simultaneously. "I feel so bad. By the time we let him out, his metabolism was really jumping. I didn't know what to say, except, 'How would you like to be in the Hotbox?'"

Lubuw's mother turned back to her work at the stereoscope. I began looking through the fruit-bat files. Several hours passed.

In the early afternoon, Lubuw entered the office carrying the toad. The boy was very excited. The toad looked considerably revived. Lubuw's small fingers were pinched in behind its ribs, and the pressure may have contributed to its demonstration of liveliness.

"Frog is feeling better!" Lubuw announced. He looked at us, from one to the other. Our faces failed to register sufficient appreciation. *"Frog is feeling better!"* he yelled at us.

I left the new Yap Institute office. Heading downhill, I paused beside the outrigger paddling canoe stored beneath. The canoe was too long for the new Yap Institute's shadow, and the prow protruded into sunshine. The canoe came, Margie had said, from Ifaluk, an outer atoll in the Yap system and a former tributary of the central Yap cluster. Her husband, Sam Falanruw, had brought it to Yap as a gift for Lubuw. In modern Yap, Lubuw's canoe is one of a kind. There were once many outrigger canoes in Yap, small paddling canoes like this one and big sailing canoes built on the same lines, but almost all were destroyed by the Japanese during their occupation. The Yapese wanderlust made administration difficult, and the canoes were scuttled to prevent the indigenes from forever sailing around to other islands. Sam's father, big Lubuw, owned the last large sailing outrigger on Yap, and Sam and Margie would like him to teach little Lubuw navigation.

Lubuw's canoe is painted red and black, colors traditional to the canoes of Ifaluk and its neighbor islands in the central Carolines. Lubuw's prow ornament, like the prow ornaments of all central Carolinian canoes, is V-shaped. The V represents, most Carolinians agree, the forked tail of the frigate bird, but the design is so ancient that no one can say for sure. The carving is stylized, simple, and clean. Its proportions are classic, like those of the Doric column or the Attic amphora or the leaf-bladed Masai spear. A day came, long ago in the history of Ifaluk, when the island's carvers realized that their prows had achieved inevitability, and there was nothing else to add. The wooden frigate's tail is more beautiful than any Western artifact on the hilltop. It is far better to look at than Margie's Jeep, or the schoolbus of the original Yap Institute, or the corrugated roof of the Falanruw Self-sufficient Home. It looks better than the Hotbox. The Hotbox has no evolutionary history to speak of and has not proceeded even halfway down the road to inevitability. The canoe's prow is sculpture of the kind that invites touch. I reached out, as I always seemed to in passing the canoe, and ran my hand over the ornament one last time.

The heat shimmered over the savannah, but under the airport thatch the shade was cool. We four travelers leaned back against the benches. Before us, bisecting Yap's brackeny, gently rolling highlands, ran the red dirt road that had brought us here. Behind us was the tarmac of the airfield. The plane waited, a twin-engine prop, its nose high. The forest bordering the far edge of the field trembled in the heat waves rising off the tarmac.

The airport felt deserted.

On a regular flight day, when the jet is due, the shade under the thatch is crowded. Old Yapese men and women sit and talk. Two or three Coast Guardsmen from the LORAN station stand awaiting the arrival of a new technician or a shipment of parts. Outer-island women in *lava-lavas* shift the babies on their hips, chew betel, and await some kinsman returning from an odyssey to the outside world. The airport's tin-walled betelnut stall is open for business then, the windows jammed with old Budweiser cartons cut in half and packed with green clusters of nuts. Today, an off-day, only four of us flying, the stall windows were empty and the benches in the waiting area looked long and bare.

From my daypack I took the square of Tahitian-chestnut cake Margie had given me as a going-away present. She had baked it in her modification of the Lorena stove. (Margie's Oceanic version burns coconut husks.) I was hungry, but the package looked too nice to open. That can be a drawback of food wrapped in banana leaf by Micronesian women and bound with sennit—it resists consumption.

"Like the root of the Tahitian chestnut" was the Yapese term for seahorse, I remembered, from Margie's fish index. That added a dimension to the cake. I was beginning to cross-reference this place, Yap—the cake in my hand, the phrase in my head. I tucked the cake back inside my daypack.

It was 2:45, half an hour past flight time. We were waiting for a medevac patient, a seaman who had suffered a stroke on a tanker passing Yap. He was now in the hospital in Colonia, we understood; when the doctors were finished with him, they would send him up to the airfield, and he would fly with us to Guam.

The pilot, who was on the phone, hung up and rejoined us. It would be another hour at least, he announced. In fact, it would be more than two hours. At 5:00, a dust cloud would appear in the distance, where the straight savannah road met the horizon. The cloud would approach very fast. At its center we would discern, first, the white police Datsun generating it, and moments later the two occupants. The police car would grow big much too quickly, and we would laugh, in spite of ourselves, at the crazy speed. If the seaman's stroke failed to kill him, then a heart attack would. At the gate, the policeman would brake hard. The seaman would climb out, an old black man from Barbados. He would give us a great white smile and stride spryly toward the plane. He would seem fine, except for his voice, which would be whispery. I would wonder, following him up the plane stairs, what this native of the Lesser Antilles made of the western Caroline betel chewers he had fallen among. I would be unable to ask, for his accent would prove too thick for me.

But that dust cloud and its passenger were hours away still. For now the savannah shimmered. The red dirt road ran straight and empty to the horizon.

The benchmate to my right was an American salesman, Dan. I had seen his face here and there in Micronesia. I had not until now learned his name, but the face had stuck, as a white face will in the islands. We had both been tenants at the Rai View Hotel. We had eaten surreal meals together at opposite ends of the stark linoleum checkerboard of the Rai View dining floor, and we had nodded on passing in the upstairs hall. We now discussed the things white men discuss in the tropics. Dan told me about competitors of his who went by different names in different archipelagos. Sometimes a salesman's name would change only slightly between archipelagos, sometimes entirely. Dan himself represented many lines, he said, but his name remained the same, independent of geography. Dan knew at least two men under indictment in the States who had sought refuge in Micronesia. The FBI couldn't touch them, he claimed. He knew a third man, a bank robber whom the FBI had tracked to a small island. The federal agents had negotiated with the robber and had struck a deal with him. They paid his way back to Guam, where he had a few days of vacation at FBI expense, then they allowed him to go to work and pay the bank off in installments.

Outside in the sun, as the salesman spoke, a Yapese boy in a bright-red loincloth emerged from the forest on the far side of the airfield and crossed the runway on his bicycle. He pedaled past the tin-walled customs shed, then off down the red dirt road. There was a strong hint in the boy's example, I realize now, but I was too dull at the time to take it. I turned to agree with something Dan had said, and when I looked down the road again, the boy was gone. He must have turned off somewhere well this side of the horizon. The red dirt road stood empty again. The savannah shimmered.

Dan and I discussed the books we could write on Micronesia—or, since he had me at a disadvantage, the modest books I had actually written and the incredible book Dan could write someday, if he ever found the time. We discussed the women of various archipelagos. Dan remembered, then, where he had seen one of my books—in the possession of a certain maid in a certain rundown hotel on a certain island. He mentioned her name, and we discovered we had a close mutual friend.

The pilot, returning from the phone again, gave us a revised departure time, 4:15. I looked at my watch. It was 3:15. We had another hour.

Suddenly I remembered mini-lesson 25 and its final suggestion: "Spend one hour, alone, in a forest, savannah, mangrove, reef, or other wild place." *In a savannah,* I thought, and I stood.

There is another handbook passage that applies, as well. "Go for a walk or swim in some wild place," says mini-lesson 32. "Just enjoy it. When you grow to be an adult and things start to get you down, nothing will lift you up like a walk or swim in a wild place! If you appreciate wilderness now, you will be able to turn to it in time of need." I did not require a mini-lesson to tell me this—I had discovered it on my own, long ago—but from time to time I need reminding.

I told Dan and the others that I thought I'd take a walk. When the pilot looked unhappy, I promised I would be back in time.

Fifty yards down the red dirt road, I pulled off my shirt. I walked on with the big friendly weight of the sun on my shoulders. I passed an old Japanese anti-aircraft gun by the roadside. Its breech was green with moss and ferns. Just beyond the gun, the Yapese boy in the red loincloth reappeared on his bicycle. He pedaled out on the road, returning from some lateral errand, and as he passed me, going back toward the airfield, he smiled and raised his eyebrows. In Micronesia, raised eyebrows are an affirmative and a greeting. I imagined now, in the high arch of the boy's brows, a look of complicity. It was like a wink, I thought, though mechanically, of course, it was the opposite. We two knew what was happening, the wink said. We two knew where. It was out here under the sun on the savannah, not back in the shade by the tarmac. I raised my eyebrows in reply—I raised the boy and called him.

The savannah was a tight-woven, chest-high wall of low-growing ferns, herbs, sedges, and vines. The tallest things in it were fifteen-foot pandanus palms, which dotted the landscape at wide intervals. Finding a break in the tight-growing wall, a gate out into the savannah, I stopped. At my feet was a stone. I turned it over. Turning stones is a bug- and salamander-hunting technique I learned on my home continent, and it worked here too, for in the pit of reddish volcanic earth beneath this island stone sat a frog. The frog must have been hiding at the edge of the stone, then fallen in when I lifted. It was small and perfect. You could have covered it with a nickel—not one of those two-ton Yapese nickels, but the small American kind. Its back was patterned in camouflage greens, and a scattering of intense rust-orange dots ran down the spine. It was just as Margie had promised. She had not promised this specific frog, but she had promised discoveries like it. I set the stone back in place. I admired the frog for a moment in my palm, then placed it beside the stone. The frog was disillusioned, just as hermit crabs are when you violate the small whorled castles of their shells. The frog no longer trusted this stone and it hopped off into the bush.

I entered the bush myself. Thirty feet in, I could no longer see the road. I was surrounded by savannah. I was happy and excited. My excitement was all out of proportion to what I was doing, I suppose, but for me this was all new country. I had driven in Jeeps through highland savannah on other Micronesian islands, but I had never walked far, and about this Yapese savannah in particular I knew nothing at all. The excitement had a lot to do, too, with my escape from the airfield. The savannah was so much better than the tarmac. The sky was blue. The savannah greens were luminous under the Micronesian sun, which is the brightest sun on earth. It was like being heir all your life to a great empire, and finally discovering it.

There were strange, round, streamless pools in the savannah, just off the road. I could not imagine how they had formed until I remembered the nearness of the airfield and that Japanese anti-aircraft gun. The airfield was Japanese once, and the holes had to be American bomb craters. The savannah was slowly reclaiming them, and that was good to see. The first bomb pool was muddy and opaque. The second was clear, but the vegetation bordering it was too thick for me to fight my way down to the shore. In the third, as Margie promised, I saw a water beetle. It was a species new to me. It dove and headed for the bottom.

I spotted a pitcher plant hidden in some ferns. The pitcher's tough, tendrily stalk was woven inextricably in amongst the ferns. I hefted the pitcher and knew from its weight that there was rain-water inside. I poured, and the contents were clear. I saw a second pitcher plant—they were growing all around, I realized, once you began to look for them. I poured, and the contents of the second pitcher were tea-colored. I raised the lid of a third pitcher and looked inside. The rosy inner throat was spotted attractively and as smooth as glass. The color and the spots were to attract insects, I guessed, and the smoothness was to keep them from climbing out again. At the pitcher's bottom I saw what appeared to be a cluster of red-brown eggs. The cluster would not pour, so with my fingers I vivisected the plant. Its green walls made a sound like paper tearing. The eggs turned out to be forty-odd miniature snails. The snails were so tiny that I could not see opercula or feelers. I could not be sure of the *absence* of opercula or feelers, either, and I had no way of telling whether anyone was home.

I opened a fourth plant. Inside was the dark, waterlogged hulk of a long-dead dragonfly, and around it wiggled dozens of pale mosquito larvae. Adult dragonflies hunt adult mosquitoes, I remembered, and dragonfly nymphs hunt the larvae. Could it have been that this dragonfly, nostalgic, craving the flavors of its previous metamorphic incarnation, had crawled down into the pitcher plant? If so, the wigglers dancing around its corpse were having the last laugh.

I opened a fifth plant. There was dark muck at the bottom. I sniffed the muck and knew the smell instantly, though I had not smelled it for at least twenty years. It was the smell of the bowl in which a child keeps green terrapin turtles and which the child has been negligent in cleaning. It was a green and guilty smell. I opened a sixth plant. At the bottom was a virulent-green algal sludge presided over by a single specimen of that tiny red-brown snail. I opened a seventh and final plant. (It was unnecessary to open any more of them, for it was obvious now that each would contain a new surprise.) The liquid inside the last pitcher was straight rainwater, clear and odorless, and in it floated a minuscule and delicate moth.

I wandered until my hour in the savannah had run out, then began working my way cross country back to the airfield. All the while I listened for the siren of a medevac ambulance, or for the sound of the airplane's propellers cranking up. The moment I heard them, I intended to run.

I came upon a marsh. The shallow marsh water was spiked

with wide-spaced clumps of grasses. The grass bunches ran south-ward nearly to the horizon, which was very close—a slight land-swell two hundred yards away. Two small cumulus clouds stood just above the landswell, and the grass-dimpled surface of the marsh reflected those cumuli and the blue bowl of the Yapese sky. It was a perfect wilderness—Yap before Man—except for the air-field's orange windsock, which stood over a slight rise to the east. I had been making for the windsock, but now I detoured. Removing my sandals, I stepped into the marsh. The water was eight to ten inches deep and unpleasantly hot.

I waded south for a while before realizing that something was wrong. I had been carefully watching the water ahead of my feet, but nothing was moving there. No living thing fled from me. Hot water is not an environment particularly favorable to life—I knew that—but *something* should have adapted to it. My own sense of the world's workings told me so, and it seemed to me that Margie had promised.

I have had difficulty, since, in finding exactly where her hand-book promised I would find life in the hot wetlands of the Yapese savannah. Any number of passages come close to promising. "How the Natural World Works," one section is titled. "Let us begin with a look at our Earth. This is how it would look from the moon; blue and green and beautiful, with swirling winds and clouds, some mountains and lowlands, big, big oceans and tiny islands. That's it, ALL of it! There are two things we must understand about our Earth: 1. *It is full of life.* [Emphasis mine.] 2. It is limited. The Earth is only so big. There is no more."

A dragonfly overtook me from behind. It was the same size and species as the moldery brown dragonfly embalmed in the pitcher plant, but it was 150 percent alive, a bright, whirring, elec-tric red. It hovered in front of me for a moment, then yawed to swoop away over the marsh. As I followed its flight, I saw two fish. They were small and drab, at first glance, but I knew they were heroic. They were freshwater fish in the middle of Oceania. They had solved the problem of life in the hot marshes of Yap. They swam slowly away from me, between the spikes of the grasses, until I lost them in the reflected cloud billows and blue of the sa-vannah sky.

# 2

# A SONG FOR SATAWAL

Satawal

The architecture at Isely Field is much too grand for Saipan. The island is just thirteen miles long and at no point wider than eight. There must be a story here: crazed ambition in the architect, or megalomania in some former ruler. The airport's ruins will puzzle future archaeologists, surely, just as our own are puzzled by Ponape's abandoned stone city of Nan Madol, or by the megaliths at Easter Island. Saipan, fifth island up in the long, northwest-trending arc of the Marianas Archipelago, is headquarters for the U.S. Trust Territory of the Pacific Islands. The governor of the two thousand islands of that territory is called "the High Commissioner." Perhaps all those islands gave him delusions of empire. Perhaps his fine title went to his head.

The terminal buildings make an imitation village under Saipan's green hills. The roofs are all identical, tight clustered, steep pitched in a generalized Pacific Island style, and shaked with cedar. The cedar shakes seem an extravagance almost Caligulan, here on an island of tropical hardwoods, so far from the latitudes that produce cedar. The supporting pillars are massive and white. The stairways and concourses are too wide for the traffic. A midday traveler hears his footsteps echoing there, as in a museum after closing time.

The check-in area is a vast and lofty ramada open on three sides to the breeze. The floor is deserted, more often than not.

Along the back wall is a row of ticket counters: Japan Airlines, Continental Air Micronesia, Island Air. Across the desert of the floor is a colonnade of white Ozymandian pillars, and beyond them the street, its two lanes empty of traffic, its curbs barren of cabs.

In the late-twentieth-century fabric of the ramada there is one large hole. At the far end of the room, opposite the Island Air ticket counter, roped off from the public, tall masted and anomalous, sits an outrigger sailing canoe.

Seen end on, from the vantage of the Japan Airlines counter, the canoe might be a giant sea bird skimming the floor straight at you. The vessel is nearly beamless, as trim-hulled as a tern. The arch of the outrigger platform makes one wing, the angle of the cantilevered lee platform makes the other. It's a broken-winged sea bird. The lee platform is much the shorter, rising steeply to the bird's elbow and ending there.

In the canoe, as in Nature, there are no straight lines. The vessel is composed all of curves; the hull, the outrigger booms, the yard and the boom of the sail, all bend to various demands of wind and the sea—even the mast, the straightness of which is broken near the top by an odd curving segment.

The mast brushes the very ceiling, and the hull and outrigger cast dim reflections halfway down the polished floor, yet the canoe has a curious invisibility. Passengers in transit don't seem to detect it. A few glance and continue on, but most fail to note the vessel at all. Perhaps nobody really looks at anything in airports. Perhaps the travelers mistake the canoe for one of those wooden sculptures that modern architects like to set out front as contrast to their sterile concrete and glass; foil sculpture that need not really be looked at. Perhaps the travelers, disembarking from jet airplanes, their heads hollow already from passage through too many time zones, are unprepared for the time *warp* that oscillates always in the vicinity of an outrigger canoe, and unconsciously shy from it.

One humid day in February, the check-in ramada was empty except for two people. One was a ticket agent, a light-brown young woman with long black hair, who stood behind the Island Air counter doing some figuring. The other was a passenger loitering by the canoe. A baggage handler entered, pushing an empty cart.

The baggage handler was a dark-brown man whose ancestors came, by the look of him, from somewhere in the central Caroline Islands. In America he would have passed for an Afro-American, among almost everyone but the Afro-Americans. He wore a yellow baseball cap held down by a pair of those hard-plastic headsets that protect ears from the roar of jet engines. He noticed the loitering passenger. Passengers show so little interest in the canoe, as a rule, that this one by his lack of movement had captured the Carolinian's attention. The Carolinian parked his steel cart beside the weathered wooden counterweight at the end of the outrigger.

"Funny to see a canoe in an airport, huh?" he asked the passenger.

The passenger agreed that it seemed strange.

"This canoe is from the island of Satawal," the baggage man explained. "Three kids and three older guys sailed it all the way up from Satawal. They teach the kids navigation—to sail by watching the currents, the stars, the birds. This canoe was supposed to be airlifted to the Tall Ships Festival, but something got screwed up. It never happened, so they put it here. It's in the way here. It sort of blocks things up."

About the Carolinian method of navigation, by currents, stars, and birds, the baggage handler was correct. About the canoe's origins on Satawal, he was mistaken. The airport canoe is not from that island, though it almost could be—its style is nearly identical to the Satawalese. The canoe is actually from Puluwat, an atoll 120 nautical miles to Satawal's east.

If the baggage handler was annoyed by the way the canoe blocked things up, the long-haired young woman behind the Island Air check-in counter was not.

"I like it," she told the passenger.

The young woman was a Chamorro. The island of Saipan, through an odd twist in its history, has two native races, and the Chamorros were the first of them, the original aborigines. They lived here from at least 1527 B.C., give or take the two hundred years' latitude necessary with carbon dating, until the early eighteenth century, when the Spaniards depopulated this island, along with all the others in the northern Marianas, resettling the people on Guam, the largest and southernmost of the chain. In the early nineteenth century, when the ancestors of the baggage man, fleeing a typhoon in the central Carolines, began arriving in fleets of canoes like this one, they found the islands deserted. "Saipan" itself is a Carolinian word. It derives from *sai*, "going to take a trip," and *pol*, "empty." When the descendants of the displaced Chamorros began returning home in 1816, they found small Carolinian settlements on Tinian and Pagan and a large one on Saipan. For the remainder of the nineteenth century and for most of this one, the two peoples did not mix, but of late on Saipan the barriers have been breaking down.

"It's beautiful," said the young Chamorro woman of the Carolinian canoe. "I could look at it all day."

That she could look at it all day is fortunate, for the canoe's cutwater rests dead even with her baggage scales, and she *does* look at it all day.

The twenty-six-foot hull is painted red above and black below. The black is still lustrous, though spotted white here and there by recaulking. The red has faded. The red and the black are a relief from the airport's modern grays and whites. Red and black are a combination that has long appealed to the human eye. Greek vases share the canoe's colors, and English freighters, and Apache war paint.

The sail, reefed now in the doldrums of the airport, is woven of pandanus palm. The canoe's lighter lashings are of sennit—string made from coconut fiber. The heavier lashings and the rigging are of coir, which is rope from the same fiber. As always with coir, the canoe's stays and halyard are bristly with split ends. Coir is Stone Age Velcro. Knots in it are unnecessary; the Carolinian sailor simply lays the rope once over itself and it holds. No rope is more convenient, no sailors rougher-handed.

The mast has a sharper rake here at the airport than it ever had on the ocean, an adjustment necessary to make it fit under the roof. A pair of birds have taken up residence in the eaves directly above the canoe, amidships. Maybe avian eyes, too, need relief from gray concrete. Maybe the birds perceive that the mast was once a tree. They use the mast as doorstep, coming and going, and it is streaked white with bird lime in two or three places.

More passengers in transit should pause by the canoe. There is a lot to deduce from it, even in a passing examination. Puluwat, the canoe's atoll of origin, would seem to be one of those sandy places where suitable trees fail to grow to sufficient girth, for the big, pontoon-shaped counterweight at the end of the outrigger is hewn from a driftwood log. The streamlined block of it is full of sea cracks and sea striations. The Pacific imparted character to this piece of wood before men ever shaped it with adzes. The decking of the outrigger platform is of much smaller driftwood; unpainted, knotty sticks of assorted diameters, lashed across the outrigger booms with sennit. The lee platform, cantilevered out from the opposite side of the canoe, looks, like its counterpoise, to be assembled of some beachcomber's kindling. The rudeness of the two platforms seems strange, joined as they are to a hull shaped and painted with evident care, and beautifully. For Carolinian canoewrights, getting the broad, functional strokes of the hull right is the important thing, apparently. Niceties of inlay are secondary. The counterweight is joined to the outrigger by a heavy yoke, four stout forked struts, and a welter of coir braces and lashings. For no other connection in the canoe have so many coconuts sacrificed their fiber, and the thickness and complexity of the lashings point to this as a crucial juncture. Strength and resilience in the outrigger would seem to be important. The outrigger must take a beating.

A few features of the canoe are more mysterious. There is the steep uphill slant of the lee platform, which looks right, somehow, but which must make it uncomfortable for passengers sitting there. There is the marked asymmetry of the hull in cross section, its lee side sheer, its outrigger side full-bellied. There are good reasons for both peculiarities. This canoe, or its type, is the highest expression of Caroline Island material culture. It held sway, with minor variations, over forty degrees of latitude, from Yap 2,400 miles eastward to the Marshalls and Gilberts. Many students of Oceanic canoes believe it to be the most versatile, best-thought-out vessel in the whole Pacific.

Several sections of the rope barrier around the canoe droop nearly to the floor, and someone has crossed over to carve his initials, "A.K.," in the gunwale near the stern.

From some unknown mainland, an uncertain number of millennia ago, the first canoe pushed off into Oceania.

No one knows how that canoe looked. Its makers were not a people who kept archives. They worked from memory, not from blueprints, and their materials were biodegradable. There is good reason to believe that the first canoe was not a canoe at all, but a raft. Whatever its design, that first vessel is now benthic ooze on some continental shelf, or in the abyss beyond. The makers lie down there too, unless they were lucky and their dust is sifted now with the sand of some coral islet.

No one knows how the crew wore their hair, or the language they spoke, or what they were running from, or searching for perhaps, as they made for that blue horizon. They were setting out, it is certain, into the last great region of the planet's surface to be explored and colonized by humans. The whole Pacific, a third of the Earth, awaited them. They were embarked on the last great demographic adventure of mankind.

They were dark men, surely. Their wide-scattered descendants would all be cautious seamen, patient for good sailing weather, and it is likely that the first sailors of the diaspora were cautious men, too. It was a sunny day. The beach they left behind, if it resembled most beaches in these parts, was composed of white sand, and in the sun the whiteness was dazzling. The beach vegetation, yellow-green and halophytic, grew thick right down to high-tideline, and the mangroves on the point were a dark viridian. Those greens burned on in the sailors' memories, out on the monotonous blue, when the horizon had come back around to meet itself and obliterate land behind them. The *smells* of land they could no longer call back, the instant the trade winds caught them.

About the first few millennia of the canoe's evolution, we can only speculate. It has not been an evolution to leave fossils. Wood, string, and paint last in desert caves and tombs, sometimes, but not on tropical beaches. Of the thousands of dead ends and wrong turns; of the ludicrous ideas that died in the laughter of wiser canoewrights; of the crazy ideas that drowned with their inventors; of the slightly imperfect ideas that revealed their flaws in gales; of the ideas good for their time but lost in the overlay of better ideas;

of the ideas ahead of their time; of the ideas right on time but frustrated by dogma; of the thousands of impasses and retrogressions, we have no record. We do know about the last stages of canoe dispersion through Oceania, for that dispersion was concluding when it met the beginnings of our own, and our own sailors carried notebooks.

By then the prow of the first canoe had plied a thousand archipelagos. The original figurehead had been transfigured. In the Admiralty Islands it had taken the shape of a crocodile's head, the jaws clamped shut. On the north coast of Papua New Guinea, the jaws came open. In the Gulf of Papua, the endpiece was the whole crocodile. In the Squally Islands, it was the crocodile's tongue. At Malekula in the New Hebrides, it was the generalized head of a bird. On the western end of New Britain, the bird was specific, an osprey, carved there as fish magic. In the Solomons, it was the head of the frigate bird. In the central Carolines, the tail. In the Ellice Islands, the prow was bifurcated to represent the open mouth of the kingfish. At Geelvink Bay the carved head was human, with cassowary feathers for hair. At Fatuhiva and Nukuhiva, atop the tall, swannecked bows of voyaging canoes, the carved heads were human again, flat and hideous. In the Marquesas, mounted atop the prows of war canoes, the human heads were not carved but real, the skulls of slain enemies, with false wooden noses, mother-of-pearl eyeballs inserted in the orbits, black-painted pupils, and boars' tusks fixed at the corners of the mouth. In New Zealand, atop the upswept eighteen-foot figureheads of Maori war canoes, grotesque semi-human faces stared through mother-of-pearl eyes and stuck wooden tongues out at the enemy.

The canoe paddle had become ovate in Fiji, approximately ovate in Hawaii, an elongated oval at the Torres Straits, and an elongated oval painted with red-and-black human faces in the northwestern Solomons. It was a fine-pointed oval painted like a fish in the southeastern Solomons and a broad oval with a beaklike tip in the Marquesas. It was obovate in Raivavai, spatulate in Tuamotu, lanceolate in Nauru, broadly lanceolate in Rapa, lanceolate with acuminate tips in the Carolines, lanceolate and plano-convex in cross section in New Zealand, lanceolate and stiletto thin in the

Tanga group of the Bismarck Archipelago, lanceolate and lightly
carved in the Mailu Islands, lanceolate and decorated with carved
snakes in New Ireland, lanceolate and inlaid with disks of pearl
shell in Manihiki. It was diamond-shaped at Cape Direction of
Queensland, heart-shaped in Orokaiva, spade-shaped in the Hermit
Islands, banana-leaf-shaped in Mangareva, and fountain-pen-nib-
shaped in the Cook Islands.

In the Palau Islands, the lanceolate paddles of the war canoes
were called *besos*, which was also the Palauan word for spear, and
the paddles may actually have doubled as weapons. They were
painted blood-red, and in some paddles that red was white-webbed
with the lines of conventionalized waves. At the tip of each blade
was a swelling that produced a keening sound as the paddle was
pulled through the water; the German anthropologist Kramer
would call it *singknopf*, "the singing knob."

On Easter Island, by the time Europeans reached the bleak
shores of that remotest and easternmost of Polynesia's outposts, the
paddle had suffered a devolution, or perhaps it was a sublimation.
The Easter Island paddle was double-bladed, like a kayak paddle,
but with hardly any shaft separating the blades. One blade of each
pair was decorated, and the other was plain. The decorated blade
was carved in low relief into a radically simplified semblance of a
human face, and in some paddles the face was painted with black-
and-white patterns identical to the facial tattoos of the Marquesas,
the ancestral homeland. The plain blade of each pair was obovate
and businesslike. With a longer shaft, and without the encum-
brance of its tattooed twin, it might actually have propelled a canoe.
It could not—it had become a "dancing paddle," useful only in ceremonies—but its impracticality no longer mattered. The great
ninety-foot vessels in which the Easter Islanders had come survived
only as murals on cave walls. No suitable timber grew on Easter
Island's rocky slopes, and when the original canoes failed, there
had been no wood with which to replace them. The art of building
voyaging canoes had died. There was no way onward from Easter
Island, and no way home again.

In Goodenough Bay of New Guinea, the Papuan paddlers
stroked in perfect unison, bending well forward at the waist and

chopping their flat, elliptic blades into the sea. They pulled the canoe up to the paddles, withdrew the blades, and rapped them sharply twice against the hull. In Hawaii, the captain rapped three times, the signal to change sides, and at the third blow his paddlers switched over. In Palau the warrior-paddlers, working double-banked and thirty-two strong, drove their spear-paddles into the sea on both sides, and as the thirty-two blades emerged again, thirty-two singing knobs sang.

When the wind blew in Oceania, the islanders of nearly every group set down their paddles and raised sail. Sails were square in the Siassi Islands, a narrower rectangle in the Hermit Islands and the Torres Straits, and oblong in parts of New Guinea and the Louisiades. Nearly everywhere else they were triangular. In Fiji, the rig was "proto-lateen"; the sail a simple triangle slung directly from the mast, apex downward. In Tonga and most of western Polynesia, it was primitive Oceanic lateen, the forward spar of the triangular sail resting in a crutch at the masthead and the mast raked forward. In New Zealand, it was degenerate lateen, very like the rig in Tonga. In Hawaii, it was the "crab-claw" sail; subtriangular, with its inverted base—the sail's uppermost margin—deeply crescentic, giving the sail the shape of a crab's open claw. In the Marquesas, it was much like Hawaii's. In the Society Islands, it was the boom-sprit sail, shaped oddly, a bit like the blade of a hunting knife, but capable of cutting close to the wind. The boomsprit sail was converging in its evolution with the spritsail of Europe, and indeed, after contact, they merged.

In Micronesia, the rig was true Oceanic lateen, the sail an isosceles triangle stepped apex downward in a foredeck socket. The triangle's two longer sides were laced to spars and slung from a mast stepped amidships but capable of being raked toward either bow. This was a superior rig, and it moved from Micronesia, where it originated, throughout much of Melanesia. In Melanesia's Santa Cruz Islands, the top edge of the isosceles triangle was deeply crescentic—the crab's claw again, its pincers nearly closed. In the New Hebrides, the pincers came wide open. At the time Europeans arrived, or until they did, the Micronesian sail appeared to be the sail of Oceania's future. When Captain Cook reached western Polynesia in 1773, the Oceanic lateen rig had not long preceded him and was in the process of displacing the primitive lateen rig formerly in use there.

If certain of the canoe's parts were prone to mutation, then some things in it changed hardly at all. The bailer, for one, was nearly identical everywhere. A few Pacific peoples made do with melon husks or coconut halves, but most used the Oceanic bailer, in which the handle is set, free end forward, within the cavity of a shallow wooden scoop. The seaman gripped the bailer inside, as a Roman boxer would his cestus, and with his fist awash he fought back the sea. Islanders from all over Oceania agreed, somehow, on the proper shape for a bailer, while diverging in their ideas on almost everything else. Perhaps there was nothing to improve in the Oceanic bailer. It was eminently functional, and beautiful too, in its simple way. There is not a lot of romance to a bailer. Perhaps island designers were less moved to apply their inventiveness there than in something else.

In its colors, the canoe changed less than one might think. Hulls were painted red and black in the Nissan cluster of the Solomon Islands; red and black in the Humboldt Bay district of Netherlands New Guinea; red and black in Truk; red and black in the Central Carolines; red and black most commonly, but sometimes also green and yellow, among the Sulka people of the Bismarck Archipelago; red, black, and brown in the Hermit Islands; yellow and black in Hawaii.

The black of Hawaiian canoes "had almost the quality of a lacquer," according to one European who saw it. Its ingredients were pandanus-leaf charcoal, the juices of banana and *kukui* trees, and the sap of a native *Euphorbia*. The underbody of the hull was rubbed down with pumice, then painted, dressed with *kukui*-nut oil, and brought to a high polish. Elsewhere in the Pacific the ingredients were similar, and nearly everywhere the black had that high shine.

The word "canoe" changed far less than the thing it described. The thing had logged millions of sea miles and countless permutations; its sailors had scattered wide across the greatest of oceans; their original few tongues had been confounded and were thousands, yet the word was recognizable almost everywhere. It was *va'a* in Samoa and *va'a* in the Society Islands, 1,700 miles east of Samoa. It was *wa'a* in Hawaii, 2,800 miles north of Samoa, and *vaa* or *vaka* in the Marquesas, 2,500 miles to Hawaii's southeast. It was *vaka* on Tonga, which is part of Polynesia, and *vaka* on Nuguria, which is part of Melanesia. It was *vaka* on Danger Island, *vaka* in Tokelau, *vaka* in the Ellice Islands, *vaka* in the Solomons, *waka* in Manihiki, *waga* at Uatom. In New Guinea alone there are more than 2,000 languages, yet in all the babble of that great island one name did not lose itself. It was *waga* in much of Papua New Guinea, *vaga* among the Massim people, *waona* among the Mailu-speaking people, *vanagi* at Port Moresby, *wa* among the Arufuma of Cape Nelson. It was *wa* in the Ninigo Islands of the Bismarck Archipelago, and *wang* in the Siassi Islands of the same group.

The word, *wa, waga, vaka,* seems to have fit the whole of the canoe—its trimness, its rake, its great speed and small draft—nearly as snugly as the Oceanic bailer fit the hollow of the hull.

While the general name for canoe changed little, the specific names for various models changed infinitely, as did their design. There were:

The outrigger canoes of Malekula, *nimbembew,* drawn through fire to drive out evil.

The big double sailing canoes of the Mailu Islands, *orou,* their twin hulls hewn from large buttress trees by inland men who had inherited magical power over the wood spirits.

The costly outrigger canoes of the Shortland Islands, *kinu,* which required one human sacrifice before they were begun, another when the tree was cut, and a third when the keel was laid.

The outrigger canoes of Buna, *nga,* built to avenge slain relatives, each vessel named for a dead cousin and addressed by that man's name, even while it stood, a tree before the canoewright's stone axe ("We are cutting you down and we are making a canoe of you to visit your slayer and to pay for you"); canoes which, when felled, were sung to ceaselessly as adzes shaped the logs, and which finally, as finished canoes, were rubbed with the burned heads of eels to give them slipperiness and with the bodies of watersnakes for speed.

The dugout paddling canoes of Hawaii, *ma*, felled and hollowed out by experts called *kahuna kalai wa'a*, "priests who shape canoes." When the time was propitious, the priest would lead a procession up the mountains, his helpers carrying pigs, red fish, bunches of a special sedge, and adzes of compact, waterworn basalt. On reaching the foot of a likely *koa*, the craftsman in the priest examined it for girth and straightness; then the priest in the priest addressed the six spirits of canoe making, each in its turn, and then he appealed to Laka, the Polynesian culture hero and greatest of canoewrights, and then to Lea Wahine, and then to all the spirits of the mountains. Then he buried the red fish and the bunches of sedge at the base of the tree. Then his helpers baked the pig. Then they cut down the tree. Then the priest appealed to all the gods and to the spirits of all the canoe builders who had preceded him. Then he and his helpers ate the pig. Then they pruned off the branches, roughed out the log with the basalt adzes, and hauled it down the mountain. If it was a big log, forty to fifty feet, the priest enlisted villagers, who climbed the mountain to help—tall and robust Hawaiian men and women who required more pigs as fuel. Down by the shore, when the hull was finished and the outrigger float had been shaped and attached, the gathering ceremonially ate a final pig. This last pig was to suggest to the canoe how it should root its way across the ocean, and it was followed by a dog, which the people consumed to teach the canoe how to tear apart the swells. Then they ate sweet potatoes and taro, not as any special lesson to the canoe, but simply because they were a people who liked to eat. Finally the priest delivered a benediction: "This is a canoe to sail in; it will not meet misfortune in the surf, nor in the deep blue sea."

There were the narrow-hulled outrigger canoes of the Santa Cruz Islands, *tepukei*, hewn by sons who inherited the craft from their fathers. Each of those sons, when near death himself, symbolically washed his own son's hands in water, thereby passing on the canoe-building art; and *that* son, when he had finished his canoe, took it down to shore, as his forefathers had since time immemorial, and he paddled it through the cathartic white tumult of the surf, driving out the ghost of the spot where the tree had stood, purging the ghost of the adze that had shaped it, and taking sole possession himself.

There were the two-masted outriggers of Aramot and Mandok, *de wang*, their timber purchased with small pigs, shell money, or dogs' teeth. There were the double canoes of New Caledonia, *huilu*, bartered for necklaces, slingstones, and daughters.

There were the double-outrigger canoes of Australia's Gulf of Carpentaria, *badra*, with hulls made from the trunks of silk-cotton trees; and the double voyaging canoes of Hawaii, *wa'a*, their twin hulls made of native *koa*, if necessary, but preferably of Oregon pine, the larger logs of which arrived at Hawaii's shores from an unknown world, just as meteors arrive at ours; and the triple and quadruple canoes of Port Moresby, *lakatoi*, their multiple hulls made from a species of enormous softwood that grows along alluvial stretches of Papua Gulf rivers.

There were the upraked and pointed outrigger canoes of Mota, *aka*, in which the holes for the lashings were drilled with the columella of a volute shell, and the mat sail sewn with a stingray's sting. There were the two-masted double canoes of the Loyalty Islands, *vaga*, their sails sewn with the sharpened wingbones of flying foxes.

There were: The high-sided outriggers of Futuna, *tavaka*, with recesses hollowed out at bow and stern to serve as fish baskets. The outriggers of New Guinea's Estuary of the Fly, *pe*, with prows worked up into basketwork shields. The neighboring outriggers of the Estuary of the Bamu, *peeri*, their ends plugged with sticky estuarine mud. The outriggers of the Stewart River, *tang'o*, their rounded bows cut away at waterline and shaped into ledges on which harpooners stood looking for dugong.

There were the war canoes of the Society Islands, with fighting platforms spanning the double hulls, crowded with warriors. There were the sailing outriggers of the same archipelago, *va'a motu*, with narrow balance platforms athwartships. (On one tack, the outrigger had to be on the lee side, and when it was, one or more sailors walked the plank on the weather side, where their weight kept the outrigger from driving under and flipping the canoe.)

There were: The outriggers of the Arimoa Islands, *waga*, their bowpieces carved into black cockatoos, their sternpieces into black birds of paradise. The forty-foot double war canoes of Mailu, their every projection flying fiber tassels or cassowary feathers, their prows decorated by egg cowries, genus *Ovulum*. The outriggers of the Atoll of Egum, adorned with *Ovulum*. The hundred-foot outriggers of Fiji, *thamakau*, decked out with as many as 2,500 of the big cowries. The outrigger canoes of Astrolabe Bay, their mastheads knobbed with nautilus shells. The double canoes and outrigger canoes of Manihiki, *waka*, their hulls inlaid with triangles and disks of mother-of-pearl. The primitive outriggers of Mawata, their hulls painted with magical Mawatan symbols of combat: rows of hearts, sinews, shoulders; a breastbone; a tongue. The outrigger canoes of Tabar Island, *tsombi*, their sides carved and painted with representations of the good spirits who protect canoes against those troublesome sea spirits who travel incarnate as sharks. The decked-over dugouts of Yela, decorated minimally—a few raised lines representing a bird flying in a high wind. The paddling dugouts of the Huon Peninsula of New Guinea, decorated maximally, each small canoe almost too busy with motifs: pigs' tusks, fish tails, stars, frogs, birds, disembodied bird wings, crocodiles holding fish in their mouths, ghosts, and others. The canoes of New Zealand, their endpieces carved into intricate scrollwork and grotesque figures and faces by the finest artists in Oceania. The plank-built outriggers of the Solomons, *ora*, their high ends curving up gracefully like a crescent moon's and tipped with red plumes, their hulls so light that two men could carry a twenty-five-foot specimen, their pale wood inlaid with nacre, the brightness of which set off the blackness of the crew.

There were the blunt-ended outriggers of Ontong Java, *va'a*, which no one but the makers admired. "Their canoe was a great unwieldy thing," complained an anonymous English visitor in the eighteenth century. "Poorly and slovenly made," wrote a man called Finsch in 1881. "Their canoes do not amount to much," wrote Wawn in 1893. The fault was not so much the islanders'. Trees grew stunted in the atoll's poor coralline soil, and the Ontong Javanese had to depend on what the current brought them. "The wood nearly always seems to have drifted a long way," wrote Parkinson in 1897, "as the planks are generally pierced by shipworm, though the holes are carefully calked. If the driftwood is not large enough, then the canoe is made of several pieces sewn together, often with very different kinds so that dark and light woods are joined together." The people of Ontong Java liked this quilted effect. Occasionally they found a log large enough to make a whole canoe, and these one-piece canoes leaked less, but the Ontong Javanese were prouder of their mosaic models, held together with sennit, sap, and ingenuity. They were working in an old and widespread Oceanic tradition—making the best of a poor thing.

There were, in that same tradition, the hundred-foot semikeeled voyaging canoes of Tuamotu, *pahi*, pieced together with great Tuamotuan cleverness from terrible Tuamotuan wood.

There were the fifty-foot, oceangoing canoe-rafts of the Chatham Islands, *waka pahii*, built of the flower stems of flax, the stalks of tree ferns, small lengths of wood from two species of native shrub, and the leaves of bull kelp. The Chatham Islands were barren of any better materials. The inhabitants, the Moriori, were Polynesians, an offshoot tribe of the Maoris of New Zealand, but, given the low-growing Chatham flora, they were unable to reproduce canoes true to type. No amount of Oceanic ingenuity could weave a sleek, narrow-hulled canoe from ferns, flax, and kelp. The *waka pahii* was of necessity a beamy, square-ended, wickerwork barge, Polynesian in name only.

In its smaller versions, called *waka korari* and used for short trips and bird hunting, buoyancy was provided by rolls of tree-fern stalks and flax stems. Tightly packed and lashed with flaxen cord to the frame, the stalks and stems served as floor. In the larger versions, intended for longer voyages and longer lives, the rolls of land vegetation were replaced by kelp floats. (Kelp is made for salt immersion; flowers and flax are not, and in the canoe-rafts they became waterlogged.) To make the floats, the Moriori raftwright punched a hole in each long, hollow kelp leaf, inflated it like a balloon, then plugged the hole. The distended leaf dried hard and gourdlike, becoming an air bladder two feet long and eight inches deep. He lashed these in large numbers to the frame and he filled the interstices with moss. At sea, the Moriori crew walked about above the inflated kelp on a wicker grillwork that confined the bladders. Supported by algae and their own imprisoned breath, they traveled the broad channels between their islands in any kind of weather.

The Chatham Islands are remote satellites of New Zealand, which was itself off the beaten track in Oceania. Chatham Island nautical design, in its double isolation and poverty of materials, developed an eerie convergence: the *waka pahii* had more in common with the framed vessels of the Old World than it had with the canoes of Oceania. In a number of details of the framing, the vessel's architecture was Atlantic architecture. The kelp floats anticipated the air chambers in European lifeboats. The canoe-rafts were propelled not by paddles or poles, as were vessels everywhere else in Oceania, but by oars, as in Europe. The oars pivoted on what English-speaking sailors called thole pins, and the rowers, like those of Europe, faced the stern. The canoe-rafts were like a prophecy. The Moriori, it turned out, were also *morituri*. Rowing about their treeless islands looking backward, they were dark simulacra of the pale race that would overtake and extinguish them.

There were the ten-foot patchwork outriggers of Rapa-nui, *vaka poe-poe*. It was with these canoes, on the austere shores of Rapa-nui—Easter Island—that Oceanic ingenuity finally exhausted itself. In 1722, the year Roggeveen discovered the island, he saw "a great many canoes of poor and flimsy construction," the last, sorry descendants of the two great vessels which, according to legend, had brought the first 300 inhabitants all 2,500 miles from Rapa. In 1773, Captain Cook saw "not more than three or four," which he described as being "very mean, and built of many pieces of wood sewed together with small line." In 1785, La Pérouse saw just three canoes. He noted that the islanders did not seem much inconvenienced, for they had learned to swim so strongly that they could travel two leagues out from shore, even when the seas were high. He predicted that soon, from lack of wood, there would be no canoes. In 1804, indeed, Lisiansky saw no canoes at all. The islanders paddled out to his ship on what he called "rush mats." In 1842 D'Urville reported islanders swimming five miles out on "planks."

In its devolution, the Easter Island canoe had now shrunk to a surf-board. In 1891, W. J. Thomson found two last canoes in a cave. The patchwork hulls, crumbly from dry rot, were serving as burial cases.

There were the primitive twelve-foot outriggers of Napuka, *maota*, their evolution pinched by that island's dangerous reef, which encircles the lagoon completely, leaving no navigable entrance. Napuka canoes were clam boats condemned to working the lagoon forever. They gave rise over centuries, in shallow parts of the lagoon, to great midden-islands of *Tridacna* shells, but they remained small themselves.

There were the eighteen-foot river dugouts of Cape York in Queensland, canoes so low-sided, as a result of their upstream evolution, that they were worthless down on their mother ocean.

There were the long, narrow swamp dugouts, *wa*, of the Agaiambo people of New Guinea, a refugee tribe driven inland to a marsh. In their exile from the ocean, the Agaiambo poled about on outriggerless, shell-thin vessels that were hopelessly tippy, to anyone but an Agaiambo.

There were the lake outriggers of Moava, *vaka*. Moava, or Rennell Island, is an upraised coral atoll with a shoreline of steep limestone cliffs encircling an interior depression. The southeastern end of the depression is filled by a large brackish lake. It was on the minor ocean of this lake, oddly, not on the major ocean of the Pacific, that the Moava canoe reached its highest development. The ocean canoe was the no-frills model, a simple paddling canoe with a straightforward three-boom outrigger. The lake canoe was fancier, with a platform atop the three booms and a pyriform sail.

There were the dugout canoes of Cape York in Queensland, paddled by black men with great manes of woolly hair, scanty beards, and bodies decorated with scars and raised cicatrices; and the outrigger war canoes of Tahuata, paddled by large brown men with faces tattooed in black rectangles; and the beamy outrigger cargo canoes of Yap, sailed by medium-sized brown men tattooed with dolphins. There were the dugouts of the Gazelle Peninsula of New Britain, paddled by the Nakani, a "finer" race in the eyes of nineteenth-century Europeans, a people with light complexions, "more cleanly cut features," and what one observer called a "Jewish look"—the most thoroughly lost of all the lost tribes of Israel.

(It is in Oceania, more than anywhere else, that the futility of "race" as a subject for science becomes clear. Pacific populations diverged in their isolation, recombined, then lost one another again, until bloodlines became unravelable. A three-race scheme helps not at all to describe them, nor a ten-race scheme, nor any racial scheme yet proposed. The vehicle for all the human speciation—speciating all the while itself—was the canoe.)

There were the problematic outriggers of Kilinailau, Polynesian-style vessels on an atoll of Melanesian people. The original inhabitants, according to local tradition, had been a light-skinned people—Polynesians?—who had been overwhelmed by colonists from Buka, in the Solomon Islands of Melanesia. No trace of light skin survived. The only evidences of a Polynesian past were a few clamshell axe blades of a Polynesian type, some Polynesian technical terms for canoe parts, and the canoes themselves. The Kilinailau canoewrights looked out, to a man, through dark Melanesian eyes, but behind those eyes, under kinky Melanesian hair, in the circuitry of Melanesian brains, the formula for the aboriginal Polynesian canoe remained.

There were the elegantly spurred outrigger canoes of Wuvulu and Aua, *wa*, strikingly divergent in form from other canoes in the area, fashioned by a people divergent from their neighbors. The people of Wuvulu and Aua were light-brown with wavy hair, like Samoans, though they lived only eighty-seven miles from the small Dark Continent of New Guinea. The canoes of Wuvulu and Aua were drawn out horizontally at bow and stern into long, sharp points—the sharpest in Oceania. From the base of either horizontal endpiece, a single tall spur rose vertically, echoing exactly the shape of its mate. The endpieces and spurs had the smooth perfection of line that one expects in smaller things; in insect mandibles under a microscope, or in the burs of a seed. The glassy horns of a mantis shrimp might almost have been their inspiration. If they had a function, it must have been fantastic—to catch a drifting canoe, like the burred seed, on some far island, or to stick in the craw of some sea roc.

There were the double voyaging canoes of Tahiti, *tipairua*, which in the tenth century carried the navigator Kupe, a man as great as Cook or Columbus, on his voyage of discovery to New Zealand.

There were the red-and-black outriggers of the central Carolinian atoll of Ifaluk, *wa*, navigated by men possessed. An Ifaluk woman's song describes one of these haunted men:

> Sleepless, the captain leaves his house.
> He cannot lie down and rest
> Beside his wife on the mat.
> A good wind springs up,
> The captain wants to be on his way.
> The gods take possession of him.
> He must away.

There were the trim outriggers of the Marshall Islands, *wa lap*, navigated by men who were matched in the accuracy of their land finding only by the central Carolinians. The Marshalls, like the central Carolines, are a mid-ocean archipelago of very small islands, and they present the navigator with the same problem: finding insignificant bits of land in a big ocean. The Marshallese were good celestial navigators, but their genius lay in interpreting the sea's surface, in the nuances of which there were no closer or subtler students on Earth. In the Carolines, navigators maintained course in daytime and on overcast nights by their feel for the direction and origin of the swells passing under the canoe. In the Marshalls, navigators did that and more. The Marshalls are a double chain that lie north-south, across the path of the trades, and the many atolls of the group break up the regular march of the swells. The Marshallese turned the apparent chaos of their seas to advantage. They learned to decipher *interference patterns*. They found clues to the location of an atoll in the disturbances it set up on the ocean's surface.

Marshallese instructors of navigation transmitted their knowledge through stick charts made from the midribs of coconut leaflets. Long, straight strips of midrib showed the direction in which various islands lay, their positions marked sometimes by cowries. Short, straight strips represented currents in the vicinity of islands. Bent strips represented deflected swells. The bent strips intersected in what the Marshallese called *buoj*, "knots," and it was in these spots, on the real ocean, that the waves by their very confusion told the Marshallese navigator most.

When the time came to apply the abstraction of the stick chart, the instructors sailed with the novice out to the open sea. The old men had the boy go over the side, float on his back, relax, and feel the waves.

No one alive remembers how that style of learning felt, but the sensation must have been something. The water was warm. The sky vaulted blue above the boy, the ocean vaulted blue below. Was he troubled at all by the bottomlessness under him? Were the teachers who waited in the canoe patient old men, or curt and stern? Perhaps the boy had to forget any fear of the depths, forget the old men, if he was to learn. He was an aristocrat, but his favored childhood could not help him now. Suspended between the two voids, he concentrated, or ceased to concentrate, and if he had the right stuff the ocean by its rhythms finally spoke to him.

There were the fast seventy-foot voyaging outriggers of Micronesia's Gilbert Islands, *baurua*, navigated by men who, like their Marshallese neighbors immediately north, were expert at detecting the "land wave." That wave—the swell deflected straight back to sea by the presence of land—was discernible as far out as twenty-five miles on the leeward side of an island, and fifty miles to windward. In "reading" this and other swells, the Gilbertese navigator, like his colleagues everywhere in Oceania, depended less on his eyes than on his kinesthetic sense of the sea and his inner ear for it. Sometimes, when the guiding swell was masked by other swells, or was for any other reason faint, Oceanic navigators were in the habit of lying on the deck of the platform, or down in the hollow of the hull, and letting themselves roll with the canoe for hours until they were sure. Gilbertese navigators added a refinement. The Gilbertese had discovered that the most sensitive organs of balance were the testicles, and those were the seismographs they used at night to detect the imperceptible shiver the canoe made as it began to pitch with the land wave.

There were the large outrigger canoes of the Reef Islands, *loju*, forty feet long, decked against the spray, white-washed with a mash of pounded calcareous algae, and commanded by star-wise navigators, perhaps the best in Melanesia. "Should the canoe be caught by foul weather," wrote W. C. O'Ferrall, who is said to have known the old-time Reef Islanders best, "the craft is soon broken up, and men will, when they have lost all hope of making land again, shoot one another with their bone-tipped arrows."

Maybe the Reef Islanders really did do that. Then again, maybe W. C. O'Ferrall, who knew them best, did not know the Reef Islanders all that well and was falling for a tall story. Mass suicide is a tendency that should not have survived long, on an ocean colonized in large part by storm-blown canoes. Did the Reef Island canoes really break up so easily? And how did the Reef Islanders, bobbing with the fragments of their broken-up canoes, brace themselves to shoot one another with bone-tipped arrows? Who shot the last man? If the last two managed to shoot each other simultaneously, who survived to tell the tale to O'Ferrall?

There were the forty-foot plank-built outriggers of the atoll of Nada, *waga*, commanded by celestial navigators and crewed by the atoll's entire population. It makes for a curious coincidence of languages, but on Nada the principal fact of life was that on Nada nothing was there. No food grew on the atoll's islands but coconuts and fish. In the northwest season, when the wind was favorable, all 160 inhabitants—or all those fit to travel—climbed into their canoes and sailed around the Louisiades, trading the mats and dresses they made from nearly nothing for sweet potatoes, yams, and sago.

There were more timid canoes: The small outrigger dugouts of the New Hebridean island of Tanna, *negau*, whose navigators sailed by landmarks, never by the constellations, which in Tanna's firmament went unnamed. The poorly made dugouts, *lo*, of neighboring Eromanga, whose navigators, on returning home from short excursions, never beyond sight of land, happily disassembled their collapsible outriggers and packed them away out of sight. The dugouts of Dobu, *waga*, whose owners disliked seafaring, were poor at it, and built their hulls heavy, safe, and slow. The Dobuans shunned the huge expanses of sail hoisted by their Trobriand Island neighbors, raising tiny expanses instead, and generally thought so ill of the whole business that wind magic on Dobu was entrusted to the women.

And then there were the behemoths: The big two-masted outriggers of Aramot, Malai, and Mandok, merchant ships with two platforms, a lower one for cargo, an upper one for crew. The great double canoes of Samoa, *va'a tele*, which served sometimes as warships, sometimes as cargo vessels, sometimes as tenders upon which two of the big fishing canoes called *va'a alo* were transported to mid-ocean reefs and there launched to pursue bonito. The gigantic multiple canoes of Papua New Guinea, *olote*, seagoing platforms built atop six huge dugout hulls, with a big mast amidships carrying a vast crab-claw sail, four smaller masts with oblong sails at each of the platform's corners, and a boulder for an anchor.

There were the modular catamarans of Mangareva, hundred-man, lateen-sailed log rafts which, on approaching the *Blossom*, the ship of Captain Beechy, Mangareva's discoverer, blossomed themselves—or budded, anyway—detaching from one another to become a fleet of smaller catamarans.

There was the great Fijian *ndrua*, one hundred feet long and more, seven years sometimes in the building, its decks washed at launching with human blood. The *ndrua* was, some think, the finest vessel ever built in Oceania. It was a hybrid: double-hulled, as in Polynesia, but with one hull shorter than the other, an apparent imitation of the Micronesian hull and its shorter counterweight. The *ndrua* was propelled on windless days by great sculling oars that passed through hourglass-shaped holes cut in the platform that spanned the hulls. It was steered by enormous paddles—one specimen in the Fiji museum is thirty-three feet long, with a fifteen-foot blade. Controlling the steering paddles required several strong men. Some helmsmen were killed by unexpected blows of the long handle, others crippled by the strain of fighting its monstrous leverage. In war, the *ndrua* became a fortress, with bamboo ramparts erected around the margin of the platform and a fighting complement of two hundred warriors stationed inside. On land, *ndrua* were stored in giant canoe houses closely resembling our blimp hangars. The biggest *ndrua* on record, a vessel reported by Thomas Williams in 1858, was 118 feet long. It was named *Rusa i vanua*,

which Williams translated as "Perished Inland," and which he took
to reflect the doubts of the makers that such a dreadnought could
ever be launched.

"Canoe" is a shapely word, but it means just "brown man's
boat" and makes for a lumpy category. A class of vessels that includes both Hiawatha's birchbark and the hundred-foot, double-
hulled, plank-built *tipairua* of Kupe, the Tahitian navigator, is a
class stretched all out of shape. The voyaging canoes of Oceania
were *ships* longer and faster than the *Endeavor* or the *Golden Hind* or
any of the other European vessels that first came among them. In
the Americas, natives may have run about shouting, "Great canoe
with white wings!," but nothing like that happened in Oceania.
The Pacific Islanders came aboard, contemplated the strange rig
with professional interest, and tried to steal some iron.

If either party was dumbfounded at these first encounters, it
was the men from the Atlantic.

"A great many canoes began to come off," wrote a Spanish
visitor to the Solomons. "They were long, and pointed at the ends
in the shape of a crescent moon, and all full of Indians equipped for
war."

At Guam in 1588, Chamorro canoes began to come off similarly at the buccaneer Cavendish, and they made a hellish apparition:
"Sixty to seventy sailes of canoas full of Savages wearing their haire
marveilous long; yet some of them have it made up and tyed with a
knot on the crowne, and some with two knots, much like unto
their images which we saw carved in wood and standing in the
head of their boats like unto the images of the devil."

In 1774, off Tahiti, Captain Cook witnessed a naval review that
he found incredible. "The vessels of war," he wrote, "consisted of
160 large double canoes, very well equipped, manned, and armed,
and decorated with flags, streamers, etc., so that the whole made a
grand and noble appearance." The fighting vessels Cook saw were
all paddling canoes. They were accompanied by a larger number of
transports and tenders—slightly smaller double canoes carrying
sails—and by several *va'a ti'i*, "sacred canoes," the largest and most
ornate of Tahitian ships, each one carrying a shrine and the image
of a god. "In these 330 vessels, I guessed there were not less than

7,760 men," Cook wrote, and George Forster, who watched at Cook's shoulder as the armada passed, added, in his own account, "All our former ideas of the power and affluence of this island were so greatly surpassed by this magnificent scene that we were perfectly lost in admiration."

In 1778, Captain Cook, anchored at Kealakekua Bay in Hawaii, several hundred yards from where he was shortly to die for our sins against Pacific Islanders, assigned two of his officers to counting the canoes massed around his *Resolution*. Both men came up with more than three thousand.

By the latter part of the nineteenth century, the fifty-foot outrigger fishing canoes of Taku, *vaka*, were confined forever to the sheds that had protected them from the sun. The Taku people were so decimated by the nineteenth century's diseases and indentured labor that the combined manpower of Taku was not enough to haul the great canoes down to the water.

By 1898, in the Torres Straits, European rigging—mainsail, foresail, and jib—had replaced the traditional rig. The mainsail was still called "younger brother sail," and the foresail "older brother sail," for that had been their relationship in the old days, but their importance was now reversed and the rig was Melanesian in name only.

In 1906, the first European whaleboat was bought at Vao in the New Hebrides, and from then on the big old traditional canoes of Vao ceased to be made. At the same time, nearby on Rano, the last four war canoes lay on the beach. From the prow of the largest, a pair of boar's jaws dangled. The canoes had not been used for a long time, and the natives of Rano were unable to recall anything of their history.

In 1915, the Sagsag and Kalingi peoples of western New Britain were decimated by smallpox. The old men died before they could impart their knowledge to the few children who survived, and the arts of canoe building and navigation died.

The last of the Samoan double voyaging canoes, *'alia*, was built on commission for the Kaiser. It proved too big for transport to Germany and stayed home to rot on a Samoan beach.

In the Gilbert Islands, where men had once navigated by their testicles, long voyaging died. With its demise, model canoe racing became a madness. The models, called *maggi*, had long single out-rigger booms and carried so much sail that the counterweight had to be loaded with young coconuts to balance the wind. At the time of the British takeover, according to canoe historian James Hornell, "Model canoe racing on Apamama, Tarawa, and Peru so obsessed the people that gambling on the performance of the models had become a public danger; men in the excitement of the hour were liable to stake all they possessed on the result, their property, houses, and even their wives. The government, because of this evil, banned the sport soon after the annexation, but in 1917 they decid-ed to allow the sport to be revived in order to give the people a renewed interest in life and so to counteract the aimless condition into which they were falling."

In 1923, a single *tira*, the last of its kind, was at work in Tahiti. *Tira* were large, double-hulled tuna canoes distinguished by thirty-foot fishing cranes named *purau*, after the tree from which the poles of the cranes were cut. When a tuna struck, the crew lifted the crane by hauling on a backstay made, as protection for their hands, from the soft inner bark of the same tree. By 1925 this last *tira* lay rotting on a Tahitian beach.

In 1943, a last Fijian *ndrua* was built by Onega Islanders. It was forty-eight feet long, less than half the length of the largest *ndrua* of old, but capable of carrying fifty men. It spent its career as a copra freighter. With its eventual decay on a Fijian beach, no one has mustered the ambition to build another. In the Fiji Museum, that thirty-three-foot *ndrua* steering oar sits on display, a killer oar, a ruiner of helmsmen's backs. It is an oar full of potential leverage and wickedness, but it has nothing left to steer.

In the early 1960s, one of the last of the claw-sailed Reef Island outriggers, *tepukei*, was wrecked in the Santa Cruz Archipelago. It was a thirty-foot vessel owned by a native of Pileni Atoll, a man called Tevake. His name means "Tropic Bird," and he was the last of the old-time Santa Cruz navigators. When his canoe broke up, Tevake did not shoot himself with a bone-tipped arrow, as a good Reef Islander was supposed to do, according to O'Ferrall. Tevake survived and continued navigating. He was an old man by then, and he was left with nothing to sail but a small, outriggerless dugout, but he had begun his instruction in navigation early, at the age of seven at his father's knee, and he was unable to break the habit. It was in Tevake's Reef Islands that a father ritually washed his son's hands in water to pass on the canoe-building art, and Tevake shook hands, through countless ablutions in unbroken succession, with his own prehistory. He could not free himself from the grip. His own hands, the last pair in the line, were exceptionally large. He was a fit, square-shouldered, graying old man, with ears pierced and earlobes pendulous from the ornaments of his youth. He had the navigator's face. In the old photographs of canoe crews, you can always tell the navigator; his is the face your attention keeps returning to. You can verify the intuition if you want by looking at the caption. It took the ocean itself to cure Tevake of his wandering. In 1970, sailing alone around his islands, he was lost at sea.

All the others: the multiple-hulled *lakatoi* of Papua New Guinea, on whose springy platforms at launching the black girls danced; and the one-boy outriggers of the Mailu Islands, *karo*, in which seven-year-olds sailed in rough weather well beyond the reef; and the *tafa'anga* of Tonga; and the *vak* of Rotuma; and the *paopao* of Uvea, are gone. On only a handful of islands in the central Carolines do Pacific men still build canoes fit for voyaging. From only two of those islands do navigators still make long voyages under the triangular sail.

The security office at Isely Field is sparsely furnished: a battered sofa, a single desk, a bulletin board, a two-way radio. Behind the desk a dark-skinned Micronesian man sits regarding the clock on the wall. The man's eyes are the brown, undangerous eyes of his race, but they are set beneath thick, black, unruly eyebrows that might go better on a slightly mad Hungarian physicist or on a Russian strongman. He wears a light-blue, short-sleeved uniform shirt and dark-blue uniform trousers with a yellow stripe. Above his right breast pocket is an identification tag showing his portrait in color. It reads "Lino Olopai." Above his left breast pocket is a burnished, pale-gold badge stamped "Chief, Airport Security." His white saucer cap sits beside him on the desk, its black visor forward.

The effect is military, with one small incongruity. Lino Olopai's right ear is pierced. The hole is not a tiny one, as in the lobes of Western women and the members of mainland motorcycle gangs; it is a hole large enough to admit daylight, the sizable slit through which the men and women of the Caroline Islands insert sea shells, sometimes, but more often flowers. Most poems and love songs of the central Carolinian atolls start with ritual references to these flowers of the ear. "Flower in my ear . . . " the singer begins, or, "Flower of the *gabwi* tree . . . " or, "He is the *remag* flower I wear in my ear . . . " Edwin Grant Burrows, one of the better-known ethnographers for the central Carolines, did not have to rack his brains unmercifully to find a title for his book. *Flower in My Ear*, he called it, *The Arts and Ethos of Ifaluk Atoll*. Olopai's ear is empty at the moment and has been for some time.

Hidden beneath Olopai's trousers, congruent with the yellow uniform stripe yet incongruous in the way of his ear, is another mark of the central Carolines. Engraved on his bare thigh, in soot with a bone needle, is an indelible second stripe, a line of tattoos from the island of Satawal.

A plane is due, and Olopai stands. He dons his white hat, tugs at the visor to adjust it, and picks up his walkie-talkie. Heading for the door, he walks by the window ledge that serves informally as the airport's lost-and-found. He passes: A camera and light meter in black leather cases. A doll. A child's purse. A squirt gun. A set of keys. A wristwatch. A pair of small sandals with gilt straps and a clear-plastic toe box painted with translucent roses. The sandals were lost, from the look of them, by a Japanese girl-tourist about eight years old.

Olopai steps outside. A rain squall has just passed, and its dark shadow is racing unevenly over the green hills after it. The Micronesian sun is hot on the street again. The wet pavement is smoking so furiously that it is hard to make out the center line.

He walks briefly through sunshine, against the flow of the steaming street, then steps into the shade of the check-in ramada.

The ramada floor is deserted. On his left is the row of check-in counters. Behind the Island Air counter stands the long-haired Chamorro ticket agent, doing her figuring. On his right, beyond the ramada's white Ozymandian pillars, is the steamy blacktop of the street, and beyond the blacktop roll the green highlands of Saipan.

From the far end of the room, through its hole in time, the outrigger canoe skims the floor straight at him. Olopai walks briskly over to meet it. He does not seem troubled by the drooping rope of the barrier, or the slight security lapse the droopiness represents. He steps in over the rope himself. Who's to stop him? He is Chief of Airport Security. Under his aegis, and made bold by his example, I follow.

"Aha!" he says. "There's that rudder I was telling you about. I've been looking for it."

From where it rests against the outrigger platform, he lifts the canoe's heavy steering paddle. The Carolinian name for the paddle, he says, is *fatul bwubwu*. This one is made of a stout five-foot branch from which, near midpoint, a smaller branch forks at right angles. The main branch is unworked except at its large end, where the wood has been planed flat to make the paddle blade. The planing has exposed, in lenticular cross section, a core of phloem. The smaller fork, which serves the helmsman as handle, remains as Nature made it. Olopai carries the *fatul bwubwu* around to the lee side of the canoe. (When an outrigger canoe is under sail, the side opposite the outrigger is always to the lee.) In the hardwood gunwale near the stern a notch has been cut to receive the *fatul bwubwu*, and a crosspiece projects to brace it. Olopai sets the steering paddle in place. A hole has been drilled at the upper end of the paddle's main branch, and through it runs a length of sennit—a safety cord. Olopai ties this to a canoe. The *fatul bwubwu* is now secure against any freak eight-hundred-foot wave that might climb the Saipan cliff and strike the airport. He points to where the helmsman sits and to the spot where the helmsman's inside foot rests, warm and dry within the hull. Then he points to where the helmsman rests his outer foot, at waterline on the *fatul bwubwu*.

"To turn right, you put your weight on your outside foot and turn the rudder like this," he says. He demonstrates, canting the back edge of the *fatul bwubwu* away from the hull, thus presenting more of the blade to an imaginary sea. "Your foot is in the water night and day," he continues. "It gets numb and wrinkled. Sometimes, when it's easy sailing, you can take your foot off the rudder and put it inside the canoe. You can hold the canoe on course just with your hand. You start massaging your leg, and just then the canoe goes off course. The navigator looks at you—'Hey!'—and you put your foot back in the water."

This system of steering had its origins in Indonesia, or, if you like your origin theories wilder, in Scandinavia, where a device very similar to the *fatul bwubwu* was used by the Vikings.

Olopai unlashes the safety cord, lifts the steering paddle from its crosspiece, and gestures as if to pass it forward to an imaginary crewmate. This is one of the quick maneuvers performed when a Micronesian canoe changes tack. Somewhere in the middle of the process, the helmsman is no longer passing the *fatul bwubwu* forward; he is passing it astern. Therein lies the great originality of the Stone Age inventors of this system. In "tacking," a Micronesian canoe does not precisely tack. Either end of the canoe can be the bow, either end the stern, and they switch alternately. The mast pivots amidships. There are sockets at either end of the canoe to receive the boom, and crosspieces at either end of the lee gunwale to brace the *fatul bwubwu*. To go on an opposite tack, the sailors rake the mast toward the new bow, swing the sail around behind it, insert the boom in a new socket, and exchange the *fatul bwubwu* between ends. The canoe leaps off in a reciprocal direction but keeps the same side—the outrigger side—to the wind. This is necessary because the outrigger "float," as it is often called, does not function as a float, but as a counterweight to the force of the wind in the sail. If, in a good wind, the outrigger should come around to the lee, the canoe would flip over. In its either-endedness, as Baron George Anson wrote two centuries ago, "the construction of this proa is a direct contradiction to the practice of all the rest of mankind."

The arch of the outrigger boom is to keep the outrigger out of the waves, Olopai explains, and the curved segment at the top of the mast is "to put more wind in there, to catch more wind."

From either prow of the canoe projects a V-shaped wooden device resembling, to reach low for a metaphor, the hood ornament of an old Ford. This is the endpiece inspired, most Carolinian authorities agree, by the forked tail of the frigate bird, or man-o'-war. The frigate is a bird that men like to implicate with their vessels. The English named it after their warships. The Marshall Islanders decorated their mastheads with its feathers. The Solomon Islanders depicted it in nacre on their hulls. The frigate is a fitting totem for a sailing ship, for bold navigators. In habits, it is a pirate and epicure, robbing other birds or plucking small morsels from the surface of the sea, never deigning to dive in itself. (The male bird's colors are pirate colors: black, with a red throat pouch—the colors of Carolinian canoes.) In construction, with a ratio of wing area to body weight greater than in any other bird, the frigate is the ultimate soarer. Its seven-foot wings sometimes provide more lift than the bird can comfortably handle, and the forked tail is often at work trimming and adjusting violently to dampen the effect. On the airport canoe, the wooden vanes of that forked tail are more than a foot long. The carving is beautiful, elemental, and strong.

"What's that for?" I ask Olopai.

"I don't know. Some people say it's for navigation—it's like a sight for aiming at a star. But we don't use it for that. I don't know what it is."

Canoe sights like this one, if canoe sight it is indeed, framed the high green island of Saipan for the fleets of Olopai's ancestors as they fled north from their low atolls. A canoe sight like this one, nearly two centuries later, led Lino Olopai home again.

Returning the *fatul bwubwu* to its resting place against the outrigger, he excuses himself and walks off to meet the plane.

The canoe, alone again, skims motionless across the perfect calm of the polished floor. One canoe sight, or whatever it is, aims into a shadowy corner of the ceiling. The other aims at the green hills of Saipan. The terminal is quiet, except for the click of someone's distant footfalls, receding. From the direction of the runway comes the sudden typhoon roar of jet engines reversing themselves.

Behind her counter, the young Chamorro ticket agent continues her figuring. The street steams in the sun.

The V of the canoe sight aimed for an open blue horizon. The outrigger rose streaming from the sea and smashed back in. Sky and ocean reverberated with light.

Olopai held a coconut frond above his head. The canoe was traveling close to that point on the globe calculated to receive the most annual solar energy of any spot on this planet, and there was little shade on the canoe to escape into. Some of Olopai's companions wore hats, some wore towels wrapped around their heads. Everyone's skin was brown-black, yet when the sun neared zenith they all pulled on shirts. No race of humans has a complexion dark enough to withstand such radiation all day.

For the Carolinian women who wait at home, the cruelty of the sun is an old preoccupation. In the songs an Ifaluk Atoll woman sings when a canoe is gone, three themes repeat themselves. First is the restlessness she remembers in her husband or lover before he sailed, his inability to sleep when the favorable wind rose, his going down to shore at dawn to study the sky. Second is her wish to walk over the waves and find him. ("While my body sleeps, can I go to him in a dream? Can I go to him like rain falling?") Third is her desire to shade him from the sun and wipe his sweat away.

The coconut frond Olopai held above his head was one of many the voyagers had brought to cover their food. From its scant protection he squinted out at a scintillant sea.

When it rained at night, the darkness was as cold as the day had been hot. The men put on all their clothes and rubbed coconut oil over their bodies for warmth. The canoe was too tightly constructed to lull them by any creaking.

"Mostly at night we hear the wind," he remembers. "Just the wind, and the constant wave pounding on the outrigger. It's very quiet, much better than on the motorboat, where you bang and bang. The canoe, it rides the waves.

"It's very hard to stand up and stretch out. We sit and sleep, but not like we would sleep at home. You're saying to yourself you're sleeping, but actually you can feel the wind and waves. When the outrigger comes up and out from the water, you can feel it even when you're asleep. You open your eyes and try to run out and bring the outrigger down.

"Sometimes the swell will come in and lift up the outrigger. The swell passes underneath the canoe and the outrigger is left up in the air. It just continues going. You look at the guy who's holding the sail, and you look at the outrigger, and you look back at the guy. Because it all depends on the guy who's holding the sail. He has to release a little—let the wind out of the sail. Just let out a *little*, otherwise the outrigger will bang down.

"Sometimes there is another swell coming. When the first swell passes under the canoe, and there's another one next to it, then you just sort of hold the outrigger up until the second one goes under the outrigger. And then put it down slowly.

"I tell you, I was just like a little boy! To sit there and be able to speak the language and know what we are talking about—and I don't know how to do it! I don't know how to go out and help them control the canoe. My job was just to bail the water out.

"The big canoe can take seven, eight. On a long-distance voyage, six. To pass the time? Oh, a lot of things we do in a canoe. We pass on stories. Sometimes we joke. Pretty good jokes—those guys are good.

"You really learn about your companions. That's when you can really tell whether this person is a good person or not. Because when you're out there for quite some time, you can tell some of the crew, they start getting tired. 'I wish our navigator will do this or that, so we can get back home.' Some people, you can tell that if they were out another week, they would start hitting people on the head.

"The stories we tell are educational stories. Sometimes stories from your own life. And sometimes we will sing. Not loud, but small songs that everybody will remember, that will relax everybody. Quiet songs. That's the respect we have for the ocean. We just don't go out there with a loud voice."

Olopai's five crewmates were natives of Satawal Island returning home. The canoe route between Satawal and Saipan had only recently been reopened, after an interlude of seventy years, and the voyage was a great event in the lives of the five Satawalese. Olopai, the lowly bailer, was returning home, too, but in a more figurative way. He was a Saipanese Carolinian with no personal memory of his ancestral atoll. His voyage was perhaps the more remarkable, for he was sailing directly into the wind of history.

For the past century a great migration has been underway throughout Oceania. It has been the reverse of the heroic outward expansion that populated the Pacific. The new migration has been in a motley assortment of motor vessels, and it has been a shrinking. Everywhere in Polynesia, Melanesia, and Micronesia, young people are leaving the outer islands and small villages and heading for the district centers. Those of school age come for Western education, those slightly older to sample the twentieth century, about which they have heard such glowing accounts. They abandon the outer islands to the very young and the very old. In Oceania, the very old are the universities. Today they find few children of educable age to whom they can open their doors, and the traditional arts and sciences, maritime and otherwise, are dying. The withering of the small places, the steady flow inward from the outer islands, is the great cultural and demographic fact of Pacific life in this century. In his canoe bound for Satawal, Lino Olopai was one man sailing counter to that stream.

Olopai was thirty before he ever saw a sailing canoe. In his youth all the Carolinians of Saipan talked of such canoes, but no one had actually seen one. This state of affairs would scarcely have been conceivable to Olopai's ancestors. "In all the villages of the Carolines exist schools of navigation," wrote Jacques Arago in 1823. "No Carolinian can marry without passing an exam in sailing. A time is chosen when the sea is rather high, the candidate is placed at the sheet, and there, surrounded by reefs, and in the midst of foaming waves, he must make his proa sail a certain distance without allowing his balancer to touch the waves."

Olopai was married and a father several times before he saw a lateen sail—before he could even contemplate testing his manhood in the way traditional to his people.

That this should have come to pass in the Marianas is another giant irony, for those islands, before Spanish priests named them after Mary, were called by Spanish sailors *Las Islas de las Velas.* "The Isles of Sails" figure in an old debate among Pacific historians over which archipelago produced the best canoes. As time goes on, that debate becomes increasingly difficult to resolve—can pterodactyl outfly archaeopteryx?—but early in this century, when canoe recollections were fresher, a kind of consensus was reached: The double canoe, everyone agrees, achieved its highest development in Polynesia, the outrigger canoe in Micronesia. Outrigger canoes were common in Polynesia, but they were used there only for fishing and short errands. All intentional Polynesian voyaging was in double canoes. In Micronesia, the double canoe was virtually unknown. All canoes, from the smallest model racers and children's paddling canoes to the largest voyaging vessels, were outriggers. Micronesian outriggers had less carrying capacity than the double canoes of Polynesia, but in all other respects performed better. The best of all Micronesian canoes—in the opinion of the early European explorers, at least—were those made in the Marianas.

"More than those of any other island group," writes James Hornell in *Canoes of Oceania,* "the sailing craft of the Marianas, by reason of their swiftness and elegance, riveted the attention and aroused the admiration of every navigator who had the good fortune to see them. Their large sailing canoes came to be known as 'flying proas.'"

"I do believe they sail the best of any boats in the world," wrote Captain William Dampier, the English buccaneer. "I did here for my own satisfaction try the swiftness of one of them; sailing by our log, we had 12 knots on our reel, and she ran it all out before the half-minute glass was half out; which if it had been no more, is after the rate of 12 miles per hour; but I do believe she would have run 24 miles an hour."

Baron George Anson, who in his *Centurion* visited the island of Tinian, Saipan's neighbor, in 1742, was similarly impressed. In the Marianas, the baron pointed out, nearly all the islands lie under the same meridian, which runs at right angles to the trade wind. To get from one island to another, Chamorro canoes had to sail well with the wind on the beam, and the flying proa was nearly perfect for that. "If we examine the uncommon simplicity and ingenuity of its fabric and contrivance," the baron wrote, "or the extraordinary velocity with which it moves, we shall, in each of these articles, find it worthy of our admiration and meriting a place amongst the mechanical productions of the most civilized nations."

Of all that uncommon simplicity, of all that ingenuity of fabric and contrivance, in the Marianas not a particle remains.

It was the Chamorros' misfortune to be discovered by Europe first of all Micronesian peoples. Magellan found them in 1521, and soon afterward the Marianas became ports of call for galleons lumbering between Acapulco and Manila. By 1700, Spanish massacres, Spanish diseases, and Spanish Christianity had reduced the Chamorro population from 100,000 to 5,000. The Spaniards forcibly removed the survivors from all but one of the thirteen northern islands of the chain—the exception being Rota, where a handful hid out—and concentrated them in Guam, where their spiritual progress could be more easily monitored. In little more than a generation, the arts of canoe building and navigation died.

If the winds and Magellan's fancy had chanced to take him farther south through Micronesia, and William Dampier and Baron Anson after him, then those men might have thought a little less of Marianas canoes and saved their highest admiration for the canoes of the central Carolines.

The Carolinian outrigger was the true flying proa. Its type sailed all Micronesia from Yap to the Marshalls. "It is difficult to conceive of any possible great improvements upon the sailing canoe design of the Micronesians," James Hornell writes of this canoe, "for it combines three inventions of the utmost utility in sailing." The Chamorro canoe had only two of those three inventions. It had the center-pivoting mast, which, stepped amidships, allowed the canoe to sail with either end forward. It had the asymmetric hull, fuller on the outrigger side along both the longitudinal and the normal axes, which offset the retarding influence that the outrigger exerted on the weather side. It lacked the third invention, the cantilevered lee platform. This addition, by greatly increasing carrying capacity, made the Carolinian canoe the better voyaging vessel, and the Carolinian canoe had a more complex and better outrigger connection as well.

The Palau Islands, southwesternmost and largest of the Carolines, were the one Carolinian group in which canoes had symmetric hulls. Palauan canoes lacked lee platforms as well. The Palau Islanders were aesthetically offended by the asymmetry they saw east of them, and they referred to the more typical Carolinian canoe as a "dish." Palau was one of those big places certain of its higher civilization. All the major islands of the group were enclosed by the same lagoon, forests and reefs were extensive and rich in resources, and the people had no need to sail across open ocean to anyplace else. Both sides of the Palauan sailing canoe, the *kaep*, were sheer, neither side more so than the other, and both were beautifully inlaid with mother-of-pearl. Of all Carolinian canoes, James Hornell writes, "none attain the slim elegance and beauty of line of this canoe, built as it was for speed. The *kaep* was the Oceanic equivalent of the large racing cutter of Europe and America: it had no cargo capacity and was used mainly by the chiefs for display and in particular for long-distance races, exceedingly popular with these islanders." The Palauan canoe was a refinement of a sort characteristic of complex societies. It was a disimprovement. In Caroline canoe evolution, it was the digital watch.

It is a paradox of the old Micronesian culture that high islanders like the Palauans were less worldly than the low islanders who paid them tribute. The Romes of Micronesia were more provincial than the Ultima Thules. Low islanders were the better sailors and navigators, they built the more seaworthy canoes, they got around more, and today their languages and their cultures have the wider geographic distribution. When a Satawalese seaman made his annual tribute voyage to the high island of Yap, he deferred to the Yapese nobility and played country bumpkin, but it must have been with a small inner smile, for in truth he had seen more of the planet.

The small islanders were travelers of necessity. Coral islands are the simplest of places ecologically, lacking usually in one resource or another. To balance his diet, or to trade for a certain fabric, or to find a mate outside his clan, the outer islander jumped in his canoe and sailed off. These have been, at any rate, the common rationales. In truth, low islanders were, and are, ingenious at living off their small bits of land and reef. Atoll life pinches the stomach less than it does the spirit. There seems to be a lower limit of acreage necessary as substrate for human happiness. Palau, with 188 square miles of forest and savannah, and extensive and varied reefs, seems to be comfortably above that limit. Satawal, with less than one square mile, seems a shade below it. Puluwat is larger than Satawal, but is still below the line. The men of Puluwat are in the habit, even today, of jumping in canoes and sailing 150 miles to Truk for tobacco, though if they waited another month or two the field ship would bring it to them. Their itch to sail owes something, probably, to the addictive power of tobacco, but more to the addictive power of travel by canoe over blue ocean, and of the new faces and unfamiliar lands at the end of the voyage.

A song from Ifaluk Atoll goes:

> The sailors shove off,
> And they set out from shore.
> From island to island they make their way,
> Visiting many lands and peoples.
> The woman says, "Ah, I am seeing everything!"
> At each island they go about,
> Enjoying its beauties and wonders.
> They see Wolaul, covered with *gaingei* trees
> And the fragrant *wareng;*
> They gather *angorik* in the mountains of Truk,
> Under the eastern star.

The coconut palm is a stately tree, but awfully repetitious on most atolls and seldom more than seventy feet tall. Beaches are beautiful, white, and continuous around most coral islets, but a resident, moving at a good clip, can circumambulate them in a few hours. Atolls are lovely places lacking in grandeur. There are no purple mountains' majesty in the central Carolines, no amber waves of grain. There *is* the ocean. There are the blue, wind-kerneled fields of the Pacific and the mountains of following seas. The canoe was the means of escape into that big country. The canoe brought drama into Carolinian lives, and heroism. It loosed Carolinians on the vastness of the planet and it kept them in touch with the rest of mankind.

Saipan was depopulated, the empty place at the end of the voyage, when the canoes of the first two hundred Carolinian colonists arrived in 1815, fleeing the typhoon that had flattened their coconut palms and inundated their taro. Famine had settled back home, and the Carolinians were sailing hungry. They had traded with the Chamorros for centuries, then with the Spaniards, and they knew the star courses north. They came for fifty years in successive waves of migration, if "waves" is the right word for human numbers so modest. They founded small settlements on Tinian, Pagan, and Guam, as well, but the largest was on Saipan. They liked Saipan's roominess, which they had all to themselves, and they liked its volcanic soil, so much more productive than the coralline soils of home.

For a time, the Carolinians served as the merchant seamen of the Marianas. The remnant Chamorros had lost the arts of canoe building and navigation, and the Spanish authorities, needing canoes for interisland commerce and communication, encouraged the Carolinian settlements. For a time the Carolinians resisted acculturation. In Saipan's Carolinian community, rank and property continued to be inherited matrilineally, as they had been back in the Carolines. The caste system remained poorly developed, as it had been back home. (Society on small coral islands tends to be as weakly stratified as the geology there.) Taboos were strong, tattoos spectacular, clothing scant, sexual customs easy. The community was close knit and cooperative. Children were passed around freely among extended families. The Carolinians became Catholics, like the Chamorros, but still took time to appease the gods of rain and storm. Back home in the Carolines, those gods could combine to erase whole atolls, and gods like that are hard to forget.

In 1899 Germany bought the northern Marianas from Spain. German Capuchins replaced the Spanish Jesuits, the German language replaced Spanish in the schools, copra plantations expanded, poll taxes went up. For the first seven years of the twentieth century, Saipan was headquarters for all of Germany's Pacific possessions.

German administrators interfered in no sweeping ways with Carolinian custom. They interfered less, certainly, than did the new American administration of Guam, three islands to the south. (In 1898, Guam had been captured by a single American cruiser. The Spanish governor had surrendered, embarrassed. In his remoteness from the world, he had not known until that moment that the Spanish-American War was on.) In 1901, under American pressure to adopt Western clothing and customs, the Carolinians of Guam all moved to Saipan.

On German Saipan, the decline of Carolinian tradition was by small erosions. German census takers continued the Spanish effort to introduce a patrilineal naming system, and in time succeeded. The Carolinians ceased naming their children matrilineally. The Germans banned the sale of hard liquor to the natives and placed strict controls on the manufacture of *tuba*, the palm wine of the islands. *Tuba*, it happens, is a beverage conducive to navigation, a fortifier of courage and resolve. The district officer for Saipan, Georg Fritz, was in favor of banning the navigation aid entirely. "Since this half-fermented drink is very deleterious to the health, especially of the Carolinians, its preparation will be entirely forbidden," he wrote. Then, with the ethnocentric obtuseness of colonial officers everywhere, he added, "Beer drinking will be introduced as a substitute. This leads to no ill effects and will be self-limiting on account of the cost." Slowly, scarcely aware of it, the Carolinians of Saipan lost Carolinianness. They remained a water people, good fishermen, better swimmers than the Chamorros, but they ceased to be canoe builders. In the memories of the sons and grandsons of navigators, star courses shone on for a time, then one by one winked out.

Back home in the central Carolines, on the islands and atolls of Pulap, Elato, Lamotrek, Ifaluk, Tamatam, Pisaras, Pulusuk, Puluwat, and Satawal, traditional navigation was alive and well. No other system of navigation had yet intruded. The central Carolines lay south of Magellan's course through Micronesia, and thus south of the sway of the magnetic compass and any deviation induced by it, for Magellan's path had become, first, the route for Spanish galleons running between the Philippines and Mexico, then cruising grounds for English corsairs preying on those galleons. No square-rigged ship had business to the south, and European influence was confined to higher latitudes. The age of motor vessels had arrived, and ships occasionally visited, but the islands were too small to excite much greed or interest, and the forces of mongrelization left them pretty much alone.

Japan seized Saipan and the northern Marianas from Germany in 1914. The Japanese language replaced German in the schools. Carolinians and Chamorros were encouraged to adopt Japanese ways. By turns Iberianized and Germanized, Saipan now became one of the most Nipponized of Micronesian islands. The Japanese switched from copra production to sugar. By the time Lino Olopai was born, much of Saipan's interior was planted to cane, Japanese sugar refineries stood on shore, and 20,000 Japanese lived and worked on the island. (It was to Saipan, in the opinion of some Amelia Earhart specialists, that the aviatrix was taken after her capture by the Japanese, and it was in a Saipan jail that she died.)

In June, 1944, the American bombardment of Saipan began. For two weeks no one governed the island. Saipan's inhabitants, Carolinian, Chamorro, and Japanese, all hid out in the hills, where many of them died. American forces landed on June 15, the American conquest was completed on July 9, and the American Epoch began. (The conquest would not be absolutely complete, as a matter of fact, for another eight years. Two Japanese stragglers would hide out atop a Saipan cliff until 1952, foraging one or two nights a week for mangoes, papayas, eels, snails, and rats. By day, while young Lino Olopai and his friends were out doing their own fishing and foraging, the two Japanese were holed up in pursuit of their hobby, which was breeding canaries.) Saipan became, despite the two-man fifth column of Japanese aviarists, the headquarters for the U.S. Trust Territory of the Pacific Islands, first under Navy administration, then under the Department of the Interior. Saipan became the center for all of Micronesia's district centers. It became the most Yankeeized of all the islands in the Trust Territory.

Lino Olopai's formal education was American. It started behind the barbed wire of the concentration camps in which native

Saipanese lived for the first two years of the American Epoch, and it went no further than elementary school. His informal education was Carolinian, at the knee of Simeon Iginoes Olopai, his father. For an informal education, it was full of attention to forms.

"My father was a very traditional man," he says. "He had all of us doing agriculture and fishing every day. He was hard-working. He likes all the family to understand the relationship to all the other families. If somebody's getting married, he makes sure that all the family comes and assists, contributes. If there's a problem, he makes sure that it gets cleared up. He is fair. He makes sure everybody gets a share. The language we use at home, we have to use it the right way."

Simeon Olopai's preoccupations with lineage and kinship are preoccupations of all Micronesian society, even today. His concern for fairness, good manners, and proper language is rarer now in Micronesia. It was part of the cultural baggage the Olopai ancestors brought by canoe to the high island of Saipan from their tiny atolls of origin, atolls made habitable by those amenities just as surely as by the introduction of coconut palms and breadfruit. The atolls were too small for inequity and rudeness. Simeon Olopai's strict adherence to what survived of Carolinian custom made him a man of stature in Saipan's Carolinian community. Whole families would visit the Olopai household, seeking counsel and staying sometimes for weeks. Lino would not realize until years later what they wanted from his father, and why the Olopai house was always so crowded.

"I learned all these things from my father at home, but when I went around with my friends and listened to them talk, I realized these things were changing. It's totally different now. Here on Saipan, even though we speak the Carolinian language, and we know our relatives and stuff, still we don't have the respect. We Carolinians are supposed to have different languages for different situations. We have a different language for the kids. We have a language to use for the womens. If a woman was here, even when she's included in our conversation, we will use a different language. More polite. On Satawal we still use the different languages. On Saipan we know them too, but here it's not being practiced."

Lino's first job was as a gate guard for the CIA, which had a facility on Saipan. He was privy to no Central Intelligence Agency secrets. In the early mornings he heard drilling noises from the restricted area, but he had no idea what the CIA was fabricating on Saipan, or what the Agency was burying there. Then he became a policeman, as his father had been before him. Then he became a linguist. His father had alerted him to the importance of words, and for a time words became his profession.

"I worked for the Peace Corps as language coordinator for the Marianas and I taught both the Chamorro and Carolinian languages. That was when I began to realize that our languages were disappearing. Then in 1971 there was a special language project of the East-West Center and the Trust Territory government. They announced the program on the radio but nobody applied—no *Carolinian* applied. They were getting ready to close up their announcement. The guy running that program told me I have to sign up, because nobody else would. So I did.

"Basically, we were trying to come up with a writing system and a dictionary. I was a compiler of information and an informant at the same time. I went to Hawaii for a year. That's when I found out about the trouble between the native Hawaiians and all the other people there. That's what motivated me to really look into our traditional system. The Hawaiians are trying to preserve the local ways, while the beachfront is being taken over by the highrise."

Hawaii, the first stop for Micronesians traveling east, seems always to be a revelation for them. The first illumination comes at the airport. Before noticing anything else about America, Micronesians notice that light-skinned people, European-Americans and Japanese-Americans, are carrying the attaché cases through Honolulu airport. Brown-skinned people are carrying the brooms. That pattern repeats itself downtown. In the streets of Honolulu, Lino Olopai saw a future he didn't like.

He kept his thoughts to himself. His employer, Dr. Donald Topping of the University of Hawaii, director of the Pacific Language Development Project, remembers no serious streak in his former employee. I met Dr. Topping in the Marshall Islands, another of the archipelagos for which his native lexicographers have compiled dictionaries, and I asked him to describe Olopai then. Dr. Topping leaned back in his chair, looked skyward, and closed his eyes.

"Good informant," he said. "Musician. Charming personality. Loose. Not committed to anything."

No archipelago is an island, in the end, and back in the ancestral homeland the outside world had finally found its way in. Field ships had begun to call regularly on the central Carolines, eliminating one excuse for voyaging, or making it look increasingly foolish. Risking one's life on a tobacco voyage to Truk became harder and harder to justify to one's wife. For the men of Puluwat, the long arm of Western law eliminated another excuse. The Puluwatans, once notorious pirates and raiders, had to give those pastimes up. Carolinian canoes grew shorter, the fleets smaller. Carolinians continued to make outrigger canoes. They continued to sail on short, forty- and fifty-mile runs to neighbor atolls and turtle islands. Occasionally a Puluwat canoe, retracing the old tribute voyage, would make the 700-mile run to Yap, with a stop at Woleai or another intermediate atoll, and occasionally a Satawal canoe would do the same, but the days of serious long voyaging appeared to be finished. The star courses for longer voyages remained in the navigators' heads, and instructors laid them out routinely during navigation class—pebble constellations on the sand outside the men's house—but those courses were destined to grow dim with disuse. The Age of Diesel had dawned belatedly in the central Carolines, and the last star courses would fade finally into the light of day.

Then, in 1969, on the verge of dying, traditional Carolinian navigation began a resurrection.

In that year, a New Zealander, David Lewis, showed up at Puluwat in his ketch *Isbjorn*. Lewis was in the middle of a 13,000-mile voyage around the tropical Pacific, searching out the last of the traditional navigators. In the Santa Cruz Archipelago he had found the navigator Tevake and had arranged for the old man to sail *Isbjorn* on two short, sextantless, star-guided voyages in the Reef Islands. On Guadalcanal he had interviewed the Tikopian navigator Ramfe. In Tonga he had interviewed a great-grandson of the blind navigator Kaho Mo Vailahi. These and other men he met all practiced traditional navigation or had knowledge of it, but none were long voyagers. He came to Puluwat to remedy that. He was hunting for a man named Hipour, one of those Puluwatan navigators who had made the 700-mile voyage to Yap by way of Woleai. Hipour was not the greatest of Puluwatan navigators, but he was the best explainer among them. He had worked two years earlier with the anthropologist Thomas Gladwin, and Gladwin provided Lewis with a letter of introduction. Lewis was taking notes for his book, *We, the Navigators*. His mission on Puluwat, he thought, was to record from Hipour and his brethren the last particulars of traditional Carolinian navigation before they were lost.

Hipour agreed to Lewis's request that he navigate *Isbjorn* the five hundred miles from Puluwat to Saipan, using only traditional methods. Traditional methods were all Hipour knew. No canoe had made the voyage for sixty-five years, but that did not trouble Hipour, for the star coordinates of Saipan are ingrained like few others in the mnemonics of Puluwatan navigation, the atoll's navigators having made that run innumerable times in the days of Carolinian emigration, and earlier, during the pre-Spanish centuries of trade. Lewis stowed his compass and sextant, not because Hipour might peek—the Carolinian was unfamiliar with those instruments—but so that Lewis himself would not be tempted. One blustery afternoon they set off, Hipour at the helm, Lewis taking notes.

The turtle island of Pikelot is the customary first stop, and the only one, on the voyage from Puluwat to Saipan. As he left Puluwat for that small island, Hipour took backsights and determined that a strong current was setting *Isbjorn* northward. He referred to his memorized instructions, and they told him that the correct alternate star course for Pikelot, when the current ran that way, was toward the setting position of the Pleiades. As night fell he steered for that spot.

At eleven, the Pleiades set. Hipour no longer needed the Seven Daughters, for by then he was familiar with how the North Star and the stars of the Great Bear aligned with *Isbjorn*'s rigging, and by maintaining that alignment he kept on course. In midmorning of the next day, he made a perfect landfall on Pikelot, an uninhabited, five-hundred-yard-long speck of sand one hundred miles northwest of Puluwat.

From Pikelot, Hipour told Lewis, Saipan's actual position lay a little to the left of the setting position of the Great Bear. He was not going to head that way, however. His instructions told him that he would encounter a strong westward-running current for the entire trip to Saipan. To compensate, he should steer for the North Star, if winds were moderate, and for the rising position of the Little Bear if winds were strong. Hipour headed for the Little Bear, for winds were strong, and six days later *Isbjorn* reached Saipan.

Hipour's 900-mile round trip to Saipan and back might have remained just an exercise, an experiment good only for a few pages in David Lewis's chapter on the last vestiges of Carolinian navigation, had not Martin Raiuk, paramount chief of Satawal Island, happened to fall ill several months later. Chief Raiuk came to Saipan for treatment. Recovering in the Saipan hospital, he heard of Hipour's voyage, and it stirred the embers of old competitive fires. In their reputations for excellence in navigation, Satawal and Puluwat had long been rivals. Chief Raiuk conferred with Dr. Benusto Kaipat, a leader of Saipan's Carolinian community, and the two men decided that more voyages would be a good idea. Renewed voyaging between Saipan and the Carolinian homeland, Dr. Kaipat thought, would bring the two communities together again and would serve to strengthen the old Carolinian claim to Saipan. Renewed voyaging from Satawal, Chief Raiuk thought, would serve to keep the Puluwatans from getting swollen heads.

In 1970, two of Satawal's best navigators, the half-brothers Repunglug and Repunglap, set sail from Satawal to Saipan. The sail this time was Oceanic lateen, the vessel not a ketch like *Isbjorn*, but a twenty-six-foot outrigger canoe.

Carlos Viti, a friend of Lino Olopai's and an occasional resident of Olopai's house, witnessed the arrival of this Satawal canoe at Saipan.

A former Peace Corps Volunteer in the Lower Mortlock Islands of the Truk District, Viti was recovering at the time from a burst appendix. That fear of every Westerner who dwells for long on an

outer island (*"What if my appendix . . . ?"*) had come true for Viti in
the Lower Mortlocks. Strolling now on the Saipan beach, after three
operations and three months in the hospital, Viti, accompanied by
his doctor's son, glad to be alive, saw a triangular sail on the horizon. A sailor himself, he recognized the rig. "That looks like a sailing canoe," he said.

"It can't be," said the doctor's son. No canoe had made the 500-
mile voyage from the Carolines since the turn of the century.

The two men ran to a Hobie Cat, rigged it, and sailed out. The
triangular sail belonged to a sailing canoe, all right. Drawing close,
Viti addressed the voyagers in Lower Mortlockese, a dialect close
enough to the Satawalese for them to understand. He asked the
sun-blackened men where they came from. Satawal, they answered. Followed by the Hobie Cat, the canoe crossed the fringing
reef through the pass off Chalan Kanoa, where, it happens, many
of Saipan's Carolinians live.

"They came there on purpose," Viti says. "They know all the
passes on Guam, too, though they've never been there. *They have
star tracks to islands that aren't there anymore.* They have myths about
why those places aren't there. It's eerie. Those guys are the real
thing. They are *the men.* And there's nothing like it left."

The canoe made landfall in daylight. Had it been night, Repunglug, the chief navigator, would have entered the pass anyway,
having memorized at the knee of his father, who himself had never
seen the pass, the stars that marked the entrance.

"When we got in, Carolinians came streaming down to the
beach," Viti recalls. "But the guys from Satawal wouldn't get off the
canoe. They just sat there. They were waiting for certain formali-
ties. It shows how cut off the Carolinians of Saipan have become
from their culture. They didn't know what was up—why these
guys were just sitting in the canoe. Finally one of the *Satawalese*
guys asks, 'What's the trouble? Why the delay?'

" 'The delay?'

" 'Where is your chief?'

"The Satawalese needed to hear certain things from the chief.
The Saipanese Carolinians were embarrassed. They just looked at

each other. 'We don't have a chief.' When the Satawalese heard that, *they* just looked at each other."

(Voyaging protocol is a tricky business. In Oceania, the passengers and crew of stray or drift canoes were sometimes adopted into the high clan of the archipelago they washed up on. Their children would grow up to rule the place. Other times, they were quickly put to death. With a range like that in hospitality, it figures that manners should be circumspect. Carolinian voyagers visiting a strange atoll would put to sea immediately, even in a gale, should their hosts let slip the suggestion that they were becoming a burden to feed, or should a crew member be hurt in a fight with locals and receive no apology.)

"Finally some Saipan Carolinians went up to the hospital and got Dr. Kaipat," says Viti. "They decided he would have to do as chief. Dr. Kaipat faked his way through it—he improvised something—and finally the Satawalese came ashore. It all happened right in front of Lino's house."

With this voyage, the contest between Puluwat and Satawal escalated. When word reached Puluwat that the Satawalese had sailed to Saipan in an outrigger canoe—that Hipour's feat in *Isbjorn* had been duplicated in a traditional vessel—it was decided that Ikuliman, Puluwat's greatest navigator, would sail his outrigger canoe *Santiago* to the Marianas, not to Saipan this time, but to Guam. The canoe renaissance was gathering steam—or gaining headway.

In 1972, Carlos Viti, completely recovered from his ruptured appendix, traveled to Puluwat to accompany the voyagers, the first white man in this century to attempt a long voyage in a Carolinian canoe. "The only place the long-voyaging still exists is Puluwat and Satawal," he explains. "It's like finding a dinosaur or pterodactyl that somehow survived. The first canoe house I ever entered—it was like entering a museum. I used to get in these time warps, sitting alone in a canoe house under one of those voyaging canoes. It's Stone Age technology, yet it's so sophisticated. There are three different ways to reef sails, for example, depending on wind conditions and the weight of the cargo. And the asymmetrical hulls— only recently have engineers begun incorporating that in modern trimarans, and that was only after experiments in test tanks and with computers. Those canoes are the end products of thousands of years of trial and error. What about all the designs that failed?

"So I'm dreaming all these things in the canoe house, and in walks Ikuliman in his *thu*. The ancient race! The anachronism!"

The canoe *Santiago*, setting off on the open sea, quickly shook Viti from his time warps and his canoe-house reveries.

"You freeze your ass off," he says. "You sit in the rain and rub coconut oil on your skin. That's part of the macho—not showing any pain or suffering. The first day out, a storm hit, and I thought I had made the mistake of my life. It really hadn't dawned on me, before I left, that this could be a life-or-death situation. We didn't have a radio. We didn't even have a Band-Aid. They were chanting all night long through the storm. The little effigy comes out of the navigator's house, and they pray to that, and then the crucifix comes out. They cover all the bases. Your ass is against the wall.

"We had to take the sail down. Even after we reefed it, it was catching too much wind. We were drifting with the current and the wind. The waves and wind were loud, like freight trains going by. The outrigger hits, *boom!* You see white water as it hits, and then it goes under. You count the seconds until it comes back up again. You couldn't see anything; you had to listen for the sound. *Whoosh.* We didn't sleep at all."

In the rain of that storm, and afterward, in the sun of following days, Viti and his crewmates donned the broad-brimmed, conical palm-frond hats traditionally worn by Puluwatan voyagers. The weave was tight, the hats waterproof. In the rain, the hats kept heads dry; in the sun, cool. Each man brought along the Carolinian portmanteau, a long green duffel fashioned of a single palm frond, its free edges stitched together. Inside, each kept his rations of fresh and preserved breadfruit. When they had finished the fresh, the sailors started in on the dry, and they ate turtle eggs collected during their stop on Pikelot. Besides Ikuliman and Viti, there were Faipi, Ponimar, Sia, and Manas. Sia's name meant "outrigger brace," a comforting name to have along on a voyage. Manas was Ikuliman's grandson, twelve years old, and for him this Guam trip was an instructional voyage.

Before departure, an immigration bureaucrat on Guam, irritated that the Puluwatans would attempt such a crossing, but unable to stop it, had informed Viti that *Santiago* would have to clear customs, like any other foreign vessel, before the crew could go ashore on Guam. It was dark, unfortunately, when the canoe reached the island, six days after leaving Puluwatan waters—the first outrigger in the twentieth century to have made that passage. Customs was closed. The voyagers debated whether they should spend the night at sea or sneak in for a night's rest, then sail out in the morning to make a proper entrance. On the one hand, the current was setting them out, they were hungry, and another storm was making up. On the other, the dark and mountainous island before them was bigger than anything they had ever seen, and spangled with electric lights, and somewhere on it were jails. The crew turned to Viti. Their job, they said, had been to navigate the canoe here; his was to deal with the white people. It was up to him to decide. Viti voted for shore.

They slipped in through the reef and headed for a beach that looked small and ideal. It proved to be Nimitz Beach, one of the most popular on the island, but no one on the canoe knew Guam, and they sailed on innocent of their mistake. As they coasted the beach, they smelled chickens cooking in beachfront houses. The aroma drove them crazy. They saw the glow of television screens through beachfront windows. None of the Puluwatans had seen television and none knew what the glow signified. For Viti, the incongruity of that glow and the aroma of the chicken had set his head to reeling. The canoe had traveled just six days and five hundred miles from Puluwat, but somewhere in between it had crossed an uncharted dateline, and had emerged several centuries later on the other side.

The voyagers saw a light on the water near shore, a fishing boat heading out. The fisherman's flashlight drew closer, and the puttering of his small outboard grew louder. The voyagers ceased their paddling. They kept quiet and let *Santiago* drift.

The fisherman, an old Chamorro, was steering for the reef as he had a thousand times before. His light swept the dark lagoon ahead. One moment, the water was yellow-green and empty in the circle of his beam. The next, a great outrigger canoe drifted there, silent, its crew, dark men in loincloths, staring at him, their paddles poised.

"Hello," said one of the apparitions.

For a moment the old fisherman was unable to speak.

"*Taotaomona?*" he asked finally. "The Ancestors?"

"No, no," said their spokesman. "No, I'm an American."

The fisherman was not inclined to believe it. Viti, an Italian-American from North Beach in San Francisco, is a dark-skinned man. His Mediterranean complexion, darkened by five years in Micronesia, then fired in the kiln of the last six days on a shadeless canoe under the brightest sun on Earth, was nearly a Carolinian chocolate. He was wearing a loincloth, besides.

Hours later, when the canoe was hauled up below the fisherman's house, and when the old Chamorro had awakened his wife and they were feeding the voyagers with old-style island hospitality, he would admit that at first he had mistaken them for ghosts. In a way, of course, he had been right.

Before dawn the next morning, the Puluwatans were anxious to be underway before they were seen, but the fisherman insisted on going to the store for coffee. Traffic began moving on Guam's roads. A schoolbus pulled off on the shoulder, and the Filipino driver stepped out to stare at the canoe. Finally, coffee finished, *Santiago* pulled away. The Puluwatans sailed out beyond the reef, turned, and sailed in again to make their second arrival on Guam, triumphant and official this time.

The crew cleared customs with a few minor hitches. The immigration officer was cranky at first, for the Puluwatans had no papers, and Guam's immigration forms proved a puzzle. The old Western incantation, "Last name first, middle name, first name last," did not apply. Each inhabitant of Puluwat has only one name.

Since the first few Caroline-Marianas voyages of the early seventies, the navigators of Puluwat and Satawal have gone wild, visiting places their grandfathers never did, sailing right off their ancestral star charts. At present, Satawal would seem to hold the lead in the contest, for in 1976 the navigator Piailug of Satawal sailed the double canoe *Hokule'a*, a "performance equivalent" replica of the traditional Hawaiian voyaging canoe, on a 2,500-mile trip from Hawaii to Tahiti, retracing the most heroic of the milk runs of old Oceania.

*Hokule'a* is the Hawaiian name for Arcturus, the star that once guided Polynesian canoes north to Hawaii. The canoe's voyage south again, a millennium later, was the State of Hawaii's bicentennial project. On board were seventeen men, among them David Lewis, caught up now in the revival he had helped begin. There were chickens, a pig, and a poi dog, Hoku. The dog, like the canoe itself, was an approximation, the result of the Honolulu Zoo's attempts to breed back to the barkless animal whose meat had fed the old Hawaiians. For historical accuracy, Hoku probably should have been eaten in the launching ceremony, as sympathetic magic to aid *Hokule'a* in biting through the swells, but the dog survived the launch, then seasickness, and lived to complete the voyage. Piailug, a Carolinian, was chosen as navigator because there had been no Hawaiian navigators for five centuries. In all Oceania, the Caroline Islanders were the only candidates left. Though not particularly famous among his colleagues on Satawal, Piailug was willing and adaptable. He stationed himself at *Hokule'a*'s stern and seldom left it for the whole month of the voyage to Tahiti. When he slept, it was briefly, in a rope hammock he made for himself and slung between the two steering paddles. In his Satawal apprenticeship, he had memorized no star courses between Hawaii and Tahiti, of course, as that Polynesian run was far outside the Carolinian realm. Carolinian navigators learn the star coordinates of their destination islands by means of mnemonic chants. Piailug, lacking a chant for Tahiti, made up a little tune from scratch. At the beginning of the trip he was supplied with the knowledge any Polynesian captain would have had: the distance to his destination; the location of reference archipelagos, which Carolinians use as aids in judging distance covered; and the currents and winds he could expect on his way. These became his verses. Humming his tune for Tahiti from time to time, he applied his dead-reckoning skills and reached his goal without technical difficulty.

The difficulties were in other departments.

"Before we sail, throw away all things that are worrying you,"

Piailug told the crew in a brief speech at the start. The crew, unfortunately, had lost that art. It may be that five centuries of dormancy are too long, and that after such a period the auxiliary graces of Oceanic seamanship cannot be revived. The crew complained about the food, disputed the decisions of the captain, and divided into factions. In the absence of watches and chronometer, they argued over the time and debated whose turn it was to be on watch. Several crew members smuggled a transistor radio aboard and listened to Hawaiian news accounts of *Hokule'a*'s progress, which were being relayed back home by the ketch escorting the canoe. No information about *Hokule'a*'s position got back to Piailug, but the radio, in the eyes of purists, might have been seen to compromise the navigator's feat. There was racial trouble between the native Hawaiians and the white men aboard, and there was a fight. Piailug conducted himself with dignity throughout. He is the only expedition member about whom all factions and all crew members speak favorably. The feeling was not mutual. In Tahiti, Piailug jumped ship, passing up the return voyage to Hawaii and flying back to the Trust Territory.

"Now I go home now," he said in a tape recording he left behind. "Why I go home? The crew no good. I sail with the first crew. The first crew no good. I not sail with the second crew, I think the second crew no good either. I not go back to Hawaii. Don't ask me to come to Hawaii ever again. That's all now. Bye-bye."

Lino Olopai, away in Hawaii compiling his Carolinian dictionary, missed the arrival of the first Satawal canoe in front of his house. He missed the other early voyages of the renaissance. In Hawaii, he was not thinking about canoes; he was worrying about the fading of Carolinian customs, of Carolinian sensibilities. He was contemplating a return to one of those outer islands where the traditional life was strong.

"I never thought about Satawal at first," he says, "because my grandfather's background is from the island of Pulusuk, several miles east of Satawal. That was the only place I had in mind. I thought, 'One of these days I'll go back and see how my grandfather's family survives.'

"About a year after I returned from Hawaii, in May 1974, my cousin Piailug came up from Satawal with two canoes. They reaffirmed all those things I had heard about my cultural background. I had always heard stories about canoes sailing back and forth. I only half-and-half actually believed the whole thing, until I saw that canoe. I didn't know my cousin Piailug. Then I find out we are related. So now I started asking my cousin what it was like there in Satawal, and whether our traditional things are still being practiced. I asked him if it was safe enough to go with them on the canoe. He said all the things that I want to hear. That made me make up my mind to go."

In November 1974, the two Satawal canoes set off for home with Olopai aboard. The men with whom he had thrown in his lot were sailing, as they had always sailed, without sextant or radar or depthfinder. They went naked except for loincloths, equipped only with their wits.

"Were you scared?" I asked him, of that maiden voyage.

"No. Before I went with them I was kind of afraid, but during the time my cousin was here, from May to November, I got to ask him things, and that sort of relieved me a little. But I was still a little scared. Several times we had to put the sail down, because of strong winds and high waves. And sometimes we would run into calm water where there was no wind. I was learning the whole time."

"Did you ever feel in danger of being lost?"

Olopai smiled and shook his head. "That was one thing I never believed we would do. Both canoes were run by experienced navigators. In the daytime the canoes stayed within sight of each other. Nighttime we were pretty close, like from here to the door. Then in the morning we sort of spread out again.

"It was a week's crossing. First we reached this small island, we call it West Fayu. It's uninhabited, a turtle island. There were some guys over there waiting for us. They had come up in some canoes from Satawal.

"It's a relief, a big relief. I know we will get there, but still. . . . We came in at nine-thirty that night, to West Fayu, and then we just drift. The next morning, when you got up and looked at that island, and you saw smoke over there . . .

"When we got to Satawal, the women are the ones that pull our canoe up on the beach. Usually the men do that. The women tied a rope to the canoe and they lined up and pulled it in. They came over to the canoe and just crashed into us. They were glad we made it. They climbed all over the canoe and grab whatever they can find and throw it up on the beach. They went up to one of their relatives, punched him, and put his head in the water."

With this rough treatment at the hands of their women, Satawal's heroes returned home, and Lino Olopai began his three years of residence on the island. It was a while before the sailors were allowed to sleep. They were red-eyed and weary from the nearly constant wakefulness of their voyage, but on Satawal there is no rest for the heroic. "The fatigue signs are there," Olopai says, "but also we are excited. We have to go to the party. It's a must to show respect for the customs. I didn't get to bed until one in the morning. Then I got up at six. On Satawal there's always something to do."

In the next three years, he would return to Saipan several times, once to fetch his wife and youngest son, again when there were illnesses in the family, but for most of those years he resided in his people's past. He exchanged his Western clothes for a loincloth. He got himself the traditional tattoo that runs the length of his thigh. He made copra to earn cigarette and coffee money. He developed a taste for *tuba*. He learned navigation.

"The hard part was trying to adjust to living without electricity," he told me. "Eating the kind of food where you don't have spices added. The food over there is pretty much natural food. We have the same things on Saipan—taro and breadfruit and fish—but it's just the way they prepare it. It's less than what I'm used to. It was hard getting used to that, to that and the kind of hard physical work they were doing."

He looked over at Vickie Olopai, his wife. She is a sturdily built, humorous woman a shade lighter in complexion than her husband. "You take a woman with high heels and stockings out there, she's going to die," he said cheerfully.

"The work is hard to adjust to," Mrs. Olopai agreed. "I think the woman has the hardest work. I thought I was going to die. The life is hard, but the people, they survive. They are healthier than any Marianas people. The island is small and crowded—five hundred people on that small island. But I was sad to leave. I really liked it, but I missed my kids. We only had Peter with us."

"It *was* crowded," said Lino, "but that didn't bother me. Privacy? That's another thing you wouldn't have, privacy. Say in the man's house. All the young mans sleep over there. You take your mat and put it anywhere you want it. Someone comes and want to sleep next to you, and talk to you about Saipan, and stuff like that. After a while you move and try to sleep over in another place. One or two other guys will come and put down their mat next to you and talk. That will go on and on, until—I don't know when—the next thing you know, the light is up, it's early in the morning.

"There's a lot of talk about Saipan in the traditional songs on Satawal, but nobody on Satawal has been there. So with me over there, they asked questions. They're asking how Saipan is different from their island. Was it pretty much flat, or sandy all around? Was it the size of Satawal, or bigger? Is there a mountain? How big is the mountain? They don't ask about cars and television. Those things comes in, but it's more about what the island looks like."

"My kids didn't want to go," said Vickie. "The school on Satawal is very small. For high school, Satawal kids have to go to Ulithi."

"They say the whole educational system came from the ghosts," said Lino. "In the *ut*—the man's house—they tell ghost stories. Ghosts get married to human beings, and they pass these things on. Some of our traditional medicines came from the ghosts. If someone is real sick, the spirits of the ancestors—the ghosts—will come to someone. Like to you. Suddenly you will be speaking, but it won't be you. You will tell us where to find the medicines.

"It was the ghosts who taught people to build canoes. When the ghosts were out on their own canoe, it flies.

"There are a lot of taboos—things you are not supposed to do before you get on the canoe. Even among the ghosts themselves, there are a lot of things they shouldn't be doing. And also before they even *build* the canoe. Otherwise, they will end up with a bad-luck canoe, a canoe that will get them in trouble, or that won't go very fast. Even the ghosts themselves, they have to watch these restrictions."

"What were some of those restrictions?" I asked.

"I don't know. My cousin, he would probably know. Anyway, in the old days, because the taboos were well practiced, the canoe itself would fly on the air. Just like a flying fish. It would come down, touch the water, and just fly up again. Canoes no longer fly like that, because a lot of the things we shouldn't be doing, we're doing them now. Now, when we ride a canoe, it stays on the water. But before, they say these things fly.

"They teach navigation in the *ut*. The chief of the people that own the navigational system puts down a mat, and that opens the class. It's a sleeping mat—any mat. When they use it for announcing the teaching of navigational art, it becomes special. But it could be any mat. It could be *your* sleeping mat. The class continues for about three months, and many people take it. I was not the oldest. Many older people are learning, brushing up on what they learned as kids. They just have to ask the families that own the navigational system for permission to take the course.

"When they take up the mat again, the class is over for most of the people. But for some it's just beginning. Certain individuals are picked by certain clans—an individual for each clan—and those are the ones that will actually become navigators. These chosen people, they can't go out. They just sit in the men's house. All the community involved brings food and whatever. If you're a teacher or a student, that's all you're going to do, one morning to the next morning. If I'm your teacher and you're my student, that's all you're going to do, is just learn. You go to sleep, and the first thing that happens when you get up, the teaching starts. The teachers take shifts, some morning to evening, some evening to midnight. Even if you sleep, there's an old man waiting for you to wake up. If you want to eat, we bring the food in to you. No women allowed. No other *man* allowed except those man that will bring food. They keep everybody away from there. This could continue on for six months or a year."

"It must really burn the lessons into them," I suggested.

"It has to," he said. "Because that's their life. And not only themselves. Once these people become navigators—once they go out on the blue water on boats—they'll be taking other people with them, womens and children. It's for the community use. That's why the community are involved during the teaching in making sure they have food."

"How would they teach a course to an island—to Saipan, say?"

"It's a list under a certain star. Take the North Star. You would learn that from here you take the North Star, and continue north until you run into a certain animal, then continue north again until you run into this kind of seaweeds, then continue until—no more, that ends it. Sometimes an island might be mixed in that list. Sometimes in the list for a star there's no island, just an animal, or maybe two animals or three. Could be no island, just the next star in the main list.

"Let's say we want to go up to Truk. You say, I'm going to go north; now I'm going to hit this, now I'm going to hit that, now I'm going to hit another thing—a different list for Truk. Different lists for every course. It takes years to memorize."

"Do old navigators ever lose their memories?"

He shook his head. "That's why the last part is the song. We have the navigational song. The song tells how this animal is related to that animal in the list. It's not hard to remember the song. There'd be a song for Truk. You'd sing some song for Truk."

The compass employed by Carolinian navigators is no small thing of metal and glass. Theirs is gigantic, encompassing a goodly portion of the galaxy, and theirs is immune to magnetic deviation. To get his bearings, the Carolinian navigator does not look down into a binnacle light; he looks up into heaven. His compass face is the spangled dome of the night sky, and his map is his memory.

The star compass or "sidereal compass" of the Carolinians, like the magnetic compass of European mariners, is divided into thirty-two points. This is not imitation, yet neither is it accident. The Carolinian compass is much the older, but both instruments were well developed by the time they met. It would seem that dividing the horizon into four cardinal points simply comes naturally to humans, the inevitable first step for an animal interested in the naming of directions. The natural second step is to divide each quadrant again, producing eight points, then to divide once more, producing sixteen, then to divide a final time. Thirty-two points, for a globe the size of ours, occupied by islands on the scale of our own, and sailed by helmsmen as sober, seems to be enough for a navigator to steer by and to find his way around.

On the Carolinian compass, each point is marked by a star or constellation. The stars are picked not for their magnitude, but for the convenience of their position around the horizon. The Carolinian navigator is friendly with many of the dimmer lights of heaven and is often guided all night by stars of the fourth and fifth magnitude. Most navigational stars are useful to him twice each night. They mark one point of the compass on rising, a reciprocal point on setting. (A star that rises in the southeast sets in the southwest.) A Carolinian navigator can steer by a star ahead of him, or a constellation astern, or stars off to one side or the other. Polaris, the Pole Star, which Carolinians call "The Star That Never Moves" (*Feusamakut*, in Satawalese), marks only one direction, north, but the Southern Cross marks five different steering points in its elliptical path across the sky. As the Earth turns, the Southern Cross nightly erects itself in the southern sky and nightly falls again. At rise, the Cross lies on its side and marks one steering point. When it has tipped up to a forty-five-degree angle, it marks a second. At zenith, and upright, it marks a third point, our south. In decline, when it has tilted again to a forty-five-degree angle, it marks a fourth. On its side again, setting, it marks a fifth. The navigator in his long apprenticeship has memorized the star bearings for all the islands his people ever wished to visit. He knows not just the star song from his home island to each of them, but the songs from each of them to all the others. He knows star courses to islands his instructor never visited, nor his instructor's teacher, nor the instructor before that. His head is as glittery with star bearings, nearly, as heaven is with stars.

> The captain recalls his sea lore,
> Remembers the guiding star for Ifaluk;
> When one is down, another rises.
> He remembers those stars
> Deep within him,
> Stars by which he can steer,
> And grows impatient to be on his way.

Repunglug and Repunglap, the Satawalese half-brothers who

in 1970 reopened the route between Satawal and Saipan, began their voyage with its traditional first leg, a fifty-two-mile trip to West Fayu, the small turtle island north of Satawal. They waited four days on West Fayu until favorable southerly winds came up, then set off again, steering for the point on the sidereal compass that Satawalese call Tupenmailepaifang—the spot where the Little Dipper sets. Repunglug, taking a backsight at West Fayu, saw that the island lay under Wenewenelupe, the Southern Cross in its up-right position, or due south. Satisfied, he held course for Tupenmailepaifang. Later in the night, when his memorized instructions and his own calculations told him that his destination, Saipan, had "moved" to a position under Feusamakut—Polaris—he changed course for that star.

Knowledge of the stars is not enough, of course, for they shine less than half the time. In the day, the Carolinian navigator steers by the sun, noting its bearing at rise and set, and checking its position over the canoe during the day's middle hours. In daytime and on overcast nights, he holds course by consulting the swells.

Swells are decayed waves generated by distant wind systems. The most reliable swells are those generated in the seasonally persistent weather of the trade winds. Recognizing the right trade-wind swell is not easy. It is hard even for a trained eye to pick out those characteristics that distinguish swells from waves generated by local winds; harder still to tell one swell from another. At a given time, swells may be arriving from four directions at once. The navigator does not "read" his familiar swell so much as he feels it. "Holding course by swells," writes David Lewis in We, the Navigators, "seems always to be a matter more of feel than sight—which emphasises the value of the art on overcast nights. Tevake told me he would sometimes retire to the hut on his canoe's outrigger platform, where he could lie down and without distraction more readily direct the helmsman onto the proper course by analysing the roll and pitch of the vessel as it corkscrewed over the waves. In distinguishing swells, he stressed, you have to wait patiently until the one you want has a spell of being prominent and discernible." Navigation in Oceania is so much a matter of feel, indeed, that famous navigators have occasionally been blind men.

The currents in the Carolines are among the trickiest in the Pacific. The islands of the group are strung out along the equator, where the North Equatorial Current, the Equatorial Counter Current, and the South Equatorial Current all flow and eddy, sometimes in this direction, sometimes in that. Current slows a vessel, or speeds it, or displaces it laterally. Lateral displacement is most bothersome to the navigator: his helmsman steers dutifully toward one star, but the current is imperceptibly setting him toward another. Compensation for current drift is more art than science. It is one of the more difficult things a Carolinian navigator must learn. Sitting on his bench at the middle of the canoe, the navigator has no sensation of the current, nor does the helmsman with his foot in the sea, for there are no reference points; everything on the surface is moving along with the current. The only remedy is for the navigator to take careful back bearings at the beginning of his trip to determine the current set, then adjust his calculations accordingly. If the current is strong, his instructions call for him to steer for a certain star. If it is weak, he is to steer for another.

"Clearly it was only through the trial and error of innumerable canoe voyages," writes David Lewis, "that the Carolinians were able to elucidate the most complex of Pacific currents for a 1900-mile east-west span—more than the distance from London to Kiev or New York to the Rockies—and about 840 miles south to north."

The navigator must also learn to estimate leeway—the lateral drift of his vessel under sail. Occasionally he is forced to estimate gale drift, as well. Gale drift is the lesser problem. Strong winds blow in Micronesian waters, and it is often necessary to drop sail and drift, yet, since an outrigger canoe drifts with its outrigger to windward, lessening the drift, the canoe seldom strays far from its "path." (On the third day of Repunglug's and Repunglap's voyage to Saipan, strong winds forced them to lower the sail. When, hours later, the wind fell sufficiently for them to raise sail again, they judged that the gale had not set them far off course. Pretending that nothing had happened, they headed for Tupenmailepaifang, as before.)

However unsettling it may seem to someone who learned his navigation in the West, the Carolinian navigator keeps track of his position through a conceptual scheme in which the ocean's islands are continually moving around on him. The Carolinian uses the concept of moving islands in two ways. The first is in the system called *etak*, by which the navigator divides his journey into segments. The second is in tacking.

In *etak*, the navigator picks an *etak* or "reference" island off to the side of the course he is to take. Ideally the reference island is the third apex in an equilateral triangle of which the island of departure and the island of destination are the first two apexes. Seldom, though, is the configuration so perfect. The first Europeans to hear about *etak* missed the subtlety of the system and misunderstood the function of *etak* islands. They assumed that these tangential islands must serve as havens in storm, and called them "refuge" islands. In fact, the reference island is often just a reef, all sharp coral—no refuge at all. The navigator never sees his *etak* island, but he knows always where it is. Making allowances for wind and current, marking time by the movement of the sun and stars and by his internal chronometer—that built-in biological clock that wakes some of us at the same hour each morning—the navigator estimates the speed of his canoe. Knowing his speed, he can, in his imagination, keep track of the "movement" of his reference island under the navigation stars. In his mind's eye, the island appears to move backward, and he speaks of it as "moving." If he is sailing east, the reference island will slide west. If, at the beginning of an eastward voyage, his reference island is under Aldebaran, it will move to a spot under the Pleiades, then under Vega, then Cassiopeia, then the Big Dipper. Its arrival under each new star begins a new segment, or new *etak*, in the voyage.

In tacking, as the navigator sails upwind toward his island of destination, he keeps mental track of its movement under the stars, just as he did with the *etak* island. Not until the very end of the voyage does he see his destination, yet, knowing his speed on each tack, he has been following its progress from star to star and knows always where it is.

This is a dead-reckoning system. It has fewer affinities with the system of Magellan and Cook than it does with the inertial navigation systems of a supertanker or an aircraft carrier. The Carolinian navigator, like the shipboard computer, constantly processes information and keeps continuous track of his position. If, for any length of time, the computer is unplugged—if for any length of time the navigator falls asleep—then supertanker or canoe loses track of its position. In the Carolines, fortunately, most men attend navigation class for a greater or lesser time, and in a given crew there are usually one or more competent men who can serve as backup computers-in-loincloth, should the principal computer-in-loincloth need a nap.

The navigator has certain capabilities that the shipboard computer lacks. The computer, for one, is no ornithologist, and the navigator has to be. Of the several techniques a Carolinian navigator has for "expanding" his target, the most effective depends on his knowledge of birds.

> He fills out the sail, taking in the sheet.
> He sees the black tern and the booby
> And the snowy white fairy tern.
> He knows he is close to shore.

Birds provide just one of the "screens" that the navigator uses to deflect him inward to his destination, or to catch him should he overshoot it. The screen can be a small island in the vicinity of his destination island. It can be a reef; either a shallow shoal upon which surf breaks, or a deep reef twenty or thirty fathoms down, detectable only by its changing the ocean's deep blue to a greenish tint. The screen can be a whole archipelago. I once asked Lino Olopai if his Satawalese instructors taught a star course to the Philippines. "The Philippines are no problem," he answered. "We use the Philippines as a backup. They are a very long chain of islands. If we miss our island in Micronesia, eventually we hit the Philippines." The Philippines, of course, are a screen of last resort. It is preferable not to miss your island so badly.

Sea birds serve to expand both the target island and any islands in its screen, if those are large and dry enough for birds to nest on. In their daily fishing sorties out, terns, boobies, and frigate birds enlarge their nesting islands by as much as twenty-five miles in all directions, thereby sometimes trebling the size of the target. Noddy terns and white terns are the species most depended upon.

At dusk, the terns head home, and the navigator, taking note of their bearing, follows. Boobies, though less common than terns in Micronesia, are even more useful when a navigator encounters them. Their range is greater, their behavior even more convenient. Thomas Gladwin, who sailed on short voyages with Hipour of Puluwat two years before Hipour's epochal voyage to Saipan, has written of the navigator's high regard for that species:

"Hipour described their habits to me in terms which were downright affectionate. He said that as the day ends and the various birds start heading for home, a booby which comes upon a sailing canoe will turn and start circling over it. He acts as though he wants to land on it, but does not. At last when the sky is almost dark he finally, perhaps reluctantly, leaves the canoe and heads straight for home. By his circling he commands the attention of even the most inattentive navigator and the course he sets at last is unerringly true. What more could one ask?"

The navigator, it must be said, has certain deficiencies that the shipboard computer lacks. The computer has no taste for *tuba*, the white lightning of the Carolines. In an inertial navigation system, this would seem to be a virtue. The computer is never drunk and seldom has a good time. The Carolinian navigator often is and does, yet he usually finds his island anyway. The high tolerance for alcohol demonstrated by Carolinian navigation—its land-finding accuracy in spite of *tuba*—is one of the wonders of the system.

Michael McCoy, Director of Marine Resources for the Federated States of Micronesia, is an outsider who has wondered at it. McCoy began his career in Micronesia as a Peace Corps Volunteer on Satawal. He is married to a Satawalese woman and he periodically returns to the island with his wife and their children. Occasionally he makes short voyages in outrigger canoes.

"Before a trip they're all completely snockered," he told me. "Cirrhosis is the main cause of death among men on Satawal. There is so much drinking on the outer islands generally that it's a principal method of birth control. I was snockered myself every night for four years. Looking back on it now, I can hardly believe it. But I was snockered every night. The treacherous thing about *tuba* is that it doesn't give you a hangover."

McCoy is a big man who once played football in the United

States. Except for the Satawalese tattoos all over him, he looks like someone whose vice should be beer.

"There are periods of abstinence," he conceded. "The chief declares the islands dry if there's a lot of fishing or breadfruit harvesting to be done. Climbing breadfruit trees is dangerous enough, even when you're sober. The chief says, 'This hurts me more than it does you,' and he declares the island dry. They all quit cold turkey. That's amazing, for an island of alkies. There's no punishment involved; it's just that no one would think of breaking the taboo. But usually on the morning of the voyage everyone's drunk. You're sitting in the men's house at 7 A.M., downing the *tuba*.

"'Why do we always do this?' I asked them once.

"'It might be our last chance,' they said. 'We may never come back.'"

McCoy was seated at his desk at the Department of Marine Resources, on the big, lush mountain island of Ponape, but there was a lot of Satawal in his office. On the walls were Satawalese pearl-shell lures his father-in-law had made. They were beautiful. The hooks were cut from turtle shell and lashed with sennit to the concave side of each iridescent pearl-shell spoon. On his person were those Satawalese tattoos. Among the papers atop one of his files was a photograph of a Satawalese woman at an outdoor fire cooking taro. A large taro leaf was serving the woman as pot lid. Her hair, cut short in mourning for a dead aunt, was just beginning to grow back and was bristly and boyish. She was bare-breasted and fine-looking. She was Mrs. Michael McCoy.

"It's a very small place," he said. "The things that make a crisis on Satawal are so small—petty things. You have big island meetings about things that are fairly trivial. But it's a *whole* place. The society is egalitarian, unlike a lot of larger places in Micronesia. The chiefs still have a sense of *noblesse oblige*.

"On Satawal I don't feel isolated, because of the canoes. You ask yourself sometimes, 'What if my kid fell on a knife?' If that happens, you just jump in a canoe and go to Saipan. It's different on other outer islands where they've lost navigation. On those places, when you see that ship go over the horizon, you really feel isolated.

"I've been to some places in the outer islands . . . they aren't as lively. Nama, in the Mortlocks, that place is dead. The people aren't engaged in day-to-day activities that are interesting.

"I've noticed that things are cyclical in Satawal. Like when you were a kid, with marbles or baseball cards—a fad will sweep through. A man builds a one-man paddling canoe. Soon every men's house is building a one-man paddling canoe. Then it burns out and they turn to something else. Sometimes an anthropologist comes for a short time and says, 'Geez, these people build a lot of one-man paddling canoes.'

"Some of the fishing techniques . . . There's one where they use a coconut for a float, with a length of line attached and baited with a piece of copra meat. For flying fish. If you look at the amount of energy put in for the protein recovered, it doesn't make a lot of sense. It's sport. But some of the fishing is very efficient. The Satawalese are probably the best in the world at pelagic pole-and-line fishing for skipjack. You use a sailing canoe, poles, line, and eight or nine guys. It's probably the best fishing on Satawal. You don't throw any bait. The splashing and the motion of the outrigger pounding down in the water and coming back up produces a lot of froth and attracts the fish. They just come up right behind the boat. No bait, no nothing. The pearl-shell lures are fantastic. The fish are small skipjack and you pull them in, *whisst whisst*. When the fish are runnin' and the wind's blowin', you can bring in a ton, a ton and a half. *Whisst whissst*, five hundred to six hundred fish in the canoe at a crack, two to three pounds apiece. You're screaming and jumping up and down. It's the most fun I've ever had in my life."

It was fortunate, McCoy added, that the skipjack fishing offshore of Satawal was so good, for reef fishing on Satawal was bad. "There's only a half square mile of reef on Satawal. Satawal is poor in reef fish. The people are very, very conscious of the limitations on that reef. Taboos close off portions of the reef in certain seasons. For the past eight months, it's been taboo to use a spear on the reef. And sometimes they ban nets. There are areas where they don't allow fishing at all. Rough areas of surf. They think of those as preserves for recruitment.

"Some of the fishing taboos are no longer in effect. At one time you couldn't take matches with you, you couldn't smoke, you couldn't have sex with your wife in particular spots. The taboos on taking pelagic species have been relaxed, and that's good. There were old taboos on skipjack that weren't really necessary. But in general the taboos were an efficient system. The turtle taboos in the Carolines *worked.* In Satawal, for example, you couldn't take a hawksbill. Margie Falanruw thinks that the introduction of Western religion meant trouble for the reef, and she's right. You've got to have a substitute for that old system."

McCoy paused, then digressed, or seemed to: "If I was president of the Federated States of Micronesia, I'd make every government official go back to his home island for three months of the year. Back to Mokil. Back to Woleai."

He paused and digressed again, or seemed to: "You can always tell what a guy's like in Micronesia by what he's got on his feet. Never trust anybody with white shoes. If he has a matching white belt, that's even worse."

McCoy gave me his other Shoe Laws, which go, as I recall them: Bare feet, man is from village. Zoris, man is from Peace Corps. Sandals, man wants to wear zoris, but has visited the outside world and thinks he should do better. Sandals *and socks,* man is something else again, I have forgotten what, except that it is unflattering.

Then McCoy told canoe stories:

One time he and five teen-age Satawalese boys set off for West Fayu with a blind-drunk navigator. The critical part of a West Fayu voyage comes first, when the navigator takes his backsights at Satawal, and McCoy watched the drunken man carefully through that stage, asking now and again if he was all right. Fine, the navigator said, perfect, and then halfway to West Fayu he passed out. The computer-in-loincloth had come unplugged. The dead-reckoning system went dead. Nothing showed on the navigator's inner screen but the static of *tuba* dreams. The Satawalese boys sailed on undaunted, convinced that they could complete this simplest of voyages in Satawal's repertoire. "We haven't seen it yet," they would admit to McCoy periodically, "but we're right on course. It should be straight ahead." Eighteen hours later, the navigator awoke with a start. "Where are we?" he asked. "Why didn't somebody wake me? Where's the island?"

For the next two days they cast about for West Fayu without success. They saw not a sign of land. "We had a lot of food," said McCoy, "but summer winds are variable, and the wind died down. It was a very foolish thing to do. I've never done it again."

At the end of the second day, becalmed, the Satawalese spotted a Japanese fishing boat. Taking off their red loincloths, they waved them in the air. When the Japanese boat turned their way, the Satawalese told McCoy to lie down in the canoe hull. They covered him with mats and coconuts. The Japanese were fishing illegally. If they saw McCoy, the Satawalese reasoned, they would take him for a government official, veer, and head away.

Buried in coconuts, McCoy listened to the conversation as the Japanese boat came alongside. West Fayu, the Japanese said, was thirty miles *that* way—McCoy in the darkness had no way of telling which. The Satawalese thanked the Japanese, but pointed out that there was no wind. Could the fishermen possibly give them a tow? The Japanese consented. As they towed the canoe slowly toward West Fayu, the Japanese passed down orange juice and rice, and McCoy, entombed in coconuts, heard his comrades eating above. He called up that he wanted out. He was hungry; he had to take a leak. The Satawalese hissed back fiercely that he should shut up.

For five hours they steamed toward West Fayu, McCoy calling out now and again like Lazarus, the Satawalese hushing him. West Fayu was drawing close, they said, and with the nearness of land the Japanese poachers seemed to be getting spooked. McCoy gathered that the atoll was in sight. He made his move. The mats parted, coconuts spilled away, and big, bearded Mike McCoy, a white man tattooed like Queequeg, rose roaring. With that materialization, the Japanese cast off.

(One of McCoy's chores now as director of Marine Resources for the Federated States is to prosecute poachers in Micronesian waters. For whatever reason, he seems incapable of working up much righteous anger toward small-time transgressors of the type who rescued him that day off West Fayu. "We recently caught an Okinawan guy with no license in Truk," he told me. "He had to go into

Tol Island with a leak, or something. We fined him a little. He wasn't one of the guys you really want to catch. He was just a little forty-ton wooden long-liner. It's a different story if you get a big U.S. superseiner with a helicopter aboard and everybody on the aft deck drinking martinis. Those are the guys you want to capture.")

Another time, said McCoy, some Satawalese in a canoe came upon a Japanese long line. As Satawalese are prone to do, they sailed along the line, taking whatever its intervals offered: bait, hooks, tuna, glass floats. Coming to the radio beacon, they cut that off too and took it along. This was a mistake. The Japanese followed the beep and overtook the canoe.

"Thank God, you've saved us!" cried one of the Satawalese, thinking fast. He explained that until this moment the canoe had been lost. Why, then, asked the Japanese, had they taken the radio beacon? Only to call attention to their plight, said the Satawalese. The Japanese were not fooled. The beep had been leading straight to Satawal, they said, and the canoe was pointed that way now.

"Ah, but we're from *Puluwat*," said the Satawalese, naming their ancient rival.

In McCoy's opinion, these occasional Satawalese thefts from Japanese long lines are not from need, but from boredom. The men want adventure, now that the days of inter-island raiding are done.

One time a Satawal canoe, driven by ennui and a brisk wind, set off for the neighboring atoll of Lamotrek with a cargo of monitor lizards. Lamotrek was the one place in the central Carolines whose inhabitants were not plagued by those big, four-foot-long, egg-stealing reptiles, and the Satawalese planned to remedy that. Nearing Lamotrek, the Satawalese dropped their sail, the traditional Carolinian signal of peaceful intent. They paddled in the remaining two miles, as custom prescribed. A short distance off the beach, they shipped their paddles and released the monitors from their cages. The lizards swam for shore in waves, big tails snaking, tongues flickering, long necks straining above the water. Lamotrek women bathing in the lagoon screamed. Lamotrek men ran down to the water and attacked the lizards as they landed. The Satawalese turned, raised sail, and headed home, not to return to Lamotrek for another two years.

Then McCoy told about the Satawal custom of suicide by canoe. Micronesian society has always spoiled its young, McCoy feels,
and he sees suicide, which is too common among young Micronesians, as a sort of ultimate tantrum. Here on Ponape, a father recently had refused to buy his son a candy bar, he said. To teach the
old man a lesson, the boy had blown his own brains out. In the
archipelago of Truk, young men hang themselves. On Satawal, the
instrument of choice is the canoe. "Once one of the guys in our
family got mad at our father," McCoy recalled. "The kid was hys-
terical. They restrained him but he broke away and ran off. Our
father took a machete and went around and cut the lashings to the
outriggers on all the canoes. It took a week and a half to repair
them."

Another young Satawal man, drunk and angry, set off for
oblivion in a twelve-foot paddling canoe with just a coconut frond
for a paddle. He woke the next morning on the open ocean, no
land in sight. For a moment he wondered what he was doing out
there. Then he remembered. Sobering rapidly, he had a change of
heart. He figured his position roughly, playing back his memory of
the night's long drunken paddle, just as a young Westerner might
reconstruct the count of a half-heard clock, or pull back from the
void a teacher's half-heard question. He saw that the wind and current were setting him west. He knew the stars, set course for Lamotrek, and reached that atoll after four days of paddling with his
frond. The incident of the monitor lizards had been forgiven, apparently, for the young man survived.

As McCoy spoke, a sailing canoe rounded a green point of land
outside his window and stood out to sea. Ponape has never been
famous for its sailors, and the canoe surprised me. I called McCoy's
attention to his window.

"That's good to see," he said, watching the canoe.

Micronesia was in the middle of a fuel crisis. The tanker that
serves the islands had been delayed by engine failure somewhere
in Indonesia and was now more than a month overdue. Ponapean
fishermen in increasing numbers were leaving their outboard engines ashore and letting the wind take them out.

Contemplating the sail, McCoy's mind jumped archipelagos.

"It was a big mistake, the Yap road system," he said. "The Yapese had a beautiful water transport system. They should have kept it on the water."

The canoe's sail was a boomed spritsail, not Oceanic lateen, but it was white and beautiful anyway against the blue. While we watched, a second spritsail rounded the point and followed after it.

Lino Olopai, back home in Saipan and the twentieth century, drives home from work at the airport. He passes the Saipan Grand Hotel, the Saipan Beach Intercontinental Inn, the Hafadai Beach Hotel, Saipan Wholesalers, Deak & Co., Boutique 101, La Boutique de Ann, Saipan Bowling Center, Pay-less Supermarket, Avis, Hertz, Bank of Hawaii, Bank of America, California First Bank, Microl Corporation, Joeten Motor Sales, Aoi Restaurant, and Kentucky Fried Chicken.

He passes the Nauru Building. This gray structure, modern and five stories tall, is a monument of sorts to one of Micronesia's several possible futures.

The inhabitants of Nauru, an island republic at the edge of Micronesia, have made the happy discovery that you can turn your island into cash. They are in the process of converting the substance of Nauru to dollars and redistributing it in Swiss and American banks and in enterprises like Air Nauru and the Nauru Building. The substance of Nauru is phosphate, phenomenally rich deposits of it, and the citizens of the island are, per capita, the wealthiest in the world. They don't mine the phosphate themselves; they hire foreign laborers to do it. Air Nauru, the republic's commercial airline, operates always in the red, but it keeps its owners entertained. Nauru boys once played with cross-boomed model racing outriggers they called *to mage*. Nauru men now play with airliners. As their island grows smaller, the Nauruans themselves grow larger. They spend much of their time drinking beer and eating, and the average Nauruan is enormous.

Atop the Nauru Building sits what appears to be a flying saucer but is in fact a restaurant named Taipei. The Taipei is the only revolving restaurant in Micronesia and is likely to hold that distinction forever. In passing the Nauru Building one day with Olopai, I had a little fantasy. Back in Nauru, I imagined, *all* structures had that circular thing on top. It was a provision of the Nauru building code. The thing would perch there, an apparent revolving restaurant but in fact a flying saucer, until the day the dollar crashed or the last of the phosphate was redeposited in Switzerland, whichever came first. Then the Nauruans would waddle or roll themselves up the gangways, the saucers would detach and fly away.

The Nauru Building fell behind. The green interval of palms or scrub acacia that separate each of Saipan's private enterprises from the next grew longer. The car left the twentieth-century stretch of the road and entered the village of Chalan Kanoa. Olopai turned off into his sandy driveway and pulled up beside his house.

"Just a typical Micronesian-style house," he said, gesturing apologetically toward his door. The apology was much too cheerful and proud. It wasn't an apology at all.

The Olopai house is not the concrete, air-conditioned, energy-intensive kind to which most Micronesian bureaucrats aspire. It is the kind of house you see everywhere in the small villages and outer islands of Micronesia. The roof was tin, the windows shuttered but without glass, the plywood floors raised on pilings three feet off the sand. In the villages and outer islands, Micronesians have been slow to understand the need for furniture, and inside Olopai's house I saw none. The door was open and Vickie Olopai was inside, lying on the floor. For Oceanic women, this is a classic pose, and was so even before Gauguin.

From the Olopais' east windows, the view seaward might have been the view from any sea windows on any small atoll in Micronesia. In the foreground stood the trunks of a few last palms—the only vertical elements in the composition. Beyond was the horizontal white of the sand, and then the turquoise and the aquamarine of the lagoon, and then, halfway to the horizon, the meandering white line of surf on the reef, and finally the dark blue of open ocean.

Lino's twelve-year-old son, Typhoon, brought us two Budweisers from the house. His father introduced us, and I smiled at the boy's name. Typhoon, accustomed to that smile, laughed. Typhoon was born in a typhoon. He is a solid boy with big legs, like a Samoan's, and he wears a permanent grin. Typhoon's name continues to amuse Typhoon and his parents, even now, twelve years after the rotating winds of his namesake abated. Part of the humor of the name may be in its inappropriateness. Typhoon is remarkably untyphoonlike. No one in the Olopai family has a sunnier disposition.

The father of Typhoon slipped out of his shirt. Carrying our beers in either hand, he directed me seaward to a thatch-roofed, high-peaked, open-air shelter he has built outside his house. Shelters like this are common in Micronesian villages. They are refuges at midday from the heat inside the house, and gathering places in the afternoons for talk and recuperation. Olopai spends much of his time out here on his own. The Olopai shelter is cool and open to the breeze. In the shade of the thatch, two picnic tables have been pushed together, end to end. We sat, and Olopai pointed up at the thatch. "We can talk about building a house like this," he said. "I can tell you about putting the crosspieces on, making the thatch, and so forth. But doing it is another thing. It's a lot of work."

A short distance seaward, the beach came to a slight crest, and there, partly shaded by a pandanus tree, rested a small outrigger sailing canoe.

The canoe was all curviform, like the big Puluwat canoe at the airport. Its lines and proportions were nearly identical, but this canoe was from Satawal and it was just sixteen feet long. The mast was gone. Rolled up with the sail and its yard and S-curved boom, it had been stored Satawal-style outside the main house, under the tin overhang of the roof. Without its mast, a Carolinian canoe has even more of that sea-bird look. This canoe was a shearwater, or an albatross, or another of those Procellariiformes whose wingtips clear the sea with the finest of tolerances. It shaved the imperceptible crest of sand as closely as the bird would shave the crest of a swell on a calm and glassy day.

The hull was painted the old Carolinian colors, red above, black below. Five inches up into the red, a thin black line ran the length of the canoe. This was the Carolinian plimsoll line. A canoe should not be so heavily loaded that it rides any deeper, Olopai informed me. Carolinians still make their own black pigment, he said. Their red and their orange they buy now in cans. Walking over, I ran my hand along the Carolinian black of the lower hull. It was still very black, still almost like lacquer, though the shine was a bit sun-dulled and cloudy now. On Satawal a canoehouse would have shaded it from the rays. The store-bought red, like the red on the airport canoe, had faded.

The Satawalese word for "sailing canoe" was *waa*, Olopai said, and he spelled it out.

"Do canoes on Satawal have individual names?" I asked.

"Yes," he said.

Canoe naming was once common in much of Oceania, I knew, and I was happy to learn that it survived in the Carolines. Canoe names were often secret, and I wondered whether I would learn this one.

"Does this canoe have a name?"

"Yeah. The kids gave it a name. They call it *U-drive*."

He laughed along with me, then explained, "They call it *U-drive* because, when this canoe was in Satawal, almost anybody can just go there and use it without asking the owner. It's an old boat— about eleven years old. It swamped a lot coming over. A canoe this size is not meant for such a long voyage."

Vickie Olopai emerged from the house, carrying the family's Satawal photo album, a cardboard box jammed with pictures. She set it on the picnic table. Flanked by the two Olopais, I began look- ing through.

There were many voyaging photographs. Some showed tat- tooed men in loincloths sitting on their outrigger platforms—mari- ners from the Stone Age. Others showed mariners dressed in odds and ends of Western clothing—mariners in transition. Most were relatives, Olopai's country cousins. There was a young helmsman on a blustery day, his foot on the steering paddle, his head hooded with a towel. There was an older man cooking on deck on a store- bought hibachi, his towel held in place by an old Army fatigue cap, which gave him the look of a Foreign Legionnaire. There was a thirsty man in khaki shorts tipping back a drinking coconut. Over my shoulder, Lino studied this thirsty man. "Before we had mod- ern containers, we just brought coconuts," he said. "We still bring coconuts: brown ones, green ones, husked ones—all kinds. But nowadays we also use five-gallon plastic containers. And sometimes we take a Japanese fishing float and make a hole in it. We fill it and plug up the hole."

I examined the photograph of the young helmsman in the towel turban. It is a gray day in the photo, and the steering paddle is sending its wave back over the young man's foot. He looks cold.

How is it that the inventors of the asymmetric hull, the cantilevered lee platform, ambidextrous prows, and so many other bright ideas could not figure a way to get the helmsman's foot out of the ocean? Maybe they didn't care. In Oceania, sailors tended to be vague about where they left off and the ocean began. In the canoes of New Guinea's Humboldt Bay, one tacking maneuver required a member of the crew to loosen a stay and jump overboard with the rope in his hand. The New Guinea man overboard did not consider this an imposition, and maybe the Carolinian helmsman felt the same way. Maybe the old designers *wanted* the helmsman's foot in the water, to keep him in touch with the ocean, or just to keep him awake.

There was a group portrait of a crew of Satawalese voyagers at Expo '75 in Okinawa. The voyagers stand stiffly, draped with leis and surrounded by their Okinawan hosts. The leader of the Satawalese is the navigator Repunglug. In 1975, as the contest between Satawal and Puluwat escalated, Repunglug had followed a star course here to Okinawa, demonstrating, the year before Piailug's Hawaii-Tahiti voyage, that journeys beyond Micronesia were still within the capabilities of Carolinian navigation. In the portrait, everyone looks grim, both Satawalese and Okinawans. Something seems to have gone sour. Perhaps opening a canoe route to Okinawa was not such a good idea.

There was a portrait of the same Repunglug back home on Satawal. He looks a little tipsy, as do the laughing men around him. Everyone seems to be having a much better time. Repunglug appears to be in his mid-forties. He is leaner than most Satawalese men that age. He is wearing a woman's dress.

The dress made me uneasy. It did not figure that one of Satawal's premier navigators should be wearing a dress. It hinted that Repunglug had spent *too* much time in the canoe—that the triumph of his voyage to Okinawa had come at a terrible cost.

"Lino, what's going on?" I asked, showing him Repunglug in drag.

Olopai peered at the photograph. "He's just fooling around," Lino said.

Repunglug, "Repung the Younger," is not the greatest navigator on Satawal. He is regarded as slightly less great than his half-brother Repunglap, "Repung the Elder." The older Repung has not sailed to Okinawa or anyplace else outside the Carolinian realm, but such voyages do not count enormously in the estimation of the Satawalese. On Satawal, navigators are measured less by what they do than by what they know. "Repunglug is a little bit braver," Lino explains it. "He goes out more in the canoe. But Repunglap knows more star courses." In Polynesia, where pure boldness in a navigator was more highly regarded, or in Leif Ericson's Scandinavia, or in the court of Queen Isabella, the younger Repung might have outranked his big brother, but not on his home island. Similarly, Piailug, despite his 2,500-mile trip to Tahiti, is considered a little less great than the Repungs. Piailug's voyage was far longer than any that either of the Repungs has pulled off, and it caused a greater stir in the world outside, but on Satawal Piailug remains somewhat less famous than either of the half-brothers. "Piailug is really a unique guy," Mike McCoy explains. "One of the most unique in the world. Though he's not even the best navigator on Satawal. What he is, is the best navigator that can handle the Western world. He could conceive what was *happening* with the stars and canoes, whereas most Satawalese navigators would be ducks out of water if you took them to the Northern Hemisphere. Piailug could perceive that his system is just part of a greater system, and he had the ability to adapt it."

(Of Piailug's genius, his cousin Lino Olopai takes a simpler view. When I asked once what personal qualities made Piailug a great navigator, Lino answered, "He just like to travel in the canoe.")

There were several pictures of Piailug in the photo box. In none of them is Piailug smiling. The navigator is a thick-set man with big legs and powerful arms. His face in the photographs is always saturnine, male, self-contained. He has a presence less animated than Repunglug's, but more arresting. The name Piailug comes up so often in Lino's conversation about Satawal that it soon

becomes apparent he is a kind of alter ego for Olopai. Piailug is the
man Olopai would want to be, had he been born on Satawal.

"He is strong," Olopai told me, as we studied a portrait of his
cousin. "He's very quiet. No, most navigators aren't like that. Only
him. A lot of the navigators, they're friendly, they fool around with
the kids, the womens, the old mans. But Piailug . . . even the chief,
when he talk with Piailug, he have to be pretty sensitive about
what he's going to tell Piailug.

"He's not a storyteller—he's a listener. He's not only a navigator, he's also a canoe builder, and he knows a lot of traditional
songs.

"There are times when the chief puts a certain kind of restric-
tion on the island. All the people confine themself to the men's
house every evening. We get up a bonfire by the men's house. All
the men and women will come to the men's house—the women, of
course, will sit around outside. And all the men, including boys—
little boys—will be in there dancing. It's a ceremonial thing. You
can really tell the difference, when we start singing and Piailug is
not there. It's not very lively. But once they see Piailug come in and
that guy starts singing and dancing, hey, everybody will just jump
around.

"And, of course, most of the time Piailug is half drunk. He
always has a good time when he drinks. When he drinks, that guy
is pretty good to talk to. When he's not drinking, that guy won't
talk.

"When he is here in Saipan, I take him out on the town. I tell
him, 'Look, there are some things here that are against our tradition, but I want you to see these things, and see the way they look,
and compare it to how we live on Satawal.' There are a lot of things
on Saipan that violate our traditions. Like we'll be sitting, and some
women, even some of the Carolinian women, will just come
straight to us—you know, they wouldn't even bend down. And
they will talk to the man when he is sitting. Chamorro women will
do that too—even though with them it's better, because they don't
understand our custom. When we're talking, they'll pass right between us. It is especially bad to do that when the chief is talking to
someone. It's especially bad when a woman does it.

"I take Piailug to bars. We take him and his crew out and see the strip shows. It blows their minds. I say, 'Well, this is just to show you what money can do. If these women don't do these things, they're not going to survive. They won't have money to pay for the same foods we are eating from the taro patch, the same food we are getting from the water. Is this the kind of jobs you want our womens to do? You decide it. I just want you to see it, what money can do.'"

In the photo box, mixed in with the voyaging pictures, were general scenes from Satawal:

A girl searching the black mass of a woman's hair for head lice. The woman is bare-breasted, the girl intent. They are engaged in a primate ritual older than *Homo sapiens*.

A man of about fifty making caulk. He is pounding sap from a breadfruit tree against a large, flat stone. His toes, prehensile, are helping to hold the stone in place.

A canoe being hauled out of the water, sliding up the beach along a slipway of palm leaves.

A canoe beached and shielded by matting from the sun.

A captured leatherback turtle on the beach with several curious Satawalese men standing over it. The leatherback is an ancient and anomalous species rare even for Satawal, whose inhabitants see a lot of sea turtles. The man most interested in the turtle is in his late middle age. He is heavily tattooed, and the lobes of his ears have been stretched into great loops to hold some ornament no longer there.

A group of women in *lava-lavas*, laughing and straining at one end of a rope. At the other end, Olopai explained, was a group of island men, and a diviner was watching the contest closely. The diviner was a specialist at predicting, from the vagaries of a tug-of-war, the quality of the breadfruit harvest that year. "You know the men are going to win," Lino said, "but it's how the fight goes."

There were other special talents on Satawal, he said. "One man makes medicine to attract the tuna. Another man knows medicine to bring in drift logs. There is a man for the current, even a man for the thunder, but they don't exercise those anymore. The knowledge is there. They could do it if they wanted to."

Of the portraits in the photo box, a large proportion were of elders, and as I flipped through, Olopai provided commentary on them. "This old man is my instructor," he said. Then, "This is the old man who tattooed me." Then, "That old man is gone already." I came to one grizzled Satawalese who, except for a new wristwatch, had to my eye a look of singular unsuccess. I could not believe that this man was a specialist in anything. "His name is Igi Ngung," said Lino. "He's the best one to bring canoes in over the reef in big waves. When *I* try that on Satawal, even in my little paddling canoe, many times I swamp it. My canoe goes over, I lose all my fish. I have to look for my fish and everything, and the people laugh at me."

Igi Ngung's talent was for reading the surf, Lino explained. He knew the rhythms of swells as they came ashore as well as the navigator knew those swells out on the open sea. He would sit in a returning canoe, just outside the reef, supervising as a rope was swum in to shore. When a group of villagers had gathered on the beach and readied themselves to pull, Igi Ngung would stand in the canoe and watch the sea behind him. When a smooth stretch of water presented itself between sets of waves, he would raise his hand, and everyone on shore would pull like hell. The rope's attachment to the canoe was rigged for quick release. Ignoring the haulers, Igi Ngung scrutinized the sea. If he saw a wave building too soon, he signaled a crewman in the bow to release the rope. It was like depressing a clutch. The people on shore continued running with the rope, but they were no longer engaged. Once the wave had broken, Igi Ngung would signal to the canoe's crew to grab the rope again.

In a number of the portraits of Satawal's men, I had noticed a peculiar thing. It was most apparent in a man named Schomai, who reappeared now and again in the photo box. Schomai looked as lithe and strong as a hurdler or javelin thrower. His eyes had the big, clear whites you see in small boys; and his dark skin was firm and unlined, as nearly as I could tell from the photographs. Yet his hair was snow-white. The effect was startling. If I had not seen the phenomenon before in Micronesia's outer islands, I would have guessed that this was a joke in the spirit of Repunglug's dress—that Schomai was a young man who had dyed his hair white.

"Look at him," I said. "His parts don't match. His body is too young for his head."

Olopai glanced at Schomai and nodded. "They all look that way," he said.

There was a single photograph from Saipan in the box. It was a beach scene snapped shortly after the arrival of canoes from Satawal. A half-naked, sun-darkened Carolinian voyager is bending over a small Saipanese Carolinian girl. They are long-lost cousins whom a peculiar twist of Micronesian history has separated until this moment. He is wearing a *thu*, she her best white Sunday dress, and their faces are close as he blows a grain of sand from her eye.

The Satawal photo album was still out on the table when one of the figures inside arrived in the flesh. Piailug's seventeen-year-old son, Tony, who lives now with the Olopais, had come home from school. Tony had sailed up from Satawal on the big canoe that accompanied *U-drive* to Saipan. He is the first student in a Carolinian exchange program that Lino wants to establish between the Marianas and the central Carolines.

Lino said something to the boy in Satawalese. Tony turned and disappeared into the house. He left wearing his school clothes, a white short-sleeved shirt and dark trousers. When he emerged a minute later, he was wearing a bright-red *thu*. He joined us under the thatch shelter, sat atop a picnic table, and prepared to spin sennit.

This was a demonstration of Satawal life for my benefit, not a daily after-school habit. If Tony preferred doing something else that afternoon, from his face there was no way of telling. He studied the pile of brown fiber he had spread on the tabletop beside him. His eyes were slow, calm, detached. The fiber had been split from coconut husks that had been soaked for several months in seawater, and the clumps of it still held the coconut's curve. After five seconds of gazing, he selected out a bunch of fiber and began rolling it against his thigh. The thigh was dark-brown and muscular. Near the knee were two raised keloid scars.

Tony seemed a genuine chip off the old Piailug block. Like his father, he was strong. His body looked older than seventeen, the muscle in his arms and shoulders hard and legitimate, the kind you see in prizefighters. In school on Saipan he gets straight A's in math, Lino boasts. Aptitude in mathematics figures, probably, in

Piailug's son, the latest in a line of navigators, but straight A's are a neat trick, just the same, in a boy who has traveled directly from the Stone Age to a modern classroom.

Tony bent over his thigh, sleepily attentive to the sennit that was forming there. When the fiber was rolled into a tight string about three inches long, he bent a little closer. Separating one end into strands, he plaited some loose fiber into it and proceeded to roll again. Three trips up and down the smoothness of his thigh were enough for each new bundle of fiber to have slimmed itself into sennit and become an increment of his growing length of line.

"It's very relaxing," said Lino as we watched. "On Satawal, young men always do it in their spare time, whenever they have a moment."

Lino went to the house and returned with the final product, some light rope coiled Satawal style into two batons. Each was about two feet long. The pattern of the coiling was simple yet elegant. The batons were light as cork and so tight-wound that they hummed in your hand when you struck them together. They were pieces of art. It was hard to imagine the islander so philistine that he could unravel one for use in something practical, though of course that must happen all the time.

It was late morning, and the airport's second-floor coffeeshop was deserted, except for the Chamorro waitress. Lino Olopai, Chief of Airport Security, could have sat at any of the tables on the terrace. He chose to walk from the shady section into the sunlight, and out to the very end of the row by the rail. "I like to sit on the end where I can watch things," he said. He set his white hat on the table and laid his walkie-talkie beside it. He ordered *asoba*. As the waitress departed he called something after her in the Chamorro language. Olopai thought it was funny. The waitress was not much amused.

I sat across from him, and for a while we surveyed the airport together. I nodded around at the over-ambitious architecture surrounding us. "Has it ever crossed your mind that someday all of this may fail?" I asked. "That canoe travel might actually come back?"

"Yes. I sort of foresee that. If all the Space Age out there ... fails. But my motivation is mostly just to have boats for the up-coming generation. To keep it alive. And not just canoes—the other traditions too. All of our eldest are now dying. They're very few now, and even those few, I'm probably as good as them in know-ing the customs. Or maybe not—maybe less. But once they're gone you won't have any more resources. We can only talk about it, then. A lot of these kids will come back from college and ask us about the clan system, and no one will know. The kid won't even know what clan he's from."

"You spend a lot of time worrying about it?"

"Yes."

"You don't want to see it go?"

"No."

"Because it's a good system?"

"Yes. It's a good system. Good only for us. If you tried to ex-port it somewhere else, like to San Francisco, it wouldn't work. But it's good for us."

"What are the good things about it?"

"The respect we have is very important. Everybody knows where they belong. Titles are inherited from the father's line. Land is inherited from the mother's side. Look at the U.S. and the elec-tions you're having. That would not be possible in our system. On Satawal you see the chief, and you know when that man dies, his son will replace him. In Saipan we are losing that. Carolinians here are beginning to follow the Chamorro system."

"And the Chamorros got it from the Spanish," I suggested.

"And the Chamorros got it from the Spanish," he agreed. He shook his head. "And it's a pretty strange system."

The waitress brought his bowl of *asoba*. Olopai made another joke with her in Chamorro. She seemed to like this one better. He sprinkled hot sauce on his *asoba*, tasted it, then sprinkled some more. I wondered how he could stand it. Lino Olopai's higher sen-sibilities may be pure Carolinian, but his palate has been subverted by the piquancy of Spanish-Chamorro cuisine. The walkie-talkie on the table crackled from time to time as we ate. For me the noise was doubly unintelligible; the Chamorro language garbled by static.

None of the messages was for Olopai, or if one was, he chose to ignore it.

"Everybody here thought I was crazy," he said. "But after I went to Satawal, they admired it. The people here on Saipan are impressed by the canoes. Every time a canoe comes up from Satawal, they have parties. Those people have been up from Satawal and Puluwat so many times, but no one thinks to sponsor one of them to stay here and to sort of revive the whole thing."

"That's why you sponsored Tony?"

"Right. What Piailug and I plan to do in the future, maybe next year, is for Piailug to come up from Satawal and stay maybe here, maybe in another area. And what we're going to do is build us a canoe, a big one, just like this one we have at the airport—a canoe for long distance. It would take us maybe a year to build a canoe here and get the Carolinians here involved in making the canoe, and to teach them to manage and control the canoe in the water. To take them out fishing and so forth. When the Satawalese go back home, *they will have a canoe from Saipan.* And then we will have a communications. In the following years when they come up again, hopefully I'll have some of the young men trained in some of these things by then, and when the canoe goes back to Satawal, those kids will go too. That's what me and Piailug are planning.

"Right now we go fishing almost every weekend in that small canoe, *U-drive,* and people see that boat on the water. They ask questions about it. Just yesterday a guy from YACC, the Young Adult Conservation Corps here on Saipan, he spoke to me. He plans to plant breadfruit trees on Saipan, and he wanted my help."

"Breadfruit," I said, puzzled for a moment. "To make canoe hulls?"

"Right." Lino smiled. "I really think in ten more years it's going to happen."

There was one thing more I needed from Olopai. I wanted to learn the song for Satawal. That mnemonic chant, in guiding his canoe on its voyage back into Carolinian tradition, had become for Olopai a sort of personal anthem, and I planned to end my story with its opening lines. I knew that declassifying the song would not be easy. Almost all Micronesian knowledge is privileged knowledge, the private property of a family or clan, and of all this secret information, none is more closely guarded than the particulars of navigation.

I had a general idea of how Carolinian navigation songs go, for on Ifaluk Edwin Burrows had succeeded in recording one, or a bowdlerized facsimile.

It gave directions from Puluwat to Satawan, an atoll several hundred miles to the east. Of the hundreds of chants that the people of Ifaluk allowed Burrows to record, only this one contained a list of guiding stars. It went:

> The star Meleilal
> Hangs over the pass at Puluwat
> And the beach Pieigore.
> The canoe goes through the pass to the beach.
> The outrigger lashing is repaired,
> Then she turns her prow toward the north
> And loads the platform with young coconuts.
> People gather to help.
> We steer for the star Mwagoliker
> Pointing toward Malrepul at one end
> And Pugulivairi at the other
> Of the crooked reef, the place to open coconuts,
> Called Truatali Velatrik.
> We steer for the star Alualu,
> Then, when nearing Satawan, for Serewalu,
> And make the pass Gepitau.
> Metaru and Metumuri,
> West-northwest, when the sun goes down,
> Hang over the pass Faleor e bwaut.

But the song for Satawan was not the song for Satawal, and that was the one I wanted. I doubted sometimes that I would get it. In certain of Olopai's answers to my navigation questions, I had already begun to hear—or to think I heard—the parts he was leaving out.

"Were there taboos you had to observe before your trip to Satawal?" I asked once.

"No, nothing. Nothing except my cousin told me I have to listen to him, watch everything he's doing, and then imitate him."

Perhaps Olopai really was unable to remember specific taboos. More likely, I thought, the taboos were none of my business. Another time I asked him if an outrigger canoe could be righted at sea if the wind flipped it.

"Yes," he answered. "That's how good these canoes are. There are several techniques. One is for everyone to just stand on the outrigger, and the weight flips the canoe back. If that doesn't work, we have a way of putting the mast on the outrigger, and we use that as a lever. Then you have to get the mast out quick, or it snaps."

"Is there a name for that first technique?"

"There's a name for it, but I don't remember. It's something like a cosign for it. But it's not a cosign, it's a name of that one method we use to bring the canoe back up. As soon as the navigator says, 'Okay, we're going to bring the canoe back up, and we're going to do it this way,' then everybody knows what he's going to do."

Perhaps Lino had simply forgotten the word, and I was imagining things. But it did seem strange that Olopai, a student not just of Carolinian navigation, but of the Carolinian language, should have forgotten a term which, uttered in a crisis at sea, informed each Carolinian seaman how he was to save the canoe and himself. In Micronesia, certain words once had power and magic in them, and it occurred to me that this navigator's command might have been one of those.

From my conversations with Carlos Viti, the photographer, I knew that prior to his voyage from Puluwat to Guam he had encountered similar blank spots in his Puluwatan crew mates.

"I asked them about *pwue*," Viti had told me. "A navigator has to have four ingredients: he has to know the stars, the wave patterns, the sea life—both mythical and what we would call 'real'—and he has to know *pwue*. *Pwue* is tying coconut shoots in knots for divination. You read the knots to predict the weather and decide whether the time is right to sail. The legend is that a canoe came down from heaven carrying gods, and every island that received the gods honorably was given this knowledge of *pwue*. We were getting ready to leave on the voyage when I asked them about *pwue*. 'Where did you hear about that?' they asked me. 'In old German books.' 'Yes? Well, that's something the old people did. We

don't do that anymore.' That's what they said. But while I was photographing the canoe preparations, I noticed that Ikuliman was doing *pwue* every day, morning and afternoon."

It was moments later, strangely, as Viti and I discussed
Puluwatan navigation, that I encountered one of those blank spots
in Carlos Viti himself.

"Tell me about the effigy," I said.

Viti had mentioned in passing, on another occasion, the effigy
to which his Puluwatan mates had prayed during a storm. I
thought this might be Aluluei, one of the Carolinian gods of seafaring, a sort of islanders' Janus. According to Edwin Burrows, who
heard about Aluluei on Ifaluk, the god had two faces. One pair of
his eyes looked forward and saw what human beings see; the other
pair looked back and saw the dangers the future held for the canoe.
Wooden images of the god were kept by certain Ifaluk navigators.
Each image had, Burrows wrote, "a manlike head and upper body,
but a sort of stand below the torso, with several prongs instead of
legs." When Burrows was on Ifaluk in 1947, he was told that none
of the images existed any longer on the atoll, but references to the
god appear now and again in the chants he recorded.

> The god of navigation descends upon the captain.
> He takes a coconut leaf,
> Waves it back and forth to moderate the wind.
> He counts the knots in a strip of leaf
> And gets a happy augury.
> The god Tegiti descends upon the captain,
> Looks down and watches over him.
> The great god Aluluei comes upon him.

"What did it look like?" I asked Viti. "That effigy they kept in
the navigator's hut?"

He looked uncomfortable.

"They had a little weather effigy in there," he said slowly. "It
was two figures, back to back. Both had faces, with the heads back
to back. Both had two legs made from the barbs of stingrays. It was
eerie. You could just look at it and you knew it was a heavy effigy.
Heavy black magic."

He stopped.

"So they had one in the navigator's hut?" I prompted.

Viti looked away and failed to answer for a moment. "Maybe I saw one on a *Satawal* canoe," he lied. "When we got in that real big squall one night, they would chant, and also they would pray—I guess maybe they were praying to an effigy like that. I'd seen one on another voyaging canoe—on a Satawal canoe. In the little hut where the navigator sits, up in the eaves of the hut. When I asked them what it was there for, they said, 'Oh, we just never bothered to take it out.'" Viti looked back at me again. "I don't want to say if we had one in our canoe," he said, and our discussion of the effigy ended.

At one Saturday-afternoon get-together under the Olopais' beach shelter, I saw my chance. If I was ever to learn the song for Satawal, now was the time. The beer was flowing, as it usually does on weekends at the Olopais'. The conversation was loud and loose. The friends were numerous. The benches of the two picnic tables were jammed with people: several Carolinians, a Yapese, a Palauan, an Englishman, a Frenchwoman, three Americans, and one American Samoan.

The American Samoan was Milton John Falemalama Coleman, who for two years had taught math on Saipan. The conversation jumped around, as conversation will when fueled by beer, and Milton Coleman was often the first to leap to a new subject. Somehow we turned to dolphins, and Coleman told us a story about the American Samoan village of Fagasa, the inhabitants of which are expert dolphin hunters. In modern times a contingent from the village traveled to Hawaii and visited the dolphin tank at Sea Life Park. With the Fagasa villagers in the audience, the Sea Life dolphins refused to jump. "Dolphins aren't stupid, they communicate real good," Coleman explained. "It's a true story. My father told me. If you don't believe me, go to the governor's office in American Samoa."

Coleman's father, Peter Coleman, is governor of American Samoa. Before taking that job, he served for a time as High Commissioner of the Trust Territory of the Pacific Islands and was stationed here on Saipan.

"All islanders are ethnocentric," the governor's son told us.

"Tahitians say Tahiti is best. Palauans say Palau is best. But do you know which islands were called 'the Navigator Islands'? *American Samoa.*"

I glanced over at Olopai to see his reaction. There was none, except perhaps for a very slight smile. He was not interested in debating which islanders were the best navigators.

We discussed the series of big waves that had recently hit the Marshall Islands. Vickie Olopai told the gathering that a similar series had hit Satawal during her time there. "Lino was away in Yap," she said. "I thought, 'Very good! You take me away from my home island to this little mosquito island, and you're safe in a concrete house in Yap!'"

Lino grinned and sipped his beer.

The talk turned to cultural diffusion. We tried to list all those archipelagos to which the custom of locking little fingers and saying *"pinge"* had spread. We discussed the custom of raising eyebrows to signify yes. I thought that this bit of body language was local to the Caroline Islands, but Lino said it was everywhere in Micronesia, and Milton Coleman told us it had reached Samoa too. Lino then told us that the only universal word in Micronesia was *bot* and its variations—the word for "nose." Except for that, he said, the languages of western Micronesia, Palau, Yap, and Chamorro were unrelated to one another and to all other Micronesian languages. Milton Coleman gave us his theory that all chiefs in Polynesia came from the same family. Study the features in the old etchings, he advised us; compare Kamehameha with the old kings of the Society Islands and Tonga and Samoa.

Coleman told us the Samoan story of the turtle and the shark. Then he told us about the small Samoan village whose men, on returning from a fishing expedition, had killed twenty-one French sailors they found fooling with their wives. He told us that the Samoan word for Europeans was *Palagi*, which meant "People from Heaven," and that Negroes were called "People from Under the Earth."

Lino's attention had wandered. He was gazing off toward the ocean. "Tomorrow we'll go fishing," I heard him say, to no one in particular. "A low tide like this, it's very tempting." He looked down at the top of his beer can and smiled conspiratorially, as if at his reflection in the aluminum.

"Piailug has sixteen kids," Vickie was telling someone.

Lino roused himself to ask, "Which sixteen kids is that?"

"Well, the sixteen from his wife."

"What about the twenty other ones?"

We talked of the Mortlock Islands, called Mordelaigong in Satawalese. Everyone at the picnic tables who knew those islands agreed that the Mortlockese were a mean people, just like the people from Puluwat. Lino told the story of the Puluwat chief saved by an Ifaluk girl after the people of Ifaluk had thrown him in a taro patch and left him for dead. He escaped by calling on the current to take him home to Puluwat.

Milton Coleman told us about the huge dead animal that some Japanese fishermen had snagged in their nets off New Caledonia. The thing proved to be a dinosaur. It smelled so bad that the fishermen threw it back, but not before they had cut off a piece. In a post mortem of the fragment, Japanese scientists verified that it belonged to a dinosaur. "You know my theory on that?" Coleman asked us. "I think it was frozen in the South Pole ice. It drifted up to New Caledonia in an iceberg."

Lino told us about climbing coconut palms on Satawal. Piailug took him up the trees to show him how to tap coconut buds for the sap from which Carolinians make *tuba*. The palms on Satawal, Lino said, were much taller than the palms on Saipan. High up the trunk, he had made the mistake of looking down. He stopped ascending and wrapped his arms around the tree. "Are you coming?" Piailug had called down. "Just resting," Lino had answered.

One of the Americans at the table, the lawyer Ed King, an old friend of Lino and Vickie, laughed hard at this story. "An all-star on Saipan," said King, "and on Satawal . . . "

"Nothing," said Lino happily. "I'm nothing compared to those guys."

Milton Coleman brought out a ukulele, and he and Lino sang, with much feeling, a song called "Princess Pupuli's Papaya." The refrain, as I recall it, goes, "You really should try a little piece of Princess Pupuli's papaya."

It occurred to me that if I was going to ask about the song for Satawal, I had better ask soon. Lino has the habit, at the height of his beer parties, of slipping away and finding a tree to sleep under.

"Lino," I said. I was careful to pitch my voice below the conversation around us. "Lino, could you navigate a canoe to Satawal?"

"To Satawal from here? That's easy."

"It is? There's a song for Satawal, then. A navigation song? I was wondering if sometime you could tell it to me."

He instantly looked unhappy.

"I better not," he said. "I could, but better not. Those informations are the last thing we have in the family. It's the backbone of everything."

There is, then, a song for Satawal. I'm happy to say I can't sing you a bar of it.

Some time later, the guests were still partying under the beach shelter. Their host had disappeared to sleep under a palm somewhere. Piailug's son Tony and Lino's two teen-age boys stood in shallow water off the beach, readying *U-drive* for one of her weekend voyages. All three young men were sober. All three wore red loincloths. A gathering of small Carolinian boys watched from the beach. One of the sailors, noticing that the bailer had been left ashore, spoke gruffly to a small boy in the audience. The boy picked up the bailer, a cut-down Clorox bottle, waded partway out, and scooted it across the intervening surface to the canoe.

The sun was bright. The blue sky scudded with small trade-wind cumuli. The lagoon scintillated. From the beach to infinity, all colors were the old colors of Carolinian navigation: The white of the sand and the turquoise of the lagoon. The dark brown of skin, the arterial red of loincloths, the capillary red of the upper hull, the lustrous black of the lower, and beyond all these the dark blue of the open Pacific. One of Lino's sons hefted the S-curved boom, carried it forward, and planted it in its socket. The canvas snapped and came alive, the canoe began to move. The sail filled, and the bright inverted triangle stood to sea again, as it had everywhere on this ocean for all those centuries before Magellan.

# 3

## RETURN OF THE NATIVE

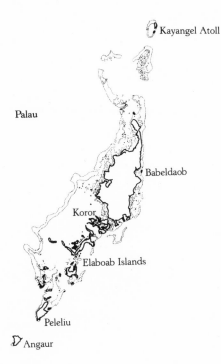

Kayangel Atoll

Palau

Babeldaob

Koror

Elaboab Islands

Peleliu

Angaur

The island of Koror, capital of the new Republic of Belau, is surrounded almost entirely by fringing reef. From the island's northwestern shore, a long causeway projects seaward over the turquoise apron of the reef, connecting land to the deep water beyond. The Chad ra Belau, the Palau Islanders, call this causeway T-dock. Running the length of T-dock and occupying most of its width is a rutted dirt road. As roads go in the Palau Archipelago, this one goes abnormally straight. There is something liberating in the straightness of the road. Driving out on it, you leave behind the tin roofs and flame trees and the jungly closeness of Koror's interior. The sky opens big again. The causeway points like an arrow toward a distant horizon. The next land in that direction is Asia.

T-dock is not a fashionable neighborhood, but it is a good place to be. It is the Cannery Row of Palau—the *old* Cannery Row, the ramshackle row of Doc Ricketts and John Steinbeck, before the smart money found it. T-dock air, like causeway air everywhere, is good air. Ten minutes after rain, the T-dock road is dusty again, like all roads in Koror Town, but where inland that pale-red volcanic dust tends to hang, never quite settling out before the next battered Datsun sends it up again, here on T-dock the sea wind quickly clears the cloud away. There is no through traffic, anyway, and few cars pass. T-dock's climate is peninsular, moderated by the ocean. Driving outward on the T-dock road, you gain honorary degrees of latitude, almost as a mountaineer does in climbing upward from the Canadian Zone to the Arctic to the Arctic Alpine. With each hundred yards or so, the T-dock traveler earns roughly a degree. Palau's actual latitude is seven degrees north of the equator; the effective latitude at T-dock's tip is twelve degrees north, or thereabouts, and each extra degree is a blessing.

At the road's landward end, T-dock is broad enough to support a single row of buildings to either side. There are several general stores, each stocked sparsely and identically, and a tiny hotel—the Paradise—and a number of tin-roofed shacks. Naked brown children play between the shacks, pausing to watch the rare and briefly dusty traffic on the road. The children watch gravely. "Small, but a man," goes one Palauan proverb. "The male child, like a small barracuda, braces against the stream," hints another. "The male heart is like a stone," suggests a third. Palauan boys get the idea. So do the girls. Less of Palau's folk wisdom is aimed directly at girls, but they too come to understand early that toughness and reserve are great virtues. Palau is not a grinning nation. Above the children, on clotheslines strung between the shacks, sheets and blue jeans and bright-colored dresses dry in the sea breeze and the tropical sun.

Toward its middle, T-dock narrows. The line of shacks continues, but only on the northern side, and their perch there is precarious. Then toward its seaward end T-dock widens again. There is substrate once more for buildings: on the northern side, the Western Caroline Trading Company Snack Bar, the Go Go Inn, and a discothèque—or a rudimentary, South Seas approximation of a discothèque—named simply Discothèque; on the southern side a small corporation yard, a bar called the Waterfront, and between them the two-story, green-painted, tin-roofed barracks that is headquarters for the Palau Community Action Agency.

Katherine Kesolei, director of that agency, stood in the second-floor hallway, shouting into the phone. She was speaking with the island of Saipan, 740 miles away, and she had a poor connection.

"We got it for thirty-four hundred dollars and we're selling it," she yelled. She laughed, and then, at the far end of the same instant, frowned. Kesolei's features are mobile, full of unconscious and half-conscious histrionics, never at rest. "We do not have a depreciation value to our equipment. I beg your pardon? This is Katherine Kesolei. We do not have a depreciation value to our equipment."

Kesolei's people looked up from their desks. There was an edge now to her politeness, a hint that the problem was more than just a poor connection in the narrow, technological, IT&T sense. There seemed to be some fault in the human at the other end. Kesolei listened for a bit, her eyes on the floor; then the physiognomic fireworks began. Her face, still aimed at the floor, in rapid succession registered irritation, amazement, irritation again, incredulity, grim satisfaction, joy of combat. All of us lingering in the hallway, and in the offices that opened onto it, were students of that face, but any stranger would have known how to interpret it. With a certain despair and a certain glee, Kathy Kesolei had certified the bureaucrat at the other end as an imbecile.

" . . . *And* the boat," she said, pitching her voice higher for our benefit. "Right on! I don't know how Paul . . . Yes, ma'am. All I know now is I'm selling the engine for three thousand four hundred dollars. If you have any problems with the *bureaucratic* end of this, you get in touch with Paul."

She hung up, rolled her eyes, shook her head as if to clear it, gave us a joke swagger of triumph, and headed down the hall to her office.

Kesolei's office is at a seaward corner of her agency's second story. Her floors are cool linoleum. The T-dock breeze enters through her louvered windows and through a large rectangular hole sawed in the plywood of her wall. The hole once accommodated an air-conditioner, but brownouts are so common on T-dock, and the breeze is such a benign influence anyway, that the machine was dispensed with. The air-conditioning provided by the empty rectangle is now entirely natural. At high tide, the sea rises to cover the reef and the rectangle becomes a blue poster low on her wall. At low tide, the sea retreats from the poster, leaving a beige-and-white composition of fringing-reef corals. When squalls blow in off the water, as they do several times a day, Kesolei can fit a plywood board over the hole, though she seldom bothers to do so.

Her windows, higher on the wall, make a kind of poster, too. They frame a line of trade-wind cumuli and a blue horizon. This was the original scene here. Through all the ages that marched by this spot before Palau's volcanoes pushed themselves up, it was the only scene. Someday surely it will be the only scene again. It is certainly among the simplest of scenes and still one of the best. The blue horizon is the Philippine Sea. Palau is the westernmost archipelago in Micronesia, and the Philippines, the next land to the west, lie six hundred miles beyond the louvered glass.

When one walks to the window and looks down, the view changes precipitately, from timeless and inevitable to low life. Below the window is the rusting corrugated-metal roof of the Waterfront Bar, a long, unpainted, one-story structure built on pilings out over the water.

On the map of a recent pamphlet for tourists, or in anticipation of tourists some day, the bar on this spot is identified as "The Blue Lagoon." Perhaps someone thought "Blue Lagoon" would look, on a tourist pamphlet, more tropical or more civilized or more inviting. Perhaps the typhoon of 1976 blew the old Blue Lagoon down. Maybe the Blue Lagoon has simply been renamed. "Waterfront," at any rate, conveys the bar's ambience much better. In late afternoons, the crisp click of billiard balls rides up from the Waterfront on the sea breeze, enters Kesolei's office, and exerts a tiny refrigerating influence. The real refrigeration, of course, is in the bar's cooler. When Katherine Kesolei gets thirsty—and she is a woman whose thirst is robust—she can drop down to the Waterfront for beers.

I followed her now into her office. She gestured toward a folding metal chair across from her, under her living poster of the Philippine Sea. I sat and opened my notebook.

Behind her desk, Kesolei was impressive, a heavy-set woman in her mid-thirties wearing a "Seattle Supersonics" T-shirt. The T-shirt was illustrated; it showed an Afro-American leaping high on her big chest to dunk a basketball. Kesolei was at least as dark as the black American. Palau lies just five hundred miles north of Melanesia, and the Melanesian racial influence is strong in the archipelago. Kesolei is one of those Palau Islanders in possession of plenty of melanin.

Flagged in my lap was the first quotation in *A History of Palau*. It read:

"They were of average stature, very straight with muscular limbs, well-formed, with a particular majestic manner in walking. Legs from ankles to mid-thigh heavily tattooed. Hair fine, black, long, and rolled behind in a simple manner close to the back of their heads. It appeared neat and becoming."

The passage had been excerpted from George Keate's *Account of the Pelew Islands*. Keate was an Englishman who in 1783 visited the archipelago that the natives called Belau, that English sailors called Pelew or Palaos, that the Japanese would spell Palao and pronounce "Parao," that modern maps call Palau, and which at last, with independence nearing, is being called Belau once more. Keate found the Palau Islanders an attractive people until they smiled. "Their skin," he wrote, "was of a deep copper colour, soft and glossy; they used no clothing what-so-ever and each chief carried a basket of betelnut with a finely polished inlaid bamboo containing their lime which they chewed with a leaf and nut. Their teeth were black and when mixed with the redden from betelnut gave their mouths a disgusting appearance."

I was interested that Kesolei had begun with that quote. *A History of Palau* was her conception. She wrote sections of it, edited the rest, and arranged for the whole to be published in three typescript volumes by her agency. She has had the odd sensation, for a Pacific Islander, of having overseen the written history of her people. Yet the savage, having finally wrested the European's pen away from him, had begun with that old line about the disgusting, betel-reddened mouths of her race. It would have been so easy to trim the last sentence of Keate's description. I asked her if she had ever considered doing that.

"I spent many, many sleepless nights trying to figure out what's best in," she answered. "I decided we have to give a picture of how other people view us. For Palauans, that quote is funny. Palauans, when they read that, say, 'Really? Is *that* what they thought? This is really very harmless stuff.'"

Kesolei grinned. In the corner of her mouth was a green wad of chewed betelnut and *kebui* leaf. Her teeth were all filmy red, as if someone had just punched her in the mouth.

An assistant entered the office, a wide-backed, light-brown woman uncertain about protocol in situations like this. Gently, as if afraid it might detonate, she set a memo before Kesolei on the desk. While the director was distracted, I looked around. The office was sparsely decorated. Tacked to the door was a poem:

> While you and I have lips and voices which are for
>   kissing and to sing with,
> Who cares if some one-eyed son of a bitch invents an
>   instrument to measure spring with?—e.e. cummings

Across from the poem was the wall of the missing air-conditioner. The empty rectangle was now blue, for the tide outside was high. Above the blue was a table of organization for the Palau Community Action Agency, and to the left was a storyboard. Storyboards are folk narratives in wood, old Palauan legends carved in bas relief. The tale this board told was unfamiliar to me. The wood itself was old and cracked, its paint faded. Behind Kesolei's desk was the preamble to Palau's brand-new constitution. "PREAMBLE," it began. "In exercising our inherent sovereignty, We, the people of Palau proclaim and reaffirm our immemorial right to be supreme in these islands of Palau, our homeland."

I was struck by several things. First was the mix of cultural influences—the Western poem in print, the Palauan legend in wood. I wondered about the word "spring" in the Cummings poem. What did that word mean to Kesolei? In Palau, seven degrees north of the equator, there is no spring, nor anything remotely resembling it. What kind of emotion could the word hold for her, or for any other lifetime inhabitant of the tropics?

Then there was the "immemorial" of the Palau constitution's opening line. That ringing declaration, "We, the people of Palau proclaim and reaffirm our immemorial right to be supreme in these islands," was whistling in the dark. Palauans have not been supreme in their home islands for a century and a half. First the Spanish, then the Germans, then the Japanese, and finally the Americans have governed Palau. "Immemorial" indeed. Never in the memory of any living Palauan had a ruling power recognized the immemorial right of Palauans to be supreme here. The American administration, after thirty-five years, was now winding down, but full independence was at least a year away.

Kesolei finished reading the memo. She addressed her assistant briefly in Palauan, then watched as the woman left the office. She apologized for the interruption and finished her thoughts on that betelnut quote from Keate. "I thought Palau history should stand for itself," she said. "It should not be defended. It's too big to be defended by just a small person like myself. I decided, just say whatever was said, and it will speak for itself."

"Did it bother you to quote Homer Barnett?" I asked.

*A History of Palau* borrows several excerpts from Homer Barnett, an American anthropologist who lived in the archipelago in 1947 and 1948, and whose conclusions about Palauan society invariably anger those few Palauans who have read him. Nowhere in his short book *Being a Palauan* does Barnett say a single complimentary thing about Palauans or their culture. ("The sanguine emotions of love, delight, hope, and yearning are shallow and constricted, outbalanced in intensity by resentment, alarm, suspicion, embarrassment, anger, shock, and surprise," he writes, of the Palauan responses to his Rorschach blots. He got similar readings from his Thematic Apperception Tests and his village observations. "Soon or late," he writes, "the child must learn not to expect the solicitude, the indulgence, and the warm attachment of earlier years and must accept the fact that he is to live in an emotional vacuum, trading friendship for concrete rewards, neither giving nor accepting lasting affection," and so on and so on, bleakly, for all eighty-four pages.)

"I still don't like Homer Barnett's *Being a Palauan*," Kesolei answered. "I think he could have been a little more responsible. The thing about anthropology—and this is why I only did it for two years—is that you go to a course and the professor says, 'Here are the four lineage systems in the world.' You go out and do your field work, and you try to fit whatever you find into this established pattern that Malinowski found in the 1920s. When the world was very big. Somehow no one has had the bravery to dispute him."

"Did you find *any* virtues in Barnett? Did you learn *anything* from him?"

She paused. "Well," she said. She paused again. "I learned something about *Barnett*," she said finally. She made a droll face, and we both laughed. "Some of the names of his informants in the book, I came across those people while I was interviewing for the Palau History Project," she continued. "I learned something about Barnett, through my interviews. And I learned about the other anthropologists. I learned something about Roland Force. I learned something about Bob McKnight. The people would ask, 'This work you're doing, it's the same as McKnight?' 'Slightly the same,' I'd say, 'slightly different.' And then they would tell me something about that anthropologist."

I wondered whether McKnight and the others had appreciated the symmetry. While they were busy compiling their ethnographies, the natives had been busy compiling ethnographergraphies.

"Can you tell me an anthropologist story?" I asked.

"No," she said firmly.

"Really? You can't tell me a story about McKnight?"

"No."

"Not even one about Homer Barnett?"

"No." Her silence on this matter was uncharacteristic, I thought, and she must have thought so too, for we both laughed. "Have you read Barnett's book *Palauan Society*?" she asked. "It's excellent. Excellent. I do not know why he wrote *Being a Palauan* the way he wrote it."

(The best anthropologist story I can offer, since Kesolei won't talk, remains one I found myself between the lines of *Being a Palauan*. In his chapter "Facing the World," Barnett writes, on more levels than he knows, of the failure of imagination:

Imagination is certain to be constrained and innovation curtailed by self-doubts, and Palauans are not in fact radically creative. They are skillful, and proficiency is considered a virtue. They greatly admire the clever manipulator of things or of men, but not the reformer, the trail blazer, or the speculator. Their novelties are rephrasings of standard themes, like American love songs, or involuted reapplications of the same device, like the committee system. They eschew flights of fancy in their art, and their story telling is a recital of events which end abruptly. They do not spin yarns; their jokes are witticisms, sharp and to the point, not build-ups with a punch line. In describing what they see in TAT pictures, they name what is rather than imagine what might be happening: "That person is Yapese, so I don't know what he is doing.")

In some respects, Kesolei admitted, *A History of Palau* had been a disappointment. "We wanted to do legends and written history together," she said, "but we found they wouldn't mix. We attempted it. We tried to put oral history on one side, and written history on the other. It wouldn't work. Palauan history had no chronology. I decided that to get the stones in place, we better do a complete history, chronologically, based on written accounts. At first I felt bad about doing it that way, then after a year I felt better. Of course, maybe this is just a rationalization of the way I did it."

Here she paused to perform, with despairing eyes, downturned lips, and a defeated gesture of the hand, a little pantomime of her rationalization and her failure. In her next breath, she withdrew all that. "But they wouldn't mix," she said flatly. "One detracted from another."

The pantomime was un-Palauan. Kesolei's acrobatic features, always mugging, always up to something, are not typical of her people. Palauan faces can be expressive, but the expression has to fight its way through the Palauan reserve. ("Palauan anxiety is chronic, but it is normally concealed behind a display of indifference," writes Homer Barnett.) Palauans are not a spontaneous folk. Their features react, but guardedly, and after a time lag.

It is possible, of course, that Palauan faces are less opaque to one another than they are to outsiders like Barnett and me, but I don't think so. Palauan society was factionalized and mutually suspicious long before the archipelago was first sighted by Don Francisco de Padilla in 1710. Palau's favorite political strategy has long been the one called *ideuekl chemaidechedui,* "the concealment of the lizard," so named for the green palm lizard and its habit of darting around to the far side of the trunk. The strategy stresses indirection, unpredictability, and a poker face.

Katherine Kesolei's face might win at poker, but not by its stoniness. It would win by mercuriality. There aren't that many cards in the deck.

Many of the faces Kesolei makes are cryptic. They may have begun as conventional representations of standard emotions, but they have since drifted off into a private idiom. In one, she stands with her face aimed downward, as if to stare at her feet, but with her eyeballs up, fixed on a spot ten feet in front of her. Her eyes commence to dart around like a cornered animal's, and she clears her throat violently. It might be pantomime of a bull who has learned, just now, to cease charging the picador, but who has strong intimations anyway that he won't get out of the arena alive. It is supposed to indicate intellectual stress. She mimics the cornered bull when she is confronted by some monstrous intricacy of human nature, or of life, or of fate. She mimicked him when I asked her some question she wanted me to know was difficult.

Kesolei specializes in various expressions of dull-wittedness. More often than not, she mimes bewilderment, stupidity, loss of the scent. Part of this seems to be the genuine humility of an ego very much under control. Part of it is probably appeasement of Palauan sensibilities, which insist that mannerly people keep a low profile, and that women exercise their power through traditional channels, or subtly ("Here I am, just a woman, whom crazy luck has placed at the head of this big agency," much of the Kesolei dumb show seems to be saying). Part of it is probably just a means of flaring excess nervous energy. But, whatever else it may be, it is not Palauan.

Of the more conventional poker face of the Pacific, the stony one, Paul Gauguin was master. He painted in Polynesia, thousands of miles from the western edge of Micronesia and Palau, but Pacific Islanders were great voyagers and miscegenators, their racial lines are hopelessly tangled, and today you see Gauguin women in the streets of Koror Town. The Gauguin woman is not a daily vision in Palau; she is rarer, more like bi-weekly, and she is not a racial type so much as an essence. With a jolt of *déjà vu* you see her, standing thoughtful in a doorway, or reclining, in a dress of some screaming hot neon color, on one of Palau's furnitureless floors, or lying asleep atop rumpled sheets, the morning too hot even for those, her torso the same dark-brown all over, her face turned away from you. It takes two or three weeks in Palau—five or six Gauguin women—

before you trace the *déjà vu* back not to any previous life of your own, but to the dead Frenchman.

Sitting cross-legged on the floor, chin in hand, the Gauguin woman, the Gauguin girl, has no fixed plan for this afternoon. She has another view of time. There is a hint, in her imperfect mask, of melancholy—a word Gauguin himself used in his diary. And the thing about melancholy in Pacific faces is how it jars with our myth. It's so unexpected in the bright sun, under palms, with the blue lagoon beyond and a sea wind blowing. There is a hint too of the thing Westerners like to call fatalism. There are hints of things nameless but paintable, if you are as good as Paul Gauguin.

Katherine Kesolei's face hints at few of those things. She is big and broad-backed, the way Pacific Islanders like their queens. She is from the high clan, and in her frame she looks it. Below the neck she is true to her geography and her tradition; above it, in her face, the Gauguin woman has died forever.

"I was a boy until I was fifteen years old. I thought it was a drag to play house. So I had slingshots, spearguns, whatever was current at that time. I had bamboo rafts. My grandfather made a canoe for me. Children in Palau know when the tide's going in and the tide's going out. We know if it's a low tide in the morning, or afternoon, or evening. Your life sort of revolves around that cycle. It dictates what kind of fishing you're going to do.

"I ran with my cousin, and some of the others. They treated me like one of the boys. It was such a drag to be a woman. But I didn't know the difference then. It wasn't quite obvious to me.

"*Until.* Until you grow up a little bit and you go swimming. Because when you're a kid, you want to save your jeans, or whatever you're wearing. You don't want to get it wet. So you take it off. That's when you begin to kind of wonder. It wasn't a question of anything lewd happening; it was just we were built differently. But really there wasn't any thought in our heads as to the difference between boy and girl. As soon as we see a high tide from around fifty feet away, we start taking off our clothes and jump in the water."

"Were other girls this way?"

"Oh, yeah, girls would easily take off their clothes."

"No. I mean, were there other tomboys?"

"There were a couple in our set. But I guess I went on for a longer time. By the time you're about twelve, thirteen, then you begin to go with your grandmother to the taro patch. And boys begin to sleep with their fathers. But I was too dumb."

"Did you *ever* learn the women's skills? Did you ever go to the taro patch?"

"The extent I went to the taro patch was just to carry my grandmother's fertilizers—leaves and the stalks of things—and drop them there. I'd watch for a while. Finally she'd say, 'Well, come back at five or so and carry the basket of taro home.' I would do that. The rest of the time it was hunting, fishing, firewood gathering.

"It was just my sister and I. We don't have a brother. My sister went with my mother everywhere, and I went everywhere with my father. I guess he wanted a son. My grandfather . . . I think he and my father were kind of amused by the way I was acting—more amused than trying to fit me into the female role. My father would say, 'Now go to Melekeok, and tell this old man so and so, and bring the message back.' That kind of thing, *boys* should be doing that. But those were my chores.

"In ninth grade at Mindszenty School, I was required to wear a uniform and stand in line with the girls. I didn't mind. *Because underneath that uniform is a pair of jeans.* And as soon as I'm off the grounds of the school, everything comes off. Topless. With a slingshot in my pocket."

"Topless?" I asked, indicating with a nod her now formidable chest. "In junior high?"

"I was a late *bloomer!* There wasn't anything to *hide!*"

The blue poster of Kesolei's missing air-conditioner had come alive. A bamboo raft was entering the picture, moving as Kesolei spoke into the patch of lagoon framed by the hole. Like most Micronesian rafts, this one was long and narrow, and it took a while for the stern to appear. When it finally came into view, there was nobody on it. The raft was unmanned. Curious, I watched a moment, then saw a young man in a diving mask surface alongside.

He dumped something heavy into the raft—a chunk of dead coral. He was gathering materials for the repair of a sea wall.

"Did your father's treating you as a son have anything to do with the role you find yourself in now?" I asked.

"I think so. I think so. Probably a little bit. My curtness, my abruptness, the way I think, it's more in the man's way of thinking.

"My father was very well educated, by Palauan standards. He went through five years of Japanese school. My mother, too. She was probably the smarter of them both. They valued education very much.

"I did pretty well in school. I skipped some grades. After high school, I spent a year in Palau doing nothing—I was too young for college. Then I applied to the Trust Territory scholarship program, and they accepted me, and I went up to Guam.

"Guam! The magnitude of things there. The number of things. The bigness of things. The roads. Paved! And another thing— Americans! The fact that there are Americans who drive cabs, who dig ditches. That's hardly the case where I grew up here. I had always had a fear of Americans. I had that politeness toward them. When I went to school at PICS [Pacific Islands Central School, on the island of Ponape], every time an American calls my name, I have to stand up and say, 'Yes, sister.' They grind that into you. A priest comes into the room, or a bishop comes in, or any visitor, and everybody has to stand up. That had become my instinct. So in those matters Guam opened my eyes. I majored in political science. That was the major everyone took."

(One of Kesolei's classmates on Guam was Margie Falanruw of Yap. "She was a tomboy and so was I, " Mrs. Falanruw remembers. "We were always on the winning teams. Kathy was tough. We were playing baseball one time and a girl twisted her ankle. We all ran over and looked. The girl was crying. Kathy was the last one to walk up and look. From her expression, she didn't think much of the girl. She seemed to think that the girl was making too much of her sprained ankle. She called me off and we started throwing the ball around to start the game again.")

"In the summers I came home to Palau," said Kesolei. "To earn money for the trip back up again to Guam, I took a job bartending at the Royal Palauan Hotel. The Royal Palauan was the in-place, and Americans were there. Every time the police came, I had to get out of the bar, because I was underage. And I did some tour guiding, besides. I drank up all the money I made.

"After two years in Guam, they kicked me out of school. I was keeping odd hours. There was a difference between scholarship students and regular students: scholarship students were supposed to be the good example. Good grades. Stay in the dormitory. Don't drink. Don't fool around. I wasn't any of those things. 'Come in at nine o'clock,' they'd say, and my individuality was saying, 'Well, why should I be in at nine o'clock, when at home I don't have to be in until . . . until whenever I *want* to be in?' After two years, they said, 'Well, we've had enough of you.' So I came home to Palau.

"It is very hard, when you're eighteen, nineteen, to order your life if you really do not know . . . if you don't have any foundation to build on. Because my foundation had always been play, fun. Whatever I wanted to do I did. And so I came back to Palau. I came and *listened* just a little bit. I questioned, basically, 'What do I want to be?' I saw people driving cars, wearing good clothes—a certain kind of lifestyle was beginning, then, that was considered 'class'— and I thought, 'Maybe I really want to be that, or . . . ?' A lot of those questions came to my head. I finally decided I had to understand a little bit more about what was happening around me. I started asking things. I didn't know anything about Palauan custom. I started coming to my senses just a little bit.

"My interest in being Palauan had begun, really, in Guam. In your classrooms on Guam you have different people, different accents, different ways of doing things. You're called upon to explain. 'Well, how do you make love in Palau?' Or 'What do you eat?'"

Remembering, Kesolei's voice gained volume and brassiness as she reproduced those old questions from the back of the class.

"'Do you have roads? Do you drive cars?' I'd never been called upon to explain myself. And, when I was called upon, I really didn't know. I'd taken everything for granted. I began to ask myself, 'Well, how *do* we make taro? How *do* we fish?'

"I was embarrassed to be a Palauan, because Palauans didn't have nearly as much as Guam had, or as Americans had. The embarrassment sparked some sort of a little bit of anger in you. Sort of a challenge. You're saying, 'Well, why am I a little bit different? Why are these people feeling the way they do toward me? My feeling toward them—toward anyone from the outside—has always been one of respect. So why are they asking me those embarrassing questions? They apparently don't have the same feeling of respect. There must be something wrong somewhere.'

"I didn't realize how little I knew about Palau until I came back here. I was a tour guide, and Americans would ask me, 'How come it's so green out there in the rock islands?' I'd ask myself, *How come it's so green?* Or they'd ask me to explain what a certain storyboard was about, and I'd wonder about that.

"That contributed to my curiosity about myself, about the things around me. Another contributing thing was that in the libraries we had books people had written about Palau. I'd read them and say, 'Hey, that's not true!'

"I got drunk one time at the bar of the Royal Palauan Hotel. The first executive director of the Palau Community Action Agency, an American, was there. We got into an argument. At that time it was so easy for me to get into an argument. To justify my existence. Just to exert myself a little bit. I was caught up in this inner turmoil. I was rebelling against many things. He and I argued about Palau history. At that time, ten years ago, no one ever worried that this history will be lost, this will be gone. I wanted to get it into the schools. Because I was rebelling against practically everything I'd learned. Why should we study U.S. history? For no apparent reason to me. And I still haven't figured that one out. So the director said, 'If you really know that much about Palauan culture and history, why don't you come up with a program, and then I'll hire you to do it?' I said, 'Sure! I'll do it!' I wasn't doing anything then, just going around antagonizing strangers, basically. So I went to his office and started preparing the papers. I said, 'I'm going to be employed! My first paycheck!' And it turned out to be something I really liked. The more I got into it, the more involved I became. The more research I did, the more reading, the more talking, the more writing, the more it built itself up.

"In Palau we have a toy—a top. When you spin a top, it circles around and around, and then it comes to its center. When a person matures, we say, 'Melalm eteloal.' That's the characteristic of a top. You finally found your central thing."

In the room catty-cornered to Kesolei's office—a dim room of metal desks and skippy, faint-ribboned old typewriters—sits a great, gray, pre-Xerox copying machine, suspicious-looking, like something Greeks might leave outside the gates of a city. Across from the machine is the green wooden door of a walk-in closet. Behind the door a naked light bulb eternally burns. Paper for the copying machine is stored in the closet, and the bulb burns in unending Promethean combat with the tropical humidity, which, if allowed to get to the paper, renders it limp and unfit for the machine. The bulb is not truly eternal, of course. There are the daily brownouts on T-dock, and there are people like me. Trying to be a good boy and turn the light off behind me, as I had always been taught, I did exactly the wrong thing until the purpose of the light was explained to me.

My business in the closet was on the floor, in a long box crammed with manila folders. Inside the folders, in longhand or typed on the skippy old typewriters, set down in Palauan and in English translation, was the history that had refused to mix with written history as set down by Europeans. It was the oral, unchronological, *Palauan* history of Palau, recorded from Palauan elders by Katherine Kesolei and the squad of interviewers she set to the task. Each folder was marked "Airai" or "Peleliu" or "Angaur" or "Ngetpang," according to the island or district from which it had been collected, but otherwise there was no order to it. Except for two thin collections of legends Kesolei had garnered from it, none of it had been published. The more manageable European accounts were the ones Kesolei decided finally to set between covers, but this history on the floor is the one closer to her heart.

The history of the floor may not have chronology, but it has sweep. It goes all the way back to a kind of Palauan Jurassic, when giant creatures roamed the archipelago:

A very long time ago, there was a monster inhabiting Irur. Meluadelchur was the name of the monster. He lived on human flesh.

The inhabitants of Irur usually ate raw foods due to their fear of building a fire. The monster always visited the spots where fires burn. The people were constantly on the run. Many unfortunate people were consumed by the monster.

Meluadelchur, the monster of Irur, had a brother monster, Meluadcheangel, who lived on Ngcheangel Atoll to the north—or perhaps they were one monster and the same, a traveling monster claimed by two constituencies, for the folder for Ngcheangel tells a suspiciously similar story:

When the population of Ngcheangel Island increased, a giant bird threatened the welfare of most of the people. It was Meluadcheangel. He was so big that when he flew over the island, it became dark. The people ate raw food for fear of Meluadcheangel sighting the smoke from the fire. Meluadcheangel ate people by swallowing them.

Time itself was structured differently, back then. The year was divided into Year-east and Year-west, according to the direction of prevalent winds. Ruluked Ngirakesau, an elder of Melekeok, describes Year-east thus:

*Tmur*, first month. The first sign of Tmur, God sleeps at Iromel and branches of *rourou* trees [Indian coral tree] blossom. It is windy and the mangrove crabs are fat and when a child is born, he will be talkative.
*Modelab*, second month. The first day of Modelab, God goes up to the hill called Ngerulkel and sits there. *Sis* trees [ti plants] and *rourou* trees blossom, and when a child is born, he will smell good.
*Elid*, third month. The first day of Elid, God goes to Imel Mengellang and stays there. This time fish get fat and leaves of *kerdeu* trees [Ixora] fall down, and when a child is born, he will be shameless and a good comedian.
*Taoch*, fourth month. The first day of Taoch, God goes to Lluul of Chol. It is windy and the mangrove clams and rabbit fish are usually fat. Flood comes and goes down into the mangrove channel and clears the channel. Clams and sea urchins get fat because the water gets muddy, and when a child is born he will be easy-going or comfortably unconcerned.
*Orengodel*, fifth month. First day of Orengodel, God goes to Techickebai and urinates on the floor and asks for moldy taro and then

goes to Barsruau and sits there. The weather is usually good and when a child is born he will be well mannered and wealthy.

*Iyach,* sixth month. God still has five more days to spend before the first day of Tmur Ngebard [first Western month]. He spends these five days in Bai re Mechau and on the first day of the Western year he will go to Ngerulbuu. The first day of Iyach, God goes to Roisingang hill and sits there and the leaves of *keiai* [betelnut palms] crack and the sea cucumbers arouse and when a child is born he will have a big penis.

The very laws of physics were different in those days. The history of the floor proceeds from the Palauan Jurassic through a sort of Oceanic age of Merlin, in which magicians bent those laws any way they chose:

Renguul heard news about an island called Ngerdekus, where the people were good at black magic. He sailed to Ngerdekus to see if the magicians could help him. When he approached the island, the magicians saw something white approaching. They used their magic, and the white thing disappeared. Renguul looked up and saw that his sail was gone. He paddled the rest of the way to Ngerdekus. When he reached shore, he saw some people sitting down with grass growing on their backs, because they had been living for countless years. They made a special paddle containing black magic and gave it to him, and Renguul sailed away from Ngerdekus. He didn't believe that the paddle had some supernatural power, so he tried it and almost turned Ngerdmau upside down. He liked the paddle, then. He turned the paddle again when he was in front of Ngerchur, thus splitting Ngerchur into two separate islands, Ngerchur and Ngerkeklau. He began laughing.

"We never really had a system," Kesolei told me, of her Palau History Development Project. "We *did* have rules regarding interviews. I would never tell one informant what another had said. We would always ask the person if he minded being recorded. We would play the thing back to him after each interview. If he didn't like it we'd destroy it right there.

"A big problem was the confidentiality of the information. 'What are you going to do with that?' they would ask. 'Well, I'm thinking of making a book out of it.' 'You're going to use my name on it?' 'Yes, if it's all right with you.' 'No, no, no! Take my name off.' That was a common response. Another question that constantly came up was, 'How am I doing in relation to others? What did so-and-so tell you?' I would say, 'We talked about other things. He doesn't know as much about this subject as you do.'

"In the good times, the good interviews, the subject would talk freely. It would be very hard to interrupt and ask questions, so we didn't. You came to the end of the tape and the machine would beep. 'What's that?' they wanted to know. 'I've got to change to the other side.' So they waited while you changed the tape, then they resumed talking. Afterward, when you played it back, they smiled when they heard their voices. 'Boy, that machine is interesting!' Finally I would ask, 'Should we keep that tape, or do you want to change anything?' 'No!' they'd say. 'As a matter of fact, I have another legend. Why don't you come back tomorrow?' Those were the good experiences."

"And the bad?"

"Some simply refused to talk to us. Flatly refused, and told us outright it was none of our business. That, or they led us through many circles and channels, simply not having the heart to say no."

In the history of the closet floor, in the folder marked "Tobi," is an interview that demonstrates the resistance Kesolei often met. The informant was Marino Fitihang, a *tamor*, or chief, of Tobi Island, the most remote of Palau's satellites, a small coral island 325 miles south of the main group. At the time of the interview, Fitihang was sixty-four years old.

Q: How was your life when you were a boy?
A: I either fished or fixed *tuba* (palm wine).
Q: Did you learn any trickery for fishing when you were a boy?
A: A small boy could fish small fish but not big ones. It was tabu.
Q: Why was it a tabu?
A: Old people were just against it. If a boy missed a large fish, and was seen by an adult, he was to be scolded. The old men did not give the main reason it was a tabu.
Q: When should a boy go fishing beyond the reef?
A: As soon as he had confidence that he knew the rules of fishing.
Q: What did you use for hook, bait, and line?
A: We used feathers or fish for bait. As for the line, we used tissue of a certain tree.

Q: How do you like the life at present?

A: It is kind of hard to say. Anyhow, thank you so much for the questions you asked, and the time you spent with me.

"We knew we were inadequate," Kesolei said. "Our knowledge of Palauan customs, our knowledge of correct behavior, was poor. During all my conscious years, I've been going to American institutions. Half of me is homegrown, and half isn't. We didn't know the etiquette. But we *knew* we didn't know, so we decided to hire an elderly person, Santos Ngodrii. One of the reasons we selected Santos was that he had been exposed to this type of thing. He had been interviewed himself. He had worked with foreigners, especially Yamaguchi, who did a music collection in Palau. Santos could appreciate some of our inadequateness and at the same time could understand what we were trying to do.

"'Can you tell us a legend?' we would ask. By his reaction, we knew we were not asking the right way. We were committing a lot of errors. Every time he saw anything that was out of the ordinary, something he's not comfortable with, he was free enough, vocal enough, to say, 'That's not the way it's done; it's done this way.'

"You don't just walk into a house and say, 'Tell me the legend of Medichebelau.' There's a long rigmarole before that. 'Talk to my wife first,' the informant will say. He wants to see what kind of questions you will ask. His wife always throws the ball back to him: 'You're just sitting there, doing nothing, *you* talk.'

"We almost always had to say, 'We work with Santos.' You can't come in from thin air. We had to introduce ourselves. We always had at least two high-school students with the interviewer, because part of the project was to give young people contact with their traditions. The high-school students transcribed the tapes, and while they learned to transcribe they were hearing their legends. I had to say, 'I am the daughter of so-and-so. This is the son of such-and-such.'"

"And when the informant didn't want to talk at all, what happened then?" I asked her. "You never got past that introductory rigmarole? The rigmarole lasted forever?"

"Yes, it did. We felt a little bit bad about that, because we believed in what we were doing."

"Were you irritated?"

"Oh, at that time we were very much irritated by the system—by the Palauanness of things. We were very much irritated. Time. Our time was important. Our egos were also very important.

"We learned. If we had not, we would probably still be propping tape recorders in front of elderly people and saying, 'I've got ten questions. Answer them, number one what is this? Number two what is that?' Basically, we learned patience. But at first, in the nature of the work, we got hurt. We felt, 'These stupid old men, can't they understand?' And so we spoke about our ideals; how we needed to get this down on paper so that future generations would understand it. *Because it was going to die.* That didn't seem to impress them.

"We learned one thing. If you interview in the morning, you can get a little information. In the afternoon, don't bother, because nobody likes to talk about anything. *But at night,* that's when you get the stories. After the evening meal, it's the responsibility of the elderly person of the house to impart some knowledge to the kids. That's when the old people are ready to talk. The kids might go to sleep in the middle of the story, but they're not *going* anywhere. They're caught on their sleeping mat. And night is the time important things are discussed. So we changed our system. We had been operating on an eight-hour basis—nine or ten in the morning, that's within working hours, so we got to go interview somebody. We changed that.

"*Time.* Time is another difficult concept. When we went to interview someone, we already had a set thing in our mind—we're going to collect *legends* this time, and all legends begin like this, 'A very long time ago . . .' *Those* are legends. And then we're going to collect clan histories. And clan histories are basically the stories of migrations—movements of people from one place to another. That's what a clan history is. That's a separate category. But when an elderly Palauan tells you a story, it's not succinct. In the middle of a story, he'll suddenly go off into half-god, half-human eras, and he'll tell it as if it happened ten minutes ago, or five minutes ago. You ask, 'How old do you think this is, before the time of Captain Wilson?' He'll say, 'Oh, waaaay back.' 'Well, at the time of the first people that came here?' 'Oh, further back.' 'How further back?' Well, it turns out it's back at the origin of Palau. So you have to coach them into this kind of time frame. Otherwise, to listen to a straight narration of a legend, it seems as if it happened yesterday."

Yesterday, as revealed by the history of the closet floor, seems to have been a better time to be Palauan. Before the spread of European diseases in Oceania, before the great Pacific depopulation, Palau was an archipelago of between forty and fifty thousand, not the fourteen thousand around today. There were many more mouths to feed, and yet, through the magic of subsistence economy, there was also more food. An old islander, one of Kesolei's informants, once told me that it was possible, just sixty years ago, to take your blowgun and hunt Micronesian pigeons among the houses of Koror Town. Nowadays you must take your .22 deep into the jungle of the big island of Babeldaob, or into *elabaob*—Palau's green maze of hundreds of uninhabited limestone islands—to bag a Micronesian pigeon, or even to hear its spooky, croaking roar. In old Palau there were land crabs and coconut crabs and surf crabs. There were mangrove crabs, the best-tasting crustaceans in any ocean. There were rabbitfish, squirrelfish, box fish, surgeonfish, rudder fish, sailfish, porcupine fish, dolphin fish, marlin, barracuda, jacks, tuna, grouper, rays, and sharks. There were clams, both giant and regular. There were sea cucumbers, octopi, sipunculid worms, and eels. There were green turtles, hawksbill turtles, and an occasional leatherback. There were salt-water crocodiles, which Palauans ate when they could spear or trap them, and which on rare occasions turned the tables and ate Palauans. There were Nicobar pigeons and jungle fowl. There were terns, if a Palauan was really hungry, though they must have made stringy fare. There were the eggs of megapodes. The megapode, a secretive, ground-dwelling bird, uses its big feet to kick up great mounds of soil and vegetation, then lays its eggs inside to incubate in the heat of the compost. There were delicacies like fruit bat. (You pluck the bat's big, grouse-sized body from the pot, its leathery, foot-long wings folded cloaklike in death, its long muzzle grinning vampirishly, and you thumb the waterlogged fur away from the good meat of the flight muscles.) There was dugong, the greatest delicacy of all. The dugong, or sea cow, was rare and elusive even then in Palau, and sea-cow meat (mermaid meat, if both Palauan mythology and the speculation of Western historians is correct) was food for aristocracy. There are still all the same creatures in Palau today, but not in their old numbers.

The Palaus are big, tight-clustered islands, and they held all the resources a people could want. Navigation skills atrophied in the absence of a need to sail anywhere else. Palau was self-contained. There were roomy interiors thick with tropical hardwoods for timber. There was topographical relief: slopes for dry taro, swamps for wet taro. There was abundant rain for cassava, yams, oranges, lemons, apples, bananas, sugar cane, coconut, pandanus, and a little breadfruit. Time was divided into Year-east and Year-west, and no other calendar existed. There was one set of verities and one set of rules. Palau was a whole world.

Palauans applied the cleverness that Homer Barnett would later mark in them to the fabrication of an impressive material culture. They built *kaep*, perhaps the fastest sailing canoes in all Micronesia, and *bai*, big, elevated, high-peaked meeting houses, with floor planks fitted so closely that the first European visitors, trying to slip pins between them, failed. They built stone fortifications, stone highways, and great stone causeways. T-dock is not a new artifact in Palau. The dock has been pointing toward its blue horizon from time immemorial.

Applying their cleverness to immaterial culture, Palauans made busy social and political organizers. Their society was matrilineal. The nuclear family, *ongalek*, was composed of a mother and her children. A number of *ongalek* of related women made an extended family, or *blai*. A number of *blai* formed a *kebliil*, or clan. The clans were organized into superclans called *klebliil*, with member clans scattered throughout Palau. In each village there were from seven to ten *klebliil*, ten being ideal. The highest-ranking male in the highest-ranking *blai* of a clan became *rubak*, chief of that clan. The *rubak* of the highest-ranking clan in a village became chief of the village. The ten *rubak* of a village met in a village council, the *klobak*. The *klobak* was divided into moieties. The chiefs representing the odd-numbered clans, those ranked 1, 3, 5, 7, and 9, were part of the faction of the village chief, who was *rubak* of the first clan. The even-numbered clans were part of the faction of the second-ranking chief, who was *rubak* of the second clan. The architects of Palauan society worked for opposition and balance, competition and compromise, in all institutions and at all levels of social organization. Women had their own hierarchy of power. Men ruled as chiefs, but councils of women approved the selection of each chief. The sea and fishing were the province of men. The land and farming were the province of women. Women did most of the cooking. Men were the artisans. Women controlled the money, not stone money, as in Yap, but glass and ceramic beads of unknown origin, which existed in seventeen categories and which required money experts to evaluate.

Palau was perhaps too perfect a microcosm. Its small world, like the world outside, was divided into federations almost constantly at war. Within those federations, villages feuded, and within those villages, clans and families quarreled. Palau's ancient social architects, those geniuses of division, were maybe a little too ingenious. There was one set of rules and verities, all right, but those rules and verities were often harsh.

Some of Kesolei's oral historians recall the violence of Palau's past apologetically:

From what I hear, a long time ago, the real cause of inter-village warfare and how they were fought did not require beheading of the enemy. It was only cutting off each other's arms.

The first fishing canoe that went out after the star to fish had the privilege to start a fight if another canoe went out later and fish beside them, or nearby them. The fight, of course, was not killing; however it was beating someone until he was weak. The people on the second canoe fought with torches; the men on the first canoe fought with coconut-husk removers.

Other accounts are less equivocal, though sometimes spelled a little strangely:

Chemeruaol was killed by Ngirachelid of Ngermid. Chemeruaol's body was brought to Ngeremlengui, and Ngiraklang, his uncle, spat on his face and instructed that Chemeruaol be sculped. He, Ngiraklang, brought Chemeruaol's sculp home and placed it by the doorway. He spat on it and used it to clean his feet.

One account is chilling, a dialogue between an Oceanic Lady Macbeth and her lord:

She told Reklai, "I want Ngeremlengui [a village] to be perished and no being shall remain." Reklai said, "This is easy. I'll think about it. Ease your mind. I'll find a way to do it."

"So you came back to Palau a stranger," I suggested to Kesolei one day.

"Very true. Very true."

"And you hadn't expected that? You thought you were closer to your traditions?"

"That's right. You speak the language the same way they speak it. You're born here. You *look* like them. That's the thing about education. They put you in when you're, what?—six?—and they begin to train you. When you confront a paper and a pencil, it's a whole different world. And then when you go home, in summertime—when you go home to your village—you do all the traditional things, but you do them marginally. You become a marginal person. Right from the start.

"As an interviewer, when you carry a foreign object with you, an instrument such as a tape recorder, or a paper and a pencil, it's just totally foreign. I coached myself by reading *Time* magazine! There's an interview section at the back, and I would look at it and think, 'That's the way to ask questions.'

"There's this attitude you develop in universities; the attitude that if you want to get information, you go out and search for it. You ask people about it. This is built into you. Because this is the way you do term papers, research. You're not going to find out unless you go to a bunch of libraries and pick it out and pore over it. That was the attitude I had in approaching this. It was a very academic task.

"But it doesn't work that way here. In Palau you're born into a knowledge and from there you cultivate that knowledge. A particular family has a specific technique of fishing, and they're the only ones privy to it. As a member of that family, you're entitled, and nobody else is. And you learn it as you grow up, perfecting it, testing it, and then you impart it to the next person down the line. Not everybody has the right to know it. It's not public.

"I was at fault in that. I believed you could go out and interview a person until you exhausted their knowledge. That's not so. It's personal. It's private property."

"The harder you tried . . . ?"

"The more I became determined to get the information, the less I was getting. *Who are you?* they wanted to know. *You have no right to know. You're a perfect stranger.* That's why you have to establish your lineage first, before you even utter your first question."

"Was your own lineage a help?" I asked. (I really wanted to ask, "Was being from the high clan a help?" but my own developing sense of Palauan manners prevented me.)

"It was a help," she answered. "It was also a hindrance, in that I couldn't get at my own clan history. If there was anything bad that people knew about it, they would color it a little better. That's why we have different interviewers. If I can't get it, somebody else can.

"The thing that gives me goosebumps when I think about it— but it's already gone, it's too late, it's already down in history—is the etiquette thing."

She picked up the purse of tightly woven palm frond that held her betelnut and lime, and she gestured with it.

"Me, I don't care if somebody grabs this and starts chewing betelnut, or sits in this chair, or that chair. But in a Palauan home you have a definite place to sit. The door close to the 'head' of the house—close to the *cheldeng*—is where the elderly men sit. The head is where most of the valuables and the gods and whatever are residing. The rest of the house is yours. But in approaching the house—even approaching the stone platform of the house—you must circle around and come through the kitchen area. To us, when we were first interviewing, whatever was open space, we sat in it. In terms of etiquette, we were way off the far end. We were just stumbling right and left.

"It pleases me that they were very patient with us. The Palauan patience. They helped teach us. They don't tell you directly, but, in relating a legend, they'll pick one that illustrates your mistake. Suddenly in the middle of it you think, *My God, I just did that!"*

Among the legends on the closet floor, there is "*Cheldechedechal a Teb ma Luk,*" "The Story of Teb and Luk." A short distance into that tale, the narrator told Kesolei:

When Teb arrived at Olengkoi's house, it was morning and Olengkoi was sitting at the *cheldeng.* Upon arriving, Teb did not, as custom demanded, walk to the side of the house and make his presence known with soft and polite gestures. Instead he moved straight across the threshold, broke the string that held the door, and entered the house without invitation.

"You thought you were learning patience with them," I suggested, "but it was they who were being patient with you?"

"They were much, much, much more patient with me than the patience I showed them."

"Your breaches of etiquette give you goosebumps?"

"Yes. When I think that by my abrasiveness, by my curtness, by my insensitivity, if you will . . ." She did not finish the thought.

"But *goose*bumps?" I asked. "To think about it now actually gives you goosebumps?"

"Aaaah," she groaned. "I really get embarrassed. I really get concerned. I don't know why. Maybe time? You've aged, and so you're a little more . . . conservative?

"When Santos teaches, or anybody teaches, they don't tell you directly what you're doing wrong, they tell you in that parable or story. If you're a little thick at the time, it doesn't quite sink in. Right then, we were very enthusiastic about what we were doing, and that overwhelmed any sort of reflection on our part. We missed lots of hints. The question you ask reminds me of mistakes I've made. I *recall* those things. During my work now as executive director, I have a lot of meetings with the village councils and chiefs—in a different capacity. Sometimes they say, 'Oh, we remember you. You came six years ago and did this or that.' And I think, *Oh God.* I have to live it all over again."

The oral history in Kesolei's closet is remarkable in that the recollections recorded there span almost the entire period of Palau's written history. Our own oral historians, in interviewing old jazz musicians and suffragettes and generals, don't get to hear memories of Babylon, the Plague, and Hannibal's crossing of the Alps. Kesolei's interviewers got to do that routinely, in a relative way. Palau is a remote archipelago, discovered late by Europe, and its written history is brief. There are elderly Palauans who recall every post-contact era but the first—that period of intermittent visits by explorers, buccaneers, and whalers. There are Palauans who remember the Spaniards:

Q:  Were there any white-skinned people here in Palau?
A:  There were people from Spain.
Q:  Were you in Spanish school?
A:  Yes, I was.
Q:  How old were you at that time?
A:  I was very young during the Spanish. I did not stay long in school, for my father did not want me to go to school. However, I learned a little Spanish, which now it's all gone out of my head.

There are more Palauans who remember the Germans, who came next:

Q:  Rubak, do you know how old you are? [The questioner was Kesolei herself.]
A:  I am really old, because I was a soldier under the command of Bingkelang (Winkler). So maybe I am around ninety-some years old.
Q:  How did they choose the soldiers of Bingkelang?
A:  They chose the intelligent and brave ones.
Q:  Did you learn to speak German?
A:  Yes, we were able to speak German. When they spoke to us, we understood what they were talking about. But now I really cannot speak it good.

There are still more Palauans who remember the Japanese:

Q:  Were the Palauan ladies still wearing grass skirts? [The interviewer again was Kesolei.]
A:  Yes, they only started to be decent in their clothings when some of us went to Japan as tourists.

Q:  Did you go?

A:  Yes, I did.

Q:  Were there any Palauan women on these trips to Japan?

A:  Lots of them went. They were really surprised to see the beautiful houses, and people with their hair cut, and the clothes they were wearing. When they returned from Japan, they told the Palauans who stayed behind of the marvelous sights they had seen in Japan. The Palauans then cut their hair and began to wear good clothes. The ones who did not want their hair being cut were punished. Soldiers went around Palau checking the ones who had long hair. Still a lot of them did not want to get haircuts.

Q:  Was this the beginning of the Japanese period in Palau?

A:  Yes. Also it was the beginning of barber shops in Palau.

Barbershops! Gunpowder, Christianity, and the barbershop, in that order, subdued the Third World. Navajo boys felt the acculturating bite of the shears, and Chinese boys. In Palauan boys, long hair was not just vanity, as the history of the floor reveals. "When the Japanese came, I did not go to school, because I had long hair," Tomisang Xavier told Kesolei's interviewers. Xavier was a seventy-seven-year-old chief from the remote island of Merir. "It was a taboo to cut one's hair short. But after my parents died, I cut my hair."

This leaves a small puzzle. Why did Tomisang Xavier wait for his parents to die before his haircut? Were they alone responsible for enforcing the taboo? The answer lies deeper in the file for Merir Island. Francisco Xavier (Tomisang's brother? cousin?) in his interview explains, "In Japanese time I didn't have a haircut, because in our custom a boy learning navigation must keep his hair long, otherwise his parents die."

All Palauans alive today remember America. For most, the United States has been simply the latest in a succession of colonial powers. For a few Palauans, the history of the floor discloses, the first real contact with Western civilization did not come until the beginning of the American epoch. For the people of Pulo Ana, a small coral island 250 miles southwest of the main Palau cluster, the twentieth century was nearly half over before it truly arrived. In 1944, an American warship steamed tardily over the horizon. When the Pulo Ana canoes went out to greet the ship, the American officers asked if any Japanese vessels had been around. Not for a year, the natives answered. Rdechor Mahobrurimalei, a man of seventy-four when Kesolei's workers interviewed him, describes what happened next:

It was a low tide and we carried our canoes on to the land. The Americans proceeded on carrying their rubber boat on to the land, too. I was surprised to see the light rubber boat for I never saw such kind, in the Japanese time. When they finally put down the rubber boat, they asked one of us to carry a round instrument which was small. The instrument was as heavy as a bucket filled with water. The top was shaped like a Palauan lamp. One of its ends was big and the other was small. The man carried that long shaped thing and I carried the one that was heavy as a bucket. The man told me to put the thing down. As he walked away that long piece of instrument began to talk. I called the man and he came to it and talked. I was scared. "Yeow." I never saw such a talking metal in my life.

Then, another thing occurred. A big boat without masts propelled its way toward the island till it got on the reef. It opened its front and a man raised his arm pointing his finger around and a surprising thing crawled out of the agaped front of the boat and knocked the rocks around. Yeow! What was that thing? It was mighty strong. I never saw such kind in Japanese time.

It was morning. Kesolei stood at the Community Action Agency blackboard in an old khaki shirt with staff sergeant's stripes on the shoulder. A decal above one pocket read, "Holmes and Narver/Saudi Arabia." The shirt must have won that one after its military retirement. Kesolei was addressing, with some animation, a gathering of her community organizers. The shirt was unbuttoned, the tails were out, the last molecule of starch had long since fled the collar. Kesolei's hair was slightly tangled. If she was a general today, it was a guerrilla general, a female Castro without the cigar.

The community organizers, men in their forties and fifties, sat erect in their chairs, not rapt, but listening with some interest and smiling from time to time as Kesolei cracked a joke. In some faces, the Melanesian influence pulled, in some the Indonesian, and in one man I saw traces of Japanese. I was sitting directly across the hallway in the room of the ancient copying machine. A folder from the history of the floor was open before me.

"Charcoal," I heard Kesolei say, then "incentive grants," then "appropriate technology." For a while she spoke in rapid Palauan, and then I heard, "The key word in this house is spin-off." The organizers laughed; "spin-off" was an in-house joke, apparently. "I think what we should do is think small," she said. "Start with what we're very sure of, and build on that." I glanced across the hallway. If the organizers saw the sense in thinking small, I could not tell so from their expressions.

"It's so hard to exist in Palau right now if you're a young person," she told the circle of weathered faces. "There's this feeling that you have to have a paycheck to amount to somebody. I may be manifesting my own insecurities from when I was young, but when a kid leaves high school, it's not the money so much, but the need to feel he can *do* something. Maybe there are some kids floating around who want to get a start in something. Maybe we can find a way of helping young people get their heads a little bit together. If they want to be farmers, then maybe there's something we can do for them, like send them to a farm for a month. Sort of as a step to personhood."

She laughed disparagingly at her own invention. *"Personhood."* The room laughed with her, more on cue, I think, than because they understood the joke. For all of Kesolei's listeners, English was a third language.

I quit eavesdropping and returned to my folder, through which I skimmed until the sound of her voice abruptly stopped. I looked up to see her leave the blackboard, walk slowly from the room, lean over the outside staircase, and spit betel juice in a bright red arc. The expressions of her listeners had not changed. They still faced the blackboard, as if some ghost of Kesolei still lectured there. Then she returned in the flesh and resumed her talk.

That the executive director had spit out the door did not impress me; I had lived long enough in Palau for spitting women to look normal and ladylike. What struck me as strange was the length of the interruption. Kesolei had left the blackboard, without explanation, for about eleven seconds. By my own internal stopwatch, that seemed to leave a big hole in the lecture. None of the Palauan men appeared to have noticed.

"Time," she mused later that morning, when we were alone in

her office. "The subject of time. When you live in a highly technologized world, you have a way of viewing time as important. Time is one thing people of differing cultures often get fumbled up with. In Palau, a deliberation might take a council of chiefs ten days, because time is nothing. It's the *consensus* that's important. The person from the outside does not see it as such. 'Where is the agenda? Where are the minutes of the previous meeting? Let's get on with it.' In Palau, we don't. Our thing is to talk around the subject as much as we can; circle it until we come to that core. Sort of like a fighting chicken. You don't approach the thing straight, but you make passes around it until you spiral into the problem itself."

"Without boredom?"

"Yes. Because in that circling you're constantly thinking. You're thinking until you zero in, and that's on the tenth day. *And consensus is better.* It's gotten so that when it comes to voting at meetings I refuse. I won't raise my hand to vote. When you vote, somebody loses; when you reach a decision by consensus, everyone wins. Or maybe everyone doesn't win, but nobody loses. It's not such a negative thing. Everybody goes away much stronger. And that's why in the villages it takes so many days to make a decision. You have to *convince* everybody."

"Or overcome them with weariness?"

"Yes. Sometimes there's that."

It was lunchtime on another day. Kesolei was wearing a T-shirt that read "Go Solar/It's Hot." We were sitting in one of Palau's ten restaurants with two of her lieutenants: Miriam Timarrong, director of Palau's Head Start program, and Karen Nero, an American who assists Kesolei in various matters. All three were big women. Now and again, one or another of them glanced toward the kitchen. Kesolei's "Go Solar" T-shirt was particularly appropriate today, for the brownout had lasted all morning. The cook was working without electricity, and our sandwiches were a long time coming.

"The sandwich," said Kesolei, "is a Palauan invention." She paused to make sure she had our attention, then continued: "For a time, according to Palauan mythology, there was no order in the world. People were getting rowdy. There was no respect for the elderly. Gods were disobeyed. It was . . . Sodom.

"There was a gate between Heaven and Earth. Uchelianged, 'God from Heaven,' put a guard there. 'You're supposed to guard this place,' Uchelianged told the guard, 'so that when people from Palau approach, you can warn us. Give us some time to hide the women.' Because at that time it was the Palauan custom to steal women from one place and bring them to another."

"And a woman from Heaven," I suggested, "would be . . ."

"Heavenly," she agreed. "Well, one night a party of men from Airai came up and took the guard's eyes out, so he couldn't see. They took the heavenly girls and brought them down to Earth. And this sort of thing kept going on, so finally Uchelianged decided the world would have to be destroyed. He sent the flood." (She pronounced it "floodth." The *d* in Palauan is like the Spanish *d*; somewhere between *d* and *th*, and occasionally Kesolei reverts to it. I liked "floodth." It sounded wetter and more disastrous.) "After the flood subsided, he sent the Tekiimelab, the Seven Messengers, down to Earth. They discovered an old woman, Milad. Milad was the only survivor."

"*Miladth*," repeated Miriam Timarrong, with affection and that Palauan lisp. "We had no Moses, but we had a Milad."

Beneath the affection there was a sisterly chauvinism, I thought. If Palau had feminists, Miriam Timarrong would be one of them.

"Milad was awakened by the seven Tekiimelab," continued Kesolei. "Their mission was to go out all over Palau and survey the damages and destruction—to see if Earth should be declared a disaster area. But first they caught some rabbitfish and left them with Milad to cook. Milad cooked the fish. Then she sliced taro and put the fish between the slices. She left the food there for the seven Tekiimelab. When the Tekiimelab returned, they saw the taro. 'That stupid old woman! She took our fish and left us only taro!' They were halfway to Heaven before they opened their sandwiches and saw the fish inside."

Our twentieth-century sandwiches arrived, looking very skimpy. Kesolei said nothing, but staring at her plate she made eloquent passing comment with her eyes.

As we ate, we discussed the power shortage. (The flow of electricity in Koror Town is far less predictable than the weather and makes a fine subject for conversation.) I observed that all the electric clocks on Koror were running on different times. Kesolei complained that, under the rationing system, T-dock's turn for sacrifice came up much too often. The reason, she guessed, was that no one on T-dock had any pull with the power department. Then we talked of Aladdin lamps, upon which many Palauans rely when the electricity fails. Kesolei's lamp at home no longer worked, she told us, because one of her sons, Doug, had shattered the glass while swinging a baseball bat.

"An accident?" I asked.

"I don't know. With Doug it's hard to say."

A game of catch had followed the bat incident, she added. The three boys were firing a hardball between the bedroom and living room when a stray throw hit the Aladdin, finishing it off.

"Your house sounds kind of . . . lively," I ventured.

She just rolled her eyes.

Then the talk turned etymological. Could I tell her, Kesolei wondered, what this word "idyllic" meant, and how it related to "ideal"? I tried. Then she asked about the difference between "satisfied" and "content." Then she told us about the confusion in Palau over the word "antiseptic." She had once repeated that word several times in conversation with an older Palauan woman. Each time she said it, the woman had made a funny face. Kesolei was puzzled until the woman asked, finally, "This 'antiseptic,' it's *good?*" At that, Kesolei understood. *Antiseptic* sounds much like Palauan slang for "your auntie's ass." A little antiseptic on a cut does not, to a Palauan, sound like much of a remedy.

She told us that Palauans who learned Japanese as children habitually confuse the *f* and *h* sounds in English. "They wind up talking about 'fuman beings,'" she said. Then, frowning, she brought up a new coinage, "Belauan." She didn't like it. "Palau" was a bastardized word already, she figured, and an alien suffix couldn't mongrelize it much more, but "Belau" was good Palauan, and "Belauan" irritated her. I suggested "Belau Islander" as a compromise, but she was not much happier with that. She saw no way around Chad ra Belau.

The conversation took a slight turn.

"We're turning 'being a Palauan' into a negative thing," she said. "I feel now that 'being a Palauan' is just—what's the word?—rhetoric. I used it a long time ago because I didn't know any better. Being a Palauan should espouse the best in being a Palauan—modesty, sharing, understanding.

"There are some things in Palauan culture I don't think are worth pursuing. I wish this clan thing did not exist. To treat someone differently because he is from such and such a clan. I ignore it. Sometimes in meetings on Babeldaob, in my introductions, I sort of forget to mention that someone is from the high clan. Afterward people tell me, 'Kathy, you should have remembered.' I have to say, 'Darn, I forgot!'"

Now, in the restaurant, she mock-forgetfully slapped her thigh.

"You can ignore it," I suggested, "but it doesn't ignore you. You can ignore it, but you can't renounce it. You're either a beneficiary of that system, or a victim."

She gave me a brief look across the table. "That's right," she said.

Our dessert arrived, ice cream soupy from lack of electricity. It was for the ice cream, mainly, that we had come to this restaurant in the first place. Again Kesolei commented wordlessly, this time by staring at her bowl without expression, which for her was a feat and spoke volumes.

After lunch, as we drove back to T-dock and the office, the etymological discussion resumed. Karen Nero was curious about the word *luchel*, the Palauan for "goosebumps," and she asked Kesolei about its derivation. That problem accompanied us down the straightness of the T-dock road, up the steep concrete stairway to the Community Action Agency's second floor, and into the room of the ancient copying machine, where Kesolei picked up the *Palau-English Dictionary* for assistance, then across the hall into the community organizers' room, where with a stick of chalk she traced the genealogy of the word *luchel* on the blackboard. Five older men, her community organizers, were sitting in there, and they became her audience—her lexical panel, rather, for as she charted each step in the evolution of the word, she looked back over her shoulder at the men to see if they agreed. Then she charted the next.

The root, she decided, was *uchel*, "angel" or "god." Descended from that was *uchelel*, "beginning," and descended from that was *uchauch*. Here she paused to refer to the *Palau-English Dictionary*, compiled by Father Edwin G. McManus, S.J., and she discovered that *uchauch* was defined as "crotch." She grimaced horribly. Father McManus's definition had gone down very sour. "Crotch" was incorrect, she said. *Uchauch* properly meant just a confined passage or hidden place. Then, before she could continue, she was diverted by another error in an accompanying definition. *Chereomel a ucheuchel* was said to mean "having a lot of pubic hair." Wrong again, she said. *Chereomel* simply meant "forest."

The dark old men of the lexical panel were tickled at this turn the scholarship had taken. Here and there among the panel great white smiles were breaking out. I began to wonder whether Father McManus's informants had been teasing the priest. But *chereomel* had another association for me, and I asked Kesolei whether that word for forest was related to *kerreomel*, which I understood to be a rough Palauan equivalent for our "conservation." I should never have done that, for Kesolei answered yes and led us clambering spiritedly off along that etymological side branch, never to find our way back. I have yet to learn how the word *uchel*, "god," came to be father of the word *luchel*, "goosebumps," though it makes sense to me somehow and I'm glad it should be so.

"As an anthropologist yourself . . ." I said to her, one day.

"I'm not an anthropologist," she replied. "I'm a . . . bureaucrat."

"But you do have the degree in anthropology, right? From the East-West Center?"

"Yes. But that was a question of meeting the course requirements and getting out of there as fast as I can. I only got it because of the constant pressure of people asking me about my degree— 'What kind of degree do you have?' It got to be a hassle."

She paused and made a face.

"In the Trust Territory there was a position called 'staff anthropologist.' A person is hired as a staff anthropologist. Now what does a staff anthropologist do? In the overall scheme of things? Other than to assure that the natives are appeased and quiet and so forth? What does a staff anthropologist do? I haven't the vaguest idea. But a lot of guys were hired on that basis.

"And I guess the tropics have a way of getting into you. It's hot, and it soften your brains a little. So you end up thinking, 'Well, I got to be useful.' You've read somewhere that if you dam the river you will be able to generate electricity, and at the same time provide a water system for the community. You yourself have no inkling of what kind of engineering is involved in that thing, but you suddenly get this whole village all excited. This is the kind of thing a staff anthropologist does.

"There was a program called CMA—'Concentrated Micronesian Anthropology,' or something like that. Anthropologists were everywhere in Micronesia in Navy times. The anthropologists were the ones with experience talking to native people, so they were put in charge of translating policies to the people. In Palau they started a piggery program. It was right after the war, and people were thinking about food. They got some piglets and distributed them throughout Babeldaob, Peleliu, and Angaur. The villagers were to raise them for six months, and then they were supposed to bring them to Koror for inspection."

She affected a thick look and shook her head sharply. It might have been her impersonation of a rhinoceros who has just collided with a Land Rover.

"Pigs. For inspection. And the best pigs would be selected to mate and have further piglets. On the day of the inspection, they ferried every pig to Koror.

"What happened next is so funny I didn't think it was possible. But everybody says it was possible. It *is* possible. *It happened.* They got the pigs all lined up. This anthropologist came and looked at the pigs. He knew the ones that were very fat, but the guy had no idea what a female pig looked like, and what a male pig looked like. So he says, 'Those two there, those are the ones we should breed.'

"They happened to be both males. And in Palau we have a thing about homosexuality. It's just . . . funny, so funny to us. So all the other piglets returned to their villages, and these two stayed in

Koror. And for days and days they couldn't get pregnant. They couldn't have babies! And all the people said, 'That stupid American! Look at him! When is he going to figure it out?'"

It was afternoon. Kesolei's T-shirt said "G.W. Huskies." The tide was low, and the sea smell of the exposed reef came strong through her open windows.

Outside, on the reef flat, small bands of women hunted clams and sea cucumbers. The tide was receding to its last silvery channels and embayments in the reef, and the women made bright points of color on a darkening plain. Some sat, their skirts awash, as they probed among the corals. Others were on the move, eyes downward, searching for a new spot. In the group nearest the causeway, one matron lost her balance and sat down suddenly. Her companions laughed, and the sound just carried to T-dock. The fallen woman remained where she sat, for dignity's sake, and began to probe with her knife.

"This month and next month, the tides are really low," said Kesolei, from her seat behind the desk. "This is no time to be in an office. We should be out fishing. We should be spending a week in the rock islands."

Outside, some of the women working the reef were slender, and a few of these wore jeans. The rest of the women were broad. There seemed to be no middle ground. Micronesia is peculiar that way: the islanders in their twenties undergo a metamorphosis, the boys entering that decade lean, the girls entering willowy, and both sexes emerging built like brick walls.

"Did you ever hunt for sea cucumbers?" I asked her.

"No," she said.

"You never look out this window at the ladies hunting and wish you were there with them?"

"No. *Sea cucumbers?* No. If they would be getting sea cucumbers, I would be spearing fish."

"You mean you never look out that window and get attracted?"

"I'm attracted to go fishing," she said. "Very much. But not the kind they are doing. More the kind with goggles and a speargun.

Or line fishing. Or just swimming long distance."

I might have been imagining it, but I thought that in spite of herself she sounded a little sad.

I found myself spending more and more time in the closet, poking through the history of the floor. Whenever Kesolei was too busy to talk to me, I would go in there and pull out another folder. It was very raw material, and I had to wade through a hundred pages of transcript to find a paragraph of any use to me. I began, inevitably, to develop a taste for the useless things. If the entire folder for the district of Ngeremlengui yielded only the information that a "Clan of Klang" lived there—and the folder did—then that was enough for me. It kept me going to the next folder.

The Palauan high-school students who had transcribed the interviews had been working in a second language and they made frequent mistakes. I developed a taste for those. Pressed like leaves inside the folders was a tropical flowering of English spelling and syntax, a flowering that made temperate-zone English seem drab. Sometimes the tropical English was good only for a smile:

There are two kinds of war tactics: surprise attack (*benged el mek-mad*), and gorilla warfare. Surprise attack is a much bigger warfare than gorilla warfare.

Sometimes it left me wanting to know more:

She was approaching her womanhood when she was stricken by the sickness called *Obechedengel ra wel* (turtle like complex) which her death was the result.

Sometimes it was almost poetry:

The girl who was in perdue came out from the hiding and said to him, "So you are the trouble maker in our house and lied that the Medorm people came. You have frightened me so from now on, the females of this house will be unfortunated."

Sometimes it was drama, dark and Sophoclean:

They wondered what kept the girl sleep late. When the covers were removed, her face was seen deadly and smirched with blood; her eyes were wide open with pupils gone, only the whites of her eyes were seen. The girl who uncovered her, screamed.

*Her face was seen deadly and smirched with blood!* The line raised the hair on my neck. Had Sophocles himself ever come up with anything to rival that? Had Shakespeare? It seemed to me, in the enthusiasm of my discovery on that closet floor in Palau, that Sophocles and Shakespeare had not.

Sometimes I liked a passage for how it confused me. In the folder for Ngeraard Municipality, there is the following explanation of the words *meang* and *mekull:*

*Meang* is a big word which may differ in meaning when said by many. Another person may define it different to others definition. It is a word that may have equal share of respect to *mekull,* in that we all must avoid not to go against what has been or who has been claimed *meang* or *mekull.* The two words may be defined as one, but the names direct to two people. From this prospect it has been used as a nice word. Mekull and Meang are two people. But when referred as words, *mekull* is *meang,* and *meang* is *mekull.*

*Meang* refers only to people, not things. But then it may refer to things. At this it would mean to be feared, or a particular phenomenon. We say a tree is *meang,* not necessarily a *meang* tree, merely because it has its particular phenomenon.

Mekull and Meang were from Ngerair. Meang was the daughter of Mekull. Mekull was born handicapped with no legs or arms. She gave birth to Meang. Meang grew up and took care of her mother.

Meang later married. She bade her husband not to bother to tidy up her mother's section of the house. "It's *mekull,* sacredly prohibited," she warned. One day Meang left the house, and her husband began to wonder with curiosity why he was banned to go to Mekull's room. He decided to take a peep. As he peeped, he saw that Mekull was limbless and naked. He stared and became agitated with lust. He wanted to rape her. He razed at her taking off floors, falling below to the ground . . .

When the electricity failed on T-dock, and the blades of the fans slowed, and Kesolei's colleagues groaned, and the fan blades stopped and the offices darkened, I would pick up my folder and step outside. Descending the stairs, I would walk seaward through the sudden heat of the sun. A pair of gas pumps rose from the dust, marking the end of the T-dock straightaway. The pumps were not for cars; they dispensed gas for outboard motors. I would turn left at the pumps and walk out along the concrete sea wall that forms the crossbar atop the T of T-dock.

The T-dock T is an odd one, in that the serifs at either end of the crossbar do not hang downward, as they should. Instead of pointing back toward land and the base of the T, they point upward, out to sea. The crossbar and serifs enclose on three sides a rectilinear little harbor of about two acres. The harbor's protected surface is almost always smooth, even when the waters outside are textured by strong wind. Because it is shallower, and because its smoothness reflects more light, the harbor is usually a lighter blue than the lagoon outside, which in turn is a lighter blue than the ocean.

I would walk a short distance out the left-hand serif. Near the serif's juncture with the crossbar, an iron capstan is sunk in the concrete. I would sit on the capstan, open the folder, and begin to read:

I faintly remember a German man who came to Ngerchur selling things. I think his name was Kaiser. "Ballet," that could be a mispronounciation, was another foreigner who was around when I was a boy. He was married to a Palauan and was tattooed. He carried a purse around like the Palauan old men. He was supposed to have had the ability to communicate with *deleb*—with ghosts.

Sometimes I had the serif to myself, but more often a small gang of Palauan boys had preceded me. They gathered near the capstan at a place where the concrete of the dock is indented by a stairway to the water. That stairway was tall or short, depending on the tides, which in Palau are considerable—the biggest in Micronesia. The stairs made a graduated diving platform, and the boys pitched themselves off, head or feet first or at crazy angles. They hit the water laughing. When their heads emerged, they squeegeed the water from their eyes and hauled out, as wet, sleek, and dark as seals. They climbed the stairs and committed themselves to the sea again. I read:

Ngiratecheboet Rebes, second-ranking chief of Imeliik, is a man of high authority of the municipality. He is renown for his great per-serverence and contained patience. Like other Palauans were, he was recruited by the Japanese, during their occupation of Palau, to join a labor force digging water-wells. This task required use of explosives which was dangerous. Once during his labor below a well, he planted dynamites and hurriedly pulled himself up the well on a rope. Un-luckily, the rope broke at midway sending him down at the midst of active explosives. With no time the dynamites would explode. Howev-er, he instantly bit off all shells on the dynamites with his teeth and they didn't explode. And nothing fatal happened and he was safe on the spot.

Through the hot middle hours of the day, the boys were the only things moving at this far end of T-dock, but in the morning and late afternoon, *yanmar* boats sometimes loaded along the serifs. *Yanmars* are local craft built in small boatyards on Koror and in slips along the mud banks of tidal mangrove rivers on Babeldaob Island. They are commonly around thirty feet long and painted gray or blue. A rude open-air cabin runs most of each *yanmar's* length, and in its engine well ponks a small marine diesel. Idling resonantly alongside the serif wall, the *yanmars* load with passen-gers and cargo for Babeldaob Island and Kayangel Atoll to the north, and for Peleliu and Angaur to the south. The women passen-gers sit crowded atop the cabin, dressed in the shocking hot prima-ry colors that only women of the darkest brown can bring off, but which on them look wonderful. When all are aboard, the *yanmars* ponk-ponk out into the blue of the Philippine Sea. The sea wall is left to the boys again.

My seat on the capstan was a good place to study the history of Kesolei's closet floor. Babeldaob was there for reference, green in the distance. The lapping of the lagoon's wavelets and the voices of the boy swimmers were accompaniment. The sky was all cobalt except, usually, for the white dome of a tropical cumulus climbing forty thousand feet into it.

We ran out to take a look. There were two planes way up in the sky. One of the Japanese said, "Don't worry, for they are only practic-ing." Suddenly a third one roared and immediately let out its bullet and had the houses flat on the ground.

How come the Japanese soldiers who were with us had radios but not guns? Ramon and Tirso went fishing on the reef spearing fish. When they returned they asked why Peleliu had huge smoke above it. One of the Japanese said it was only a practice. The following day, a small boat came and reported that Peleliu was hit. Just then, the American planes came and shot at our soldiers. The guns we fixed were useless. The operator of them was aimless and so the planes returned and shot at the Japanese soldiers and got them killed.

Looking up from that page, I could stare across at Babeldaob, where those Japanese soldiers had got themselves killed. From the perspective of the capstan, the war was both easier to imagine and harder. Why would the black motes of warplanes ever want to buzz above the green swell of that old volcano, so far from any continent and any legitimate business of the world's? And how could those motes have been lethal? The narrator seemed to have wondered those things himself.

From where I sat on the capstan, a skewed vantage, maybe, it seemed that Kesolei's peasant history of the Pacific War was more powerful than any American combat history I could remember.

We didn't know that there would be a war. We were very surprised when lots of warships arrived and crowded Ngemlachel all the way to Ngibtal. Unfortunately, there came a war, so everyone fled to the woods to seek a safe place. The residents of Ngeraard dug pits for people to hide themselves in, because the bombers were very strong. The war came again on April and continued until May. That was in Angaur and Peleliu. They just dropped down bullets to kill anyone they saw on the sea, or just any walkers. We were left in the wood. Most of us were killed; some fled on canoes to the American ships. The Japanese found out that we could flee on our canoes, so they made holes in our canoes and sank them. Sometimes we could find people looking for moray eel to eat; we went around the mangrove swamp looking for crabs to eat. Maybe some people had a good living, but not us. Poverty was on us.

There was a single drawback in fleeing the browned-out office for the capstan and daylight. If the office was a little too dim, then the daylight was much too bright. Micronesia receives the highest annual insolation of any place on earth. The same giant sun that had blackened the boy swimmers reflected from the white concrete around the plug of the capstan and into my eyes. It turned my pages incandescent. I hunched over the folder to make a shadow, but the sun soon bled all the dark from the pitiful, round-shouldered pool I had made, contracted my pupils to pinpricks, and drove me inside again.

One day, returning blinded from the capstan, I was about to mount the stairs to the office when I noticed a woman on the reef. It was Kesolei. The tide was low, and she had climbed down the sea wall, removed her shoes, and waded a short distance toward Asia. Her hands were clasped behind her back. She was bent slightly at the waist and moving slowly forward, studying the corals at her feet. She looked a little like a female professor of marine science returning to old haunts. She looked a lot like a Palauan woman hunting sea cucumbers on a reef.

She looked up and saw me, and her shoulders sagged. For a moment she stared out to sea. Then she looked around her wildly. At her feet glinted a soft-drink can someone had thrown off the causeway. She stooped, grabbed the can, and threw it at me. She has a good arm, and the can just missed. It occurred to me that people must get tired of journalists following them around all the time. I retreated up the stairs. Inside, I resumed reading by a window, and my pupils returned to their normal size.

When the sun has passed over the rim of the Philippine Sea, the light dies quickly at T-dock. Temperatures drop into the seventies, night advances, and the discothèque named "Discothèque" and the Waterfront Bar begin to jump with amplified music. Headlights jiggle outward along the dark causeway. Young Koror men park their cars at the end of the dock, under the southern constellations. They sit on the car hoods or on the ground below, in T-shirts or shirtless, five or six to a vehicle, and they drink beer. They get their music free this way, and their beer at liquor-store prices. The stars are thrown in for nothing.

Most of the tunes are country-and-Western and rock-and-roll. Of all music exotic to the islands, country-and-Western is most popular by far in Palau, as it is across much of the tropical Pacific. Ten years ago, in district-center jukeboxes throughout Micronesia, every third quarter played "Okie from Tuscogee," and that song is still a Micronesian standard. The big song of the eighties has been "Coward of the County" by Kenny Rogers. On a given night at T-dock, Rogers will sing, over and over again, "Promise me, son, not to do the things I've done; stay away from trouble if you can. . . ." To that advice from Nashville, the last, tardy terns wing home from the sea, the young men sip their beer, the Southern Cross slowly rights itself in heaven.

Japanese songs still have a vogue in Palau, and occasionally someone will play one on the jukebox or will sing it himself. Palau is full of good amateur singers who volunteer at nightclub microphones. Kesolei's assistant, Miriam Timarrong, is one of the best of them. ("I have this observation about the Palauan infatuation with the microphone," says Kesolei, apropos of her oral-history collecting in the villages. "You give a mike to a Palauan, and he has more fun. . . .")

The Palauan ear, after so many different foreign administrations, is catholic. The songs from Tennessee and Japan have little in common, except perhaps for a certain twang and plaintiveness, yet the volunteers and their audiences are able to shift easily between.

Occasionally a volunteer will sing a Palauan song. It has always been my fancy that the bar falls more silent for a Palauan song. It seems to me that the drinkers listen harder, while pretending not to. The Palauan song, almost always sad, its bass notes vibrating over a loose speaker, thumps outside into the warm T-dock night. The southern stars wheel slowly. The young men sip their beer.

Palau Culture Week began May 1, and for the next seven days Kesolei was seldom in her office. She was one of Culture Week's organizers, and her obligations during the week were heavy. To pass the time, I consulted the mimeographed schedule of Culture Week events. A photo-judging contest was being held at the Palau Museum. That looked interesting, so I made my way up there.

The Palau Museum sits atop the highest hill on Koror. The view is fine: to the west, the tin roofs and taro gardens of town; to the north, the dark-green of mangrove forest; to the east, the big convoluted cove called Iwayama Bay, its still surface broken by the sheer, jungle-green, Alice-in-Wonderland shapes of a scattering of *elabaob*, Palau's raised-limestone islets. The museum in Japanese times was a weather station. The cups of an anemometer revolve still on the museum roof, but their data are fed to the *new* weather station—the American station—separated from the old by forty yards of lawn. The museum looks much as it did in photographs from the Japanese epoch, except that cracks are beginning to ramify in the walls, and the door, as befits a national museum, is now grander, a heavy plank of tropical timber carved with Palauan storyboard figures.

At his desk inside sat Charlie Gibbons, Palau's most celebrated artist. Gibbons is eighty-six. He specializes in scenes recollected from his boyhood in another age: feasts, canoe races, first-childbirth ceremonies, pigeon hunts, fruit-bat hunts, reef fishing, taro gardening. Occasionally he will attempt a subject like the Apollo moon landings, but always from the perspective of old Palau. His verbal accounts of the old days are as sharp as his watercolor accounts, and he has been one of Kesolei's better informants. It was Gibbons who, along with Santos Ngodrii, gently steered her toward better manners at the beginning of her history collecting. He holds the title Rechucher, fourth-ranking chief of Koror Island, and he works on the staff of the Palau Museum. Today he sat exactly as when I first saw him, nine years before; bent over his drawing board, applying detail with a fine brush. He was balder than Picasso, and his brown eyes were young and amused behind his glasses. He directed me to the museum's thatch-roof outbuilding, where the photo-judging contest was being held.

Walking over, I passed a rusty Japanese cannon, a Japanese antitank gun, and a bomb I took to be American, all lying on the grass. In nine years, not one of these relics had moved an inch. The museum hilltop was the right place for them, someone had thought, but the next step in their disposition had not been decided.

I arrived just as the last class of schoolchildren were finishing their turn at the contest. The photo-judging contest, it turned out, might better have been called a "chief-identification contest." The little thatch-roofed shelter had become a Hall of Palauan Elders. Black-and-white portraits of ninety titled islanders hung in high panels where the walls would have been, if the shelter had possessed walls. The children were to identify as many of their traditional leaders as they could. Karen Nero, Kesolei's American assistant, was helping to run the contest. The contest was Kathy's idea, Karen said, and she explained that the competition was not among individuals, but among school classes. This was partly because Palauans traditionally have competed in groups, and partly because no one student could be expected to recognize more than a few of the chiefs. Working collectively, each child naming the titled elders from his or her home village, the students could watch the lists fill fast.

I picked up a list compiled by an earlier class. "Yutaka Gibbons/Ibedul/Oreor (Koror)," it began. "Lomisang/Reklai/Melekeok. Charlie/Rechucher/Oreor." (Name, rank, and island or district.) The leading class so far had identified thirty-five of the ninety elders. The kids were not wild about the contest, Karen said, but they were interested. From time to time someone would shout, "That's my grandfather!"

I recognized the portraits as the work of Carlos Viti, the photographer who had sailed from Puluwat to Guam in the canoe *Santiago*. Kesolei, wanting faces to go with the transcribed voices of her Palau History Development Project, had commissioned Viti to do the job several years before. Viti's gallery of old faces, frozen in black and white, looked down from their high panels. The troop of young faces, murmuring and fidgety, in living browns and *cafés au lait* and chocolates, looked up. It was hard to see a connection. It did not seem possible that these young faces were those old faces in the process of becoming. The eyes below were clear and easy to read. The eyes above were cloudy and fixed on something I could not see. The high faces had the ambiguity of great age; they could have been Oriental or Mestizo or African. They belonged to a different race, or to no race at all.

Katherine Kesolei arrived just as the last of the children were leaving. Karen and the two Palauans running the contest were glad to see her, for a problem had just occurred to them: Who *were* these old people? Had the children identified them correctly? Karen knew certain of the elders of highest rank, and the two Palauans knew the titled people from their home places, but most of the others were unknown to them. Kesolei sighed dramatically, but sat and began a master list of correct answers. Warming to the chore, she provided an intermittent commentary. "That's his name," she would say of an old man, jotting his name down. "He doesn't have a title. He's completely blind." She would scribble a few more names, then say, "Number fifty-six is Serafina's father." The list grew quickly. Kathy Kesolei, who at nineteen had known nothing of her native tradition, now knew the names, at least, of all its important guardians. I doubted that any other Palauan of her age class knew so many of those names and faces.

"Number sixteen," she said, looking up. "Who is that guy?" We all stared up at number sixteen, as if staring could help jog her memory. We failed, and the nameless old chief remained anonymous.

It happened that Carlos Viti, the portraitist, was in Palau for Culture Week. He worked now for the *Pacific Daily News,* Guam's newspaper, and his editor had sent him down to photograph the festivities. One night toward the middle of Culture Week, I ran into Viti at Bai Ra Metal, the nightclub owned by Ibedul, paramount chief of Koror Island, and I asked him about his photographs.

"It was Kathy's idea," Viti said. "Not many Micronesians—or Americans, for that matter—would have thought of using photography that way. It was very farsighted. Many of those old people are dead. Everyone appreciates those photographs, now. 'There's my grandfather!' But she's the one who realized it then, eight years ago.

"I got no salary, just my expense money down. We started in 1972, photographing several people on a small scale, then in '75 there was a big push to do everyone, and that year I spent three weeks doing it. We took off from Koror. It was like a full-scale expedition, with camera gear and supplies. Kathy had planned it really well. She had a good schedule that we were able to keep to. We went with her community organizers to the people's houses.

We visited and explained who we were. Sometimes we spent the night first and photographed them the next morning. We would sleep at the *bais*.

"There was a lot of hiking. We would hike in for three or four hours, really beautiful walks. Gorgeous. We would walk for hours on the traditional stone paths. Raised paths, really efficient. It would rain, and there would be mud on either side, but not on the paths. People in the villages brought us delicacies to eat and sleeping mats. That was the first time I saw the megaliths. Kathy liked to sleep out. She really got a kick out of it.

"Some of the hamlet chiefs were very shy. They didn't know why we wanted to photograph them. Kathy put everyone at ease. She's unique in that she's truly bicultural. She's good with people like you and me, but she also shined when she met old folks. Old people thoroughly enjoyed talking with Kathy, gossiping with her. She was very good at just being a Palauan woman.

"Some of the informants, the people themselves—their backgrounds—were really moving. I remember one old crippled man, he'd been shot by American planes. And there was this old man named Ngiraibuuch. Ngiraibuuch had an aura about him, an aura of peacefulness. He was blind. He had been blind since birth. I hadn't known that at first when I started photographing—he was just returning from collecting firewood. When he was young, he had been a great canoebuilder and carpenter. Now he traded with people for firewood. He could still go through the jungle and collect the right wood.

"One old man had a white Stetson—he wanted to wear his favorite hat in the picture. It wasn't quite what we had in mind, but that's what he wanted. This old guy went in to get his hat. There was an old lady. She couldn't stand up. She had long, flowing hair to her waist, but for the picture she put it up. She had a big black belt on, the kind they got from whalers.

"It's moving to me now to look at those photographs. I remember sitting on the step with them, chewing betelnut. I felt that for a while I was a part of Palauan life. Kathy is the one who brought me in and let me see that tradition. I would have never seen it otherwise.

"It was strenuous. It was all done with available light. It had to be carefully controlled, and the concentration was exhausting. While Kathy talked, I was looking around for the right setting. I think it was the best work I've done.

"I'm getting out of photojournalism. I keep thinking, you know, 'Tomorrow's fish wrapper?' That first dawned on me during the Chief's Project. I realized I should be doing more things like this. What's going to go down in the Big Book? Whatever the Big Book is. What will be left after Carlos has gone?"

Culture Week ended, and I drifted back into the history of the floor and its voices of old people.

I am Tkedesau Mad, born at Ngerubesang in Melekeok when the Spaniards were in Palau. I recognized their only concern in Palau was to spread Christianity. At about age thirteen, the Spaniards left the island, and the Germans came in. Later, the First World War broke out, putting the end of the German regime on the island and the Japanese took over.

Within these different eras, I have noted that the kids of the earlier eras were more respectful and well-behaved as compared to the kids today. In this case I yearn to live the life of the past rather than the life today.

My name is Ngiraibuuch. And I'm ninety years old. I have never been employed in office during each foreign governmental rule on Palau. I was always on my own making thatch roofs, producing coconut oil, and digging water-wells. I never did go to school. Nevertheless, I had knowledge in figures. In events where money problems arise, my people come for me. People didn't know arithmetic at that time. And Boat Purchase for a village was an event that required someone who knew arithmetic. So I was much needed in that kind of service. Today I have laid down all the burden of the past, except I've remained collecting firewoods.

"Some of the interviews were entertaining and exciting," Kesolei had told me. "One tape, the students played that *rubak* over and over again. I asked them, 'Haven't you transcribed this yet?' They said, 'No, we're just listening.'" Now I was doing that myself: just listening, unsure where in my story the voices would fit, or whether they would fit at all.

My name is Matlab. My title is Ngiraked. I know few of the earlier Ngirakeds. The late Ngiraked was Tmenang. There was Ngiraked Remeskang. My father was Ngiraked Ngecechei. And the first Ngiraked to be buried on a hill is Kerai. When I first assumed the title Ngiraked, I was seventy-six years old. Today I'm seventy-eight years old, which means I have been Ngiraked two years. I assumed the title from my father who held it before me.

In brownouts, I continued to adjourn to the capstan. Headed there one day, the old voices temporarily stilled in closed folders under my arm and the sky to the west dark with thunderheads, I saw that the waters outside the harbor swarmed with canoes. The canoeists were young boys, the canoes sheets of corrugated metal bent into a V at the keel. At either end, the edges of tin were pinched together and fitted into blocks of wood that served as cutwaters. That was all there was to them. They were more like Indian birchbarks than like the traditional Micronesian outriggers, but they were good, fast boats.

One boy, digging alternately with a double-bladed paddle, more like an Eskimo than an islander, flew away from T-dock. He headed northwestward, well out beyond the other vessels in the fleet. He turned west, as if he intended now to make for the Philippines. He looked very bold, against that long horizon.

In the old days, according to Kesolei's *A History of Palau*, Palauan war canoes called *kabekl* had sprinted across this same lagoon. *Kabekl* were dugouts fifty or sixty feet long, with hulls inlaid with pearl shell, painted red, rubbed with oil, and polished. The warrior-paddlers, armed to the teeth, worked double-banked, one row seated on thwart bars across the hull, the other row seated on the outrigger. The lanceolate blades of the paddles pulled in perfect unison, the singing knobs whistling through the water on the upstroke. White strings of cowries swung, in time with the stroke, from the projecting tips of the thwart bars, and dark, decapitated human heads swung from the outrigger. Howling fiendishly, the warrior-paddlers paid unneighborly calls on adjoining villages. The *kabekl* went fast but never far. Palauans were not interested in subjugating total strangers on some tiny coral atoll across the ocean; they were interested in whipping their cousins across the channel, and the *kabekl* was just the warship for that.

A corrugated canoe came ashore for a change of paddlers. While it was beached on the concrete, I bent to examine it. The paddlers were tolerant. They sympathized with my admiration. One boy laid his brown hand on the metal bow, and in English boasted, "Very good."

The canoe shoved off, and I walked back to the capstan to read.

I was born in Merir, and while still a child I was brought to Sonsorol due to a small tidal wave that flooded Merir. Later, at Sonsorol, I and some of our people were transported by German ship, *Esther*, to Palau. Therefore, I began my first grade in the German school at age ten in Palau.

As I read, the thunderheads moved in from the sea. The effect, from the vantage of the capstan, was that the big, rain-dark summits of cumulus were growing vertically, billowing higher and higher. T-dock fell into shadow. Big tropical raindrops began pocking the greenish water of the little harbor and smoking on the concrete of the dock. Tucking the folder inside my shirt, I retreated to the office. Safe inside, I withdrew the folder, found a desk, and resumed reading.

I am Rengiil Beches, born at Ulimang, my home village in Ngeraard. I tried my best to perform the hardest and most arduous tasks for the public. For example, I was the one who would empty the large outrigger canoe, *kabekl*, when it is at the brink of shrinking, a task which was not easy and handy to do. When it comes to track racing, I run my best even to the point of having my loincloth (*usaker*) torn. But I always tried my best for the reputation of Ngeraard. I follow my father's footsteps of being best in everything when it comes to physical matters. My father Ngirabas is known for having stopped a running karibou by holding its tail.

I was curious about this strong man, Rengiil Beches. Born in 1894, he had been seventy-nine at the time of the interview. I wondered if any vestige had remained then of the young runner so fast he had torn his loincloth; son of Ngirabas, famous for having stopped a running carabao by holding its tail.

"Could you tell, looking at him as an old man, that he had been an athlete?" I asked Kesolei, when I had the opportunity.

"Oh, yeah. Palauan men nowadays are out of shape, but then it was just muscle and bone. The old men are bent, but you can see the muscle."

"Like Bandarii," I suggested.

She nodded, and for a while we discussed Bandarii, the weather magician for Ngcheangel Atoll, in the north of Palau. I told Kesolei how strange it had been when I first saw that magician, a dark young man in a straw hat coming down a sandy path toward me, his stride bouncy, his torso lean and muscular as a prizefighter's, and my realizing only as he passed that the young man was not young; that the hair under the straw hat was white.

She nodded again, more emphatically. "A lot of the old men— as a matter of fact, my grandfather—there's not one inch of fat there. It's old, but it's strongboned. They're stooping, but it's not because of sickness, or weight, or anything. Rengiil is a runner and diver. He took the title very young."

Thanks to Carlos Viti's portraits, I now had faces to match with the voices of Kesolei's history. One of these illustrated voices, after translation by descendants several generations removed and working in a second language, sounded like this:

Ngirangetkaeb rescued the lady and one of the men and started paddling toward the warriors from Ngeraard. After they were close enough, he started firing his gun. Some of the warriors were wounded and were taken to be hospitalized at that moment. The others kept coming. Ngirangetkaeb reloaded the gun, and went toward the warriors and started to shoot again. The guns at that time were bad, because you have to load them by putting in many things, including coconut husks. While he was shooting, the warriors were throwing spears back. The woman was hit by one of the spears, because she was sitting at the back. A spear was thrown and hit her organ.

After the war, Ngirangetkaeb took the wounded lady. He applied medicines to the lady which made the lady almost survive. But he couldn't help himself, because he kept seeing the lady's organ every day. He tried to control himself, but he can't help it so he made love to her. After the love affair, the lady died.

The recollector of this sad romance, Tet Ngirangeang, faces Viti's camera without expression. Ngirangeang was born December

12, 1883, which makes him eighty-nine at the time of the photograph, yet there is still plenty of dark hair mixed in with his gray.
His white mustache is sparse. His ears are pierced and the holes
stretched a bit—in his youth he must have inserted sea shells or
flowers, the old custom. His eyes, in this picture at least, are the
cloudy sort that seem to have gone off somewhere else. His age is
mostly in his hands and feet, which are darker than the rest of him,
having seen more sun and work. The photograph needs no caption,
for on the subject's arm TET NGIRANGEANG is tattooed in block let-
ters. It's a long name, and it runs from shoulder to elbow. On his
wrist he wears the *klilt*, a bracelet fashioned from a dugong verte-
bra and worn by chiefs. It's an old *klilt*. The spinous and transverse
processes of the bone have been worn nearly even with the rest.

Q:  What do you call that bracelet in your hand?
A:  This is the dugong's bone called chelecholl. This bracelet is hard
    to put on, because they had to tie your hand real tight and it takes
    many people to put it on.
Q:  What is that bracelet for?
A:  It is just a decoration. I didn't like it in my hand, but my wife
    wanted it in my hand.
Q:  How old were you when you married?
A:  I was twenty-some when I married. I don't like this bracelet for I
    can't climb or split logs, because it will crack.
Q:  Can you tell in what part of a dugong fish is this bracelet located?
A:  It is located in its abdomen.
Q:  Did you put it in your hand right after you took it out of the fish?
A:  No, this was Olmetelel's bracelet. Olmetelel was the son of Ibe-
    dul. Ibedul who had two walking sticks, had two wives. My fa-
    ther bought it at a much higher price. It was too big for Olmete-
    lel's hand so he had to put a piece of cloth in it in order to make it
    tight. My father spent too much money for it, so I don't want to
    lose it.
Q:  Do you think it is getting smaller?
A:  Yes, because its ears are being chipped off.

For nearly seventy years, Tet had been bugged by the bracelet,
but never could bring himself to get rid of it, his father having paid

too much for it at the turn of the century.

"I photographed Tet in 1972," Viti would tell me. "I went back again in 1975 and looked him up. I was shocked. He was dying. He was in bed and couldn't get up. He could only get to his elbow. He was so dignified. He had a bullet wound, you know, that went back to German times. It was in his arm, near that tattoo.

"'Aaah,' he said, 'you're the one who took my picture.' He saw I was upset. He said not to worry. Don't feel bad. He said he was very old, and this was how life goes. He told me his wife was there to take care of him. He had a high, birdlike voice—hardly any voice left at all. I had seen him in his prime, in the twilight of his manhood. I wanted to photograph him again, but I couldn't. I just started to cry."

*"Ngak a ngklek a Sochai,"* begins one voice from the floor even older than Tet's. *"E chelecha e a dui el kuluchel er ngii a Spis. . . ."*

"My name is Sochai, with hold of the title Spis—Chief of Ngchesechang Hamlet in Airai. I am ninety-seven years old. I was born before the Spaniards came."

The Spis Sochai of Viti's portrait stares fiercely off in semi-profile. He is graying now, finally, at ninety-seven, and his hairline is beginning to recede above the temples. His neck, frailer than it once was, but still strong, leans forward at a belligerent angle. His collarbone is prominent. Against the left side of the collarbone rests a Palauan adze, its blade bound to its wooden handle by hundreds of turns of sennit. The line of the chief's mouth is long and stern, his face as stony as the basalt adze. The Palauans have a proverb, "Like the core of the mangrove," that they apply to people of great age, especially those who, like Spis, bear titles. The core of the mangrove log is soft and workable when green but becomes very hard with age. Of all the faces in Carlos Viti's gallery, none looks more like old mangrove than Spis's.

"Spis was very animated," Viti told me. "He spoke a lot with his hands—threw them around. He knew how to make a striking pose. He'd done this before. He knew how to jut his jaw out and look imposing. He was a ham."

"Ah, Spis," Kesolei remembered, fondly. She thought about

him for a moment. "Spis was an expert on weather. He was one of the people in possession of information. There are fourteen thousand people in Palau, but which of them have the information? If you're curious about the origin story of Palau, for example, there are only a few people who know it, who can piece it together. If you're curious about seasons, tides—again, there's only a few people who know it. Spis knew about weather. I thought, 'We've got to get these things Spis knows on tape.'

"But Spis never really explained it all. I listened, and it was always legendary. He never gave us the *interpretations*. And it was disjointed. I began to realize that the links had already been transferred. He had passed it on. It was someone else's property.

"I remember an old woman from when I was very young, a knowledgeable woman who was always consulted, like Spis. She died. I thought, *Why does someone die?* To the granddaughter of this woman, I said, "Isn't it too bad that all your grandmother knew is lost?'—a typical Western reaction. She said no. I said, 'You mean . . . ? You mean someone knows?' She said yes.

"Someone had been living with the old woman for several years. In Palau, when someone is going to die, he picks a younger person in the clan whom he takes a liking to. The young person spends all his time with the old person, until the end. That way, there's someone to take care of the funeral, and there's someone to pass information along to. My grandfather has eight children, but he's living with only one child. The person selected learns everything the old person has to deal with. The old person deals with things in a minimal way, but the younger person takes care of the rest. That's one reason adoption is so important in Palau. Throughout your life you're looking at your children, evaluating them. Which will be the one?"

If Kesolei's intuition was right and Spis had passed on his information, then his face masked the transfer nicely. In Viti's gallery of Palauan elders, there are a number of faces that do look vacant, as if they had indeed passed on their real substance, but Spis's is not one of them. He seems, with that adze on his shoulder, to be guarding something. It may be, of course, that he's just a rear guard, that the fierce brows and jutting jaw are all decoy, but if so, the ham in Spis is enjoying the role.

"Couldn't you have *asked* Spis?" I asked her. "When you suspected that the links were missing—that they already had been transferred—couldn't you have asked him if that's what had happened?"

She looked surprised and a little disappointed, as if I had missed the lesson. "Actually, not," she said. "Because it was his property. It would have been rude. You'd have to be awfully inconsiderate to do a thing like that."

That Kesolei's history of the floor should remain on the floor seemed to me a great waste. Many of her taped interviews with Palauan elders had gone untranscribed and remain so today. Those set safely down on paper sit in the closet, where for several years they gathered dust, seeing no light but the closet bulb until I began taking them outside to the capstan. I asked Kesolei one day if that state of affairs pleased her.

"I've often been asked, 'What will you do with the tapes?'" she answered. "I've asked myself that many times. I don't know. You transcribe it, and it goes on the shelf. There's the problem of retrieving it. It becomes a kind of rich man's thing. I guess I'd like to keep them as tapes. Duplicate them, maybe. The files you're reading are duplicated now in microfilm at the University of Hawaii."

"Are you happy with what you've recorded?"

"Oh, no. What we have, Ken, is just the tip, the very tip of whatever looms under there."

The afternoon was bright after a morning of rain. A few small trade-wind cumuli lay on the horizon. A strong wind was blowing from the northwest, and within the containing arms of the T-dock serifs, the water was choppy. The intimate little aquamarine harbor looked strange, tossing that way—a storm in a fishbowl. The chop was translucent, and the sun glinted from the peaks. Outside, the lagoon was making up small whitecaps, but the harbor lacked fetch enough for that. I walked out toward the capstan, against the wind, with a folder from the history under my arm.

Four boys were swimming off the inner wall, beneath the capstan, their sleek black heads bobbing in the chop. Two others had
hauled out. Of the two boys ashore, one was still wet. He lay on his
stomach on the gray-white concrete of the dock, his head gone over
the edge. His face must have been very close to the water, for the
tide was high, nearly on a level with the dock. The second hauled-
out boy was smaller and nearly dry. He lay on his side, facing
inland, singing.

I walked across the singing boy's line of sight, but his eyes,
half-lidded, did not move to track me. Without missing a note, he
raised his volume, as if to erase me. He was singing a Palauan song.

I sat on the capstan, opened the folder, and read:

I am going to recount the history of the Udes Clan, starting from
the first Reklai up to present time. I am the seventeenth Reklai of the
Udes Clan. The title "Reklai" started with a group of people from
Ngeruangel who later moved to Kayangel. This group of people entered a passage called "Waingtuul" and from there proceeded on to
Ngeruuds. They did not stay long, for they moved again to Klubas,
then on to Ngerkebang. Ngeriungs in Rengoor was their next destination, and they stopped there briefly before they went on to Ngerbelas,
Orak, then on to Ngerechur.

The wind was trying to fill and flip the folder's pages, so I held
them down with a thumb. Now and again I looked up at the harbor. The same gusts struggling under my thumb had swept a windrow of eelgrass against the harbor wall. Here and there among the
blades of eelgrass a mangrove leaf floated. The undulating raft of
sea vegetation had flattened the chop along the entire length of the
T-dock crossbar, except at this end, where the boys in their diving
had blasted a gap. The boys were providing chop of their own. The
two smallest stood on the third stair, beating the surface with
boards, little mad Caligulas declaring war on the ocean. The older
boys were jumping off the dock with chunks of Styrofoam clasped
to their chests.

The singer continued to sing. His partner rolled suddenly into the water, and the singer was alone.

His songs were all Palauan, and he sang them one after another. He did not attempt a snatch of Japanese or American song, though those songs were all you heard at night here on T-dock, propagated by speakers loud and unbalanced and escaping through the open doors of the discothèque and the Waterfront Bar. Palauan songs are wonderful, sad songs. Nothing, unless it is the fragrance of chewed betelnut, evokes Palau faster for an expatriate than a few notes from one. The boy singer had the pleasant, husky voice common to many Palauan children. It went nasal, flat, and mournful in the spots where the Palauan singing style requires that.

For the other boys it was a siren song. The swimmers hauled out, one or two at a time, to lie alongside the singer. They never stayed long enough to get very dry, but they kept returning. At one point, three of them lay around him at odd angles. They looked as indifferent to terrestrial music as three seals on a rock, but they must have been listening. The singer faltered only once. A larger boy began to wrestle with him, the song stopped, the larger boy broke off abruptly, the song resumed.

I realized it was all up to the singer.

Katherine Kesolei's elderly informants, when told that their lore would die if it went unrecorded, had been unmoved. They were right to be. They had understood better than their young countrywoman, despite her degree in anthropology, where the life in oral literature lies. Kesolei herself, ten years wiser now, was right in wanting to keep the interviews as tape. In that form, the old songs and stories and legends were one step less removed from relevance. On tape much was still missing: the weave of the sleeping mats upon which the new generation lay, captive audience to the old voice; the stars through the window; the consanguinity of the tale teller and all his old man's gestures, but at least a voice remained. Kesolei was not negligent in leaving the history where it lay. The floor was as good a place as any. The history was just taxidermy. The boy singer was the real animal.

He turned over on his back and shielded his eyes with both hands, interlocking the fingers. He was entirely dry now. The salt had stiffened his hair at crazy angles. Below the hot concrete of the dock, the windrow rose and fell. The floating eelgrass was olive-green, the mangrove leaves were yellow. Now and again the boy's fingers flexed, as if their owner were dreaming. In the nimbused shade of his two hands, his eyes were nearly closed. He sang his Palauan song.